SECRETS OF A TOP SALESPERSON

How Emotions Make or Break the Sale

Secrets of a
Top Salesperson

*How Emotions
Make or Break the Sale*

PAULA PAGANO

BOOKSURGE PUBLISHING
Charleston, South Carolina
2009

Copyright ©2009 Paula Pagano
All rights reserved.

Library of Congress cataloging in publication data

Pagano, Paula
Secrets of a Top Salesperson: How Emotions Make or Break the Sale

ISBN-13: 978-1-4392-3479-2
1. Pagano, Paula—Biography. 2. Women real estate agents—United States.
3. Real estate business—United States. 4. Sales—United States.

Library of Congress Control Number: 2009903340

First edition
Printed in the United States of American
Set in ITC New Baskerville

Visit www.booksurge.com to order additional copies

Secrets of a Top Salesperson
How Emotions Make or Break the Sale

Acknowledgments

First I would like to thank those managers who allowed me to teach their salespeople, especially Eileen Mougeott and Jay Costello, Aldo Congi, Kip Oxman and Charlie Moore, Cathy Scharetg, Ilse Cordoni, Mark Best and Betty Carr Walton. Also, thanks to Tommy Hopkins for his inspiration. Special thanks to Joanna Phillips, owner of Real Estate Power Training, who hired me to teach negotiation and contracts to various MLS organizations throughout California. The experience of teaching and coaching gave me the courage, confidence and tenacity to become the author I have always wanted to be.

Next I would like to thank my fellow best selling author-mentor-friends, Carol Adrienne, Joyce Maynard, Frank Jordan and Ray Brown who have supported my writing over the years. Also thanks to Ellen Roberts, Barbara Johnson, Tracy O'Neill, Daniel Altman and Doug Wink for their excellent design and editing work. Final thanks to my Laguna Beach and San Francisco colleagues and clients who gave me the crazy situations, challenges and lessons to tell such vibrant stories.

To my husband, Gralen Britto,
the most patient person on this planet
who accepts my Sicilian-Irish-Mohawk Indian devil part of me
as well as the angel.

INTRODUCTION

IT WAS OBVIOUS FROM THE BEGINNING of my sales career that I was not a natural-born salesperson. I came into real estate not having any business experience, so I had to endure humiliations and heartache. By recounting my struggles for success in this book, I hope to spare others from suffering a similar fate. Hopefully, my experience will help smooth your path to a successful sales career.

I believe that most people, like me, have a plan. Usually, however, it is not that plan but an opportunity that shapes career choices. After graduating from college, I became a medical researcher. It was not until I had to experiment on animals and actually kill them that I realized I needed to find another profession. I traveled to California looking for some answers. When someone suggested real estate, I thought it would be a good fit because my father was an architect and I loved houses. Passing the licensing test and getting hired by a company was fairly easy. But real estate is not about houses. It is about sales and those sales come out of solid relationships. I was only a young, immature biologist with few communication skills, little life experience and an emotionally challenged Irish-Italian background. Could I now assist people in one of the most important investments in their lives? No way! My customers were making an important life decision and I had nothing to offer aside from my impatience. (Oops! I forgot to mention the Mohawk Indian on my mother's side only added to my impetuous nature.) The truth was my clients' anxieties, emotional outbursts, and dawdling drove me crazy.

Although there are plenty of books and seminars available about systematic business plans, scripted sales techniques and ramped-up positive thinking, these skills did not show me "the underbelly" of sales—*how to get along with anxious clients, their overprotective friends and family and pushy colleagues.* What I needed—and which most struggling salespeople need as well—is an understanding on how to hold boundaries, communicate effectively and change limiting belief patterns. And sure enough, these skills can be learned just like contracts and building codes. Changing negative habits is hard work, but it can be done.

As a scientist I understood something about human physiology. For instance, changing the neural pathways of learned behavior, like impatience and worry, offers the same choreography as changing a career. First, I had to identify the negative habit and understand why I was addicted to that behavior. Then, I had to let that negative habit go and replace it with a positive one. For instance, I learned to talk to myself soothingly when clients whined at me. I learned to have faith through the weeks and months a buyer waffled about putting a realistic offer on a property. I learned that if I assisted incompetent mortgage brokers and title officers in getting their job done, the escrow would eventually close. And I learned that if I listened patiently while a seller railed incessantly about not getting the price they hoped, we forged a trustful binding relationship which could last for a lifetime. For whenever I faced the challenges placed before me, I would not only get my clients repeat business but their recommendations as well. With this arsenal of skills for controlling my old emotions, I enhanced my self-esteem and became the number one top producer in my office during a recession with 17% interest rates and remained successful for three decades.

It takes emotional strength, personal awareness and courage to deal with people's roller-coaster emotions. Their new house will change their lives. It is the biggest investment they will ever make, so of course they are stressed out! A new agent at one of my ClientConnect seminars said it best—"I knew that my clients would be emotional. What I didn't consider was my reaction to all their emotions." *Secrets of a Top Salesperson—How Emotions Make or Break the Sale* will explain exactly how to develop healthy and creative ways of communicating and connecting with clients while being in a variety of situations.

Secrets of a Top Salesperson—How Emotions Make or Break the Sale contains all the virtues necessary to be a top producer and the behavioral practices, or "vices," to avoid. Since my case histories are about actual people, the reader can see how much our own issues color our interaction with others.

For example, if you do not believe you deserve success, you will probably miss the obvious opportunity of getting a referral from a satisfied client or from an over-booked office-mate. Good salespeople recognize the importance of taking time for themselves and will need help in maintaining their client base. Another powerful rule is to be present in the moment. When you observe the nuances of what customers say, you can discern the real ones from the unmotivated. Take this a step farther and develop the sixth sense of intuition and you can avoid the pitfalls of failed transactions.

For best results, go slow. Read only one chapter a week and take the time to integrate the rules into your business practice. If you want to delve even deeper, there are detailed success exercises on my teaching website, ClientConnect.us.

In spite of all the stress and drama clients bring, sales can be tremendously fulfilling—emotionally, intellectually and financially. I have tried to include the wisdom within these pages to make you the successful salesperson you always hoped, while showing that life is more than making money. Enjoy my journey of personal transformation as I grow as a person, help others along the way and make a life-long dream, a reality.

PART ONE

The Eight Essential Virtues

CHAPTER ONE

COURAGE

Being True to Who You Are

IT IS A YEAR AFTER THE BICENTENNIAL and I am planning to move to the other side of the world. My job as a medical researcher in New York has turned into a bit of a disaster. Not only is it isolating—I am stuck in a dark, dank laboratory most of the day—but it is also heartbreaking. For when I'm not reading research articles, I'm hunched over furry little hamsters and doing all sorts of terrible things. Sometimes I have to slit their throats to collect blood samples. Other times I have to implant cancers into their cheek pouches, wait for the tumors to grow and then irradiate them. When co-workers see me crying, they scold me as they shake their heads. "Paula, if you want to be a scientist you are going to have to learn not to be emotional."

So the end justifies the means? I find myself resisting their logic. I have always loved animals, which is the main reason I chose Biology as my major in college. Being a doctor or veterinarian was out the question. I did not have the funds or the commitment, and no way did I want to be a nurse and push bedpans. Full of optimism and hope that I might be part of a team who discovers a breakthrough cure for cancer, I told myself medical research was the job for me.

But it isn't. As my colleagues shrug their shoulders and continue torturing small animals, I have violent nightmares. I hate walking up the six flights of stairs to the floor where they house the mice, rats, hamsters, guinea pigs, rabbits, and monkeys. Each time I clutch the handling gloves tightly to my chest and say a prayer, knowing that the animal I choose will die. I keep thinking my frame of mind will change. I will become hardened and strong like the rest of them. But I don't. Every new day is as hard as the first which is still imbedded in my memory.

When Dr. Nelson, one of the PHD's in the Radiology Department, tells me to collect a hamster for an experiment, I am more eager than afraid. I have been reading research articles for a month and want some "hands on" action. I feel I am ready and he agrees. I am halfway down the hallway when he calls to me. "Paula, aren't you forgetting something?" Dr. Nelson holds up a pair of gloves.

"Oh, I don't need those," I say.

He walks them over to me. "Trust me. You will."

When I unclasp the lock to the cage, a group of hamsters shrink en masse to the farthest corner, standing on their hind legs with front claws drawn, ready to sink their teeth into anything that comes close. "Oww," I yelp, banging my ungloved hand on one of the metal bars, trying to get it out of harm's way.

The loud clanging noise causes high-pitched screeching from the hamsters which alerts the other animals who add to the clamoring chorus. Surely, people on one of the other floors can hear all this commotion. Hopefully, no one will bother to check on what's happening. Being new, I don't want any unwanted attention or criticism. So what to do? Gloves are a definite must. I put them on making sure none of my flesh is showing. As I reach inside, the screeching starts all over again. I talk to the small creatures in a low soothing voice, almost humming. Animals always love me, I tell myself. I creep my hand in slowly, millimeter by millimeter, but lose confidence when the animals rush toward me, determined not to let me take one of their own. I am forced to withdraw.

Dr. Nelson insists that animals do not have emotions. But these animals seem pretty angry—and isn't anger an emotion? I wonder if they know their fate. Do they have some secret language and talk amongst themselves? Or do they just notice that when one hamster leaves, he never returns?

I am a big proponent of medical science, but does the end justify the means? I thought Hippocrates said "First, do no harm." Or did he just mean no harm to us, the evolved species on the planet? Then there's the rational logic of the seasoned researchers echoing in my head, insisting that the experimentation on animals is necessary for the benefit of mankind. I wonder if the macho men who design these research projects have ever been on this floor. It is unlikely that they've ever risked losing one of their hands.

But I'm stuck. I need this job to pay my rent. I won't be dependent on my parents—that's for certain. And being dependent upon a man is just not my style. I am determined to make it on my own—no matter what. Even before I heard Gloria Steinem speak at New York State University at Oswego I had made that decision. Yet torturing small mammals is not my forte. I try one more time. Another try and another after that. I am up in that horrible lab most of the morning before my mission is accomplished.

The reason I got into Biology in the first place was because of my love of all living things, but now I experiment on them. I force myself into work, day after day, but after many months of implanting cancerous tumors in hamsters' cheek pouches, irradiating them, taking their vitals and eventually killing them, I am looking for a way out. When Ted Martin, my current boyfriend at the time, receives a job offer to teach at the University of California campus in Irvine, California, I decide to move with him. Just like The Mamas and the Papas, I hoped "I'd be safe and warm if I was in L.A." I leave the cold blistery winter days in upstate New York behind. California could be my ticket out of hell.

We settle in Laguna Beach, a small artistic beach town which reminds me of the French Riviera, except without the small pebbles which are so hard on my feet. Here the beach is fine sand; there are few men in bikini Speedo trunks and no woman without a top. This is United States after all, but it feels like a slice of paradise to me. The small town center is filled with the usual coffee shops, restaurants and stores and a city hall, fire/police department and library. Unlike the polished sophisticated nearby beach towns of Newport, Corona del Mar and Balboa Island, Laguna is quaint and charming, nestled between grass hills and the Pacific Ocean. There are no high-rises on the beach (the hotels had been built in the twenties and thirties) and not a chain store in sight (except for an Albertson's tucked away from the city's center where people buy their groceries). The houses surrounding the town, where we're looking for a rental, are mostly small beach cottages, some of which have been renovated and expanded into more substantial homes. However, even the smallest cottage is too expensive for us. We find a tiny one bedroom apartment in a four plex located on a busy commercial corner. It is curtain-less, dingy and in desperate need of a paint job, but the beach is so close I don't really mind.

A knockout beauty with sparkling eyes and a distinct East Coast accent is Bette Mae, our landlady, who has lived in Laguna most of her adult life. Her chestnut brown hair is tied up in a tight bun, which, to me, is a bit old fashioned, but it does not take away from her strikingly good looks. I figure she's approaching fifty because she introduces three robust well-tanned men as her sons. I wonder if time will be as kind to me should I decide to stay in California. Her smile and open manner welcome me and she takes me in like I am her long lost daughter. There is always a pot of homemade soup on her stove, a warm smile and a listening ear for anyone who needs to talk. Since I feel so safe with her, I confide that I am in a quandary of what to do for a career. She suggests I get my real estate license, telling me her inspiring story of how she was widowed twice before she was thirty and left with three young children. She invested the money she received from her husbands' life insurance policies and bought two houses—one for her family and the other for income. Real estate has literally been her savior. Perhaps it could be mine as well.

> RULE #1-1: RESEARCH YOUR OPTIONS If your career path is not working, summon up your courage to try something else. Evaluate different vocational options by talking to people who actually work in the field. If you think real estate may be the profession for you, interview successful salespeople. Ask them how they got started, what made them successful and how long it took.

I know nothing about business, sales, or dealing with the public. I am new to California and know no one. Real estate is enticing, because my success would depend entirely on me. On days that I have surplus energy, which I often had, I can work as long as I want and have a good chance of benefiting from the fruits of my labor. I had been in the medical field long enough to know that the men got the promotions. Coming in early, filling in for my less ambitious colleagues and working on weekends to finish an experiment got me nowhere. No overtime pay. No bonus. No extra day off. No acknowledgment, "Paula, you're doing a good job." Not even a pat on the head.

"Ambitious salespeople are amply rewarded for their success," Bette says. "It actually helps being a woman, because the average person trusts us more than the fast-talking men who might just as well be selling used cars."

In sales I could be my own boss and come and go as I pleased. The freedom would be liberating. No more feeling boxed-in by a life which is not harmonious with the person I really am. No more living someone else's dreams. Wanting to be the good little girl, I did what other people told me to do rather than taking the time to find out what I wanted. "Get a science degree. You can always do something with that," I heard said to me over and over (It reminded me of the advice, "get into Plastics," given to Dustin Hoffman in *The Graduate*). Well, if I did not want to be a nurse and did not have the money or brain power to be a doctor what could I do? I know—be a medical researcher and torture defenseless animals in the name of science!

I walk to the beach with a notepad in hand to think this all through. Finding a place of solitude, I let the soft pink sand sink between my toes as I make two columns on my paper. I close my eyes, concentrating on the soft lapping sound of waves on the surf. I feel the healing rays of the sun on my face and open my eyes only to write a negative or a positive under the appropriate column. When I am done my list has many more pros than cons. I know the analytical life of a scientist is not for me; there is nothing else on the horizon, and I may have the qualities it takes to be a salesperson. I like people, I like houses and I like my freedom. I have been stuck in a suffocating role too long. Since I would essentially be an entrepreneur, I can do this profession my way on my terms. The thought gives me a liberating feeling inside. I feel my heart opening wide—the possibilities enticing. For me it is worth the gamble to give real estate a try.

RULE #1-2: DISCOVER WHAT YOU WANT I find the best way to view a situation is through the process of writing it all down on paper. The simple process of writing envelops the complete picture and will bring you closer to attracting the success, goals and dreams you secretly crave.

When I tell Bette of my decision to get my license, she warns me about the fate of other people she knew who had tried real estate and failed. "First of all you need a minimum of six months savings in the bank." I check my finances. I have a good nine months and, if I am frugal, a year—enough time to get my business rolling. She then explains that real estate is cyclical. "You have to be prepared for the dips and valleys. Real estate is 100% commission based. If you don't make a sale, you don't get paid. Not one dime."

"That's okay," I say.

"And you see those successful agents driving around in their fancy cars? Most of them live on the edge—just one step ahead of creditors. They make a sale and then spend, spend, spend, thinking that the good times will never end. But they do. My question for you is— do you have the courage to hang in there when things get tough?"

I think it over carefully the next few days. Only two months ago I left my familiar East Coast surroundings and moved here. That took some guts. I also had the bold courage to put myself through college when my parents gave me no emotional or monetary support, probably hoping I'd take the easy marriage route. After graduation I procured a job in another city and even though I did not like what I did I stayed with it day after day. Then I remembered my childhood.

Mother has guests over for an afternoon lunch. As I run through the living room to the back stairs and the freedom of the outside, Mother grabs my arm with a firm grasp and leads me to a chair. "You remember Lois and Ernie don't you?" I shake my head slowly side to side. "It is impolite not to say hello," Mother says.

"Hello," I say. I smile only slightly, knowing that a big gapping hole shows where my front tooth used to be.

They say something I don't understand.

"Paula, they just asked you a question. Answer them."

"Huh?" I say.

"Oh, so the tooth fairy got a hold of you recently," one of them says.

I nod without looking up. I don't want them to think I want to be here. Instead I drift into my own thoughts. I look outside where my brother is playing. I wish I was out there with him. There is nothing to do in here. Just adults talking. I am supposed to look pretty for them, Mother said. So I'm all dressed up—now what? I know—a quick walk around the room to see what there is to eat. I try the onion dip and then the seafood one and am on to the Swedish meatballs when I notice Mother motioning me to sit down next to her. I quickly stuff two meatballs in my mouth and gulp them down fast. Sitting is not what I do best, but I really don't have a choice.

I glance down at my brightly polished black patent leather shoes, wishing I had the black and white saddle shoes that are so much more popular with the kids at school. I notice that the lacey ankle socks are starting to slip down my heel so I pull them up—careful to fold them over like Mother likes—an attempt to be the sweet angel girl Mother wants me to be. I need to try harder, I tell myself. It would make life so much easier. I can hear Mother's voice in my head asking over and over again. "Why can't you be more like your cousin, Noreen?" I squinch up my face and wrinkle my nose, trying hard to remember what is so special about my cousin who I hardly ever see.

Mother gives me one of her looks and pulls me closer to her. "Be still", she says. "No wiggling around."

I have all this energy bottled up inside and now I don't know what to do. I want to be outside with the birds, the butterflies and the blue sky. I imagine rolling around on the grass like my dog, Daisy—the scent of the freshly cut lawn going way up inside my nose, making me feel happy inside. I get out of my chair, heading for the back stairs and to the field behind our house.

Mother sees me and shakes her head, "No."

Hanging my head, I walk back and sit down, making sure I sit upright in the chair. I wish I could be the picture she would like me to be, but it's hard. I cross my feet at my ankles—just like she taught me. I put on a pretty smile, but it's not real. I try harder. I force my lips to curl up, but it's not real. It is all fake.

Fake. Fake. Fake.

I imagine sneaking outside to our big backyard with the pear and berry trees. The birds love that berry tree. I don't know what type of berries they are. I've asked several times, but no one tells me. Maybe they don't know. I've tasted the berries. They're really not that good, but I taste them anyway. The birds love them. Maybe I'll acquire a taste for them someday like Daddy's coffee. I've tried Daddy's coffee too. It's not that good, but Daddy explained that the first time we try something we might not like it, but if we keep trying we can change our taste for things.

Change. *Can I change?*

Can I change?

I start to cry. Then I stop myself. No, I can't go outside. I'll get my pretty white dress with the red strawberries and ruffled sleeves all grimy with green grass. Daddy loves this dress. Besides, I don't want to get in trouble. I have to be strong. No, I need to sit here and act like a lady. More words echo in my head. Be quiet. Be good. Be the perfect daughter But I don't want to. I want to be outside! I can hear my brother playing out there. Why can he play and I can't? Rough-housing—that's what they call it when I do it. They say nothing when he does it. Boys can. Girls can't. I don't want to be a little lady and just be pretty! It isn't fair! I want to throw myself on the floor and beat my fists into the rug until my hands ache. I take a deep breath and grab some courage, slowly walking over to Mother.

"May I go outside now too, please?"

She doesn't answer.

"Mother, can I? I promise I won't get dirty." I can hear the whining in my voice. Mother hates it when I whine.

"The answer is no."

"It's just not fair that Peter's outside and I can't go."

"Paula, we've been through all this before. Life isn't fair. The sooner you understand that, the better. You're not going and that's that. Do what you're told and behave yourself!" Mother's voice is getting louder and meaner. I go back to my chair.

I love to catch the grasshoppers in the field behind our house. They hop really high on their hind legs among the wildflowers and Queen Anne's Lace. My God, there must be a trillion of them.

Some of them are brown.

Some are green.

Some in-between.

I like to catch the big green ones the most.

The chair is hard on my bottom. I keep shifting in my seat hoping Mother won't notice my fidgeting. I wish I could swing my legs and arms like I do when I'm outdoors.

Instead I feel like my arms are pinned down and I'm being suffocated. Not being able to be me. I look around at all the people sitting in their chairs and talking quietly—no one I can have fun with. I take small gasps of the stale inside air, hoping I don't faint. The box is definitely closing in. I move my arms from side to side and open my mouth wide to let more air come in. I close my eyes for a few seconds, hoping it will make this feeling go away. It doesn't. I swing my arm around to give myself more room. My glass of lemonade lands on the carpet spilling its contents on our living room rug.

I jump up. "Mistake—it's just a mistake," I say.

Mother comes flying across the room.

I run to the kitchen for the paper towels. "It's okay—I'm wiping it up myself."

She leads me back to my room. "You're hurting my arm," I say.

"As usual you can't sit still for five minutes. How many times do I have to tell you to watch what you're doing? You're always knocking things over, because you're not paying attention!"

Tears start streaming down my face and I reach for her, promising, "I'll be good. Please don't leave me alone in my room. Please."

She takes my hands off her and turning her back, walks away. "You can stay in your room the rest of the afternoon—maybe next time you'll be more careful."

I feel my eyes overflowing and dribble coming out of my nose. I use my sleeve to wipe it all away.

The wetness.

The disappointment.

The sadness.

I'm being forced inside a box which is not meant for me. Now I want outside the box. Yes, Bette, I will drum up the courage to hang in there when things get tough.

I wonder why I hadn't chosen this career path before. It certainly is in my genes. My great-uncle's real estate firm, Pagano Real Estate, had For Sale signs everywhere in Delmar (where I grew up). And although I wasn't popular in school, everyone always commented on how beautiful our house was. It certainly was different. A Post-Modern Ranch—Dad was an admirer of Frank Lloyd Wright—perched high on a hill on a full acre parcel. A row of regal pine trees lined the front of the lot with a long gravel drive to the garage. A stone walkway with steps cut across the lot to the front door and a four foot retaining wall encircled the house. Both were hedged with ornamental bushes and colorful long-stemmed flowers. A huge paned picture window was the focal point with flagstone siding bordering each side. The house door and under-hanging soffit were painted turquoise. This was a daring choice on my father's part, which might have seemed gauche, but he knew the bright iridescent color against the flagstone would be spectacular. I bragged to all my school mates that Dad designed our house and built it himself (which was no exaggeration). It was the one obvious thing I could boast about my family. The rest of the stuff I'd just as soon keep to myself.

Telling my parents I am leaving the medical field will not be easy. Any conversation, other than weather always proves to be a test of wills. No wonder I moved so far away. I know—I'll mention the Sunday drives we took, looking at the neighborhood architecture. From Dad I learned the difference between a Dutch Colonial, a Cape Cod and a Georgian Colonial; the difference between a split level, bungalow and ranch; the difference between a cross gabled, a front gabled, a gambrel and a mansard roof; the difference between a Doric, Corinthian and Ionic column (For the latter I also got a mini-demonstration at Dad's drafting table complete with T-square, triangle and slide rule). Maybe he'll be empathetic if he thinks he inspired me. Without thinking further, I grab the phone. Mother picks up.

"I have some exciting news to tell you," I say, all enthused. "Is Dad around?"

Mother calls for Dad to pick up on the other line. She chirps, "I know—you're finally getting married! I hope not to that Ted person. His head is always stuck in a book. But I guess something is better than nothing. At least you won't be an old maid."

"No, Mother. Something much better than that. I've found a new profession! Something I think I'll be really good at—real estate! I'll be selling houses, meeting new people, always on the go and doing something I enjoy. You've always said how I can't sit still. I hate being cooped up in a laboratory all day doing one rote experiment after another. It's soooo boring." (Plus, I won't have to kill animals. But I don't say that.)

"Paula, your Dad is an architect, which is a respectable occupation." (Mother enunciates the syllables of the last two words so I'll really get the point.) That's a lot (again more enunciations) different than selling houses." In her most critical voice, she adds, "Life isn't always fun and games—you need a real job."

"But selling homes is a real job," I counter. "I'll be writing contracts, finding people their dream home, negotiating offers… " I hear a loud sigh on the other side of the phone and prepare myself for the emotional backlash.

Her voice raises an octave higher. "Now you want to be a common salesperson, after all that money and time spent on getting your BA in Biology? What a waste!" As usual, Dad hasn't been able to say a word.

Yeah, but it was my money and my time and now I want to do something else. What I'm doing right now isn't working. I take a deep breath and try again. "Real estate is something I feel passionate about," I say, continuing on with my reasoning. "Since I will be working as an independent contractor, my success will be measured on how well I do my job. You know what a hard worker I am. As a medical researcher, I never got recognized for all my accomplishments. All the promotions passed me by and went to the men. My real estate success will depend only on me."

Mother keeps on talking as if she has not heard a word I said, trying to convince me to continue living my life of quiet desperation. Perhaps Dad will understand. I turn my attention to him, recalling all our fun drives looking at homes. His response: "Listen to your mother."

I have to live my own life, I tell myself as I hang up the phone, wondering why the many miles between us cannot give me the emotional distance I crave. I turn on my stereo and choose a record album to match the raw emotion I am feeling. Not the Beatles—they're too happy, the Stones—too raunchy... Ahh—Janis Joplin, that's the one! Didn't she have to struggle to break free to be who she really was? I place the needle on her record as it blasts through the rooms of my apartment, repeating my new mantra: "Each time I think I've had enough, I know I can be strong. I know I can be tough." I turn the volume up some more, realizing I'm essentially an orphan who wants to help others find their home.

RULE #1-3: GO AFTER WHAT YOU WANT Do not rely upon what your family, your neighbors, or what Corporate America thinks you should do. You are the only one who holds the key to create the life you want.

Bette Mae lends me the Anthony School Instruction Book, which she had gotten for her older son Mark, hoping he would choose a more steady career than just washing cars. He had taken the test three times and given up. Bette assures me the material is not all that hard. I tell her I'm not worried. If I can pass my Organic Chemistry final, I can take just about any test. For the next month I spend my days and evenings at the library. Escrow, trust deed, amortization, equity, leverage are all words I have never heard before, but I study hard and pass the test the first time.

The interview process is more difficult. Bette gives me the names of the two best firms in town. I make the appointment, dress the part and talk myself into being calm. It's a piece of cake, I tell myself. I laugh—always the sweet eater. The first firm is Nolan Real Estate so close to Bette's apartment I can walk. A secretary ushers me into a private office where I am to wait. It is only a few minutes, but it feels like all afternoon. It is hot and stuffy with the sun beating through the window in the middle of the day. The minutes crawl by. I am beginning to perspire. Finally a middle-aged man with a brisk manner and high opinion of himself walks in, shakes my hand and takes a seat at the desk opposite my chair. My hands are folded neatly on my lap. No fidgeting, I tell myself. No dramatic talking with the hands. And speak slowly. He asks me the same question I had asked myself. "Where will you get your clients? You just moved here. You have no sphere of influence."

"What's a sphere of influence?" I ask. I did not catch that phrase studying for my real estate exam.

"A sphere of influence is all the people you know—family, friends, past business associates, your doctor, lawyer, hairdresser and then all the people they know. To get started you need a minimum of one hundred contacts. Then each of them has a hundred and so on. Real estate is a contact business. Your success depends upon who you know."

"I just moved here," I say.

He thinks for a moment. "We find that many of our successful women agents meet their contacts through their children's schools. Do you have any children?" Before I have a chance to answer, he says, "I'm sorry. I should ask first—are you even married?" When I say no, he ends the interview and gives me the "good luck" handshake.

The second company is Lingo. The sales manager asks me what model car I have within minutes of meeting me. Proud to even own a car, I answer, "A Chevette," and immediately get shown the door. For them, a Realtor's image is most important. I figure it is not just the car; I am too young, inexperienced and poor. When Bette's suggestions for jobs didn't pan out, I realize I need to make my own plan. I decide to try Newell Associates, the real estate office on Pacific Coast Highway which had helped me find my rental. Okay, so they are not the most prestigious office in town. But they do have a good reputation, are in a visible location and are an established family-run business.

On the day of the interview I convince myself this is my lucky day. I take my time getting ready, choosing my best dress, pulling on my pantyhose—though it's warm outside—and heels. I carefully apply my make-up. Not too much rouge or lipstick or dark eye liner, but enough to look mature. I check myself in the mirror. Do a quick turn around. Not bad for someone who is not into fashion. As I look at my reflection I say: "Today is the day," convincing myself the third interview is the charm. All I need to do is to believe in myself. I waltz through the door, smiling with anticipation.

Paul Newell Jr., the owner's son, is a Laguna native, an amber-tanned well-dressed man in his mid-thirties who has a perpetual smile. I guess he has a lot to be smiling about if his family owns a real estate firm on Pacific Coast Highway. We get in his immaculately kept, champagne-toned Cadillac Seville with cushy leather seats. This is the nicest car I have ever ridden in. I am taking Paul Newell's decision to take me to lunch as a good sign. He chooses the historic Laguna Hotel right on the water. As soon as we pull up, a valet opens the car door for me. I act like I do this every day. I get out with the graceful ease of a model. Today, I have decided, I am queen for the day. The hotel has a restaurant deck which overlooks an azure blue ocean with blazing indigo sky. We sit underneath a green-and-white stripped umbrella. I notice all the wealthy vacationers enjoying themselves—women in oversized sun hats and dark glasses sipping strawberry daiquiris while athletic men with bulging biceps down ice cold beers. Over the railing I can see surfers gliding atop the waves and it is the middle of February! I am feeling relaxed, confident and assured. I just assume I have the job. Even when Paul Newell says, "We haven't hired you yet." I ignore his comment and keep proceeding forward as if he has. He's the type, I surmise, that has a hard time saying no to young attractive women. After a lingering lunch, we go back to the office. My charm, my courage and my chutzpah pay off. He shows me my desk and I join Newell Associates that afternoon.

CHAPTER TWO

CLARITY
Determining What Matters Most

AFTER I SPEND FOUR MONTHS of learning the basic tools of the trade, Paul Newell thinks I am ready for a referral. The client is a high-profile lawyer with two teenage sons who has just gotten divorced and is currently staying in a short short-term rental—all the signs of the perfect client—financially qualified and under a time restraint. When he walks through the door that Monday afternoon, he is so stunningly handsome—tall and lean with dark almond eyes and a bronze-toned complexion—that I almost trip over myself trying to shake his hand. He has the same exotic look as Omar Shariff in Dr. Zhivago. I gain my composure and introduce myself.

"I'm Paula," I extend a hand. I wonder if they shake hands where he comes from. Who knows? Maybe he is even from the States. He takes my hand. "Paul Newell tells me you are looking for a home. Why don't we step into our conference room and you can tell me what it is you're looking for. Coffee?" I hand him a cup. I notice my hands are shaking. I will them still. "Sugar?"

He takes his coffee black. I bet he doesn't eat quiche. And in the bedroom he...

"I need a three-bedroom family home for my two sons," Omar says, interrupting my lust-filled daydream. His voice is soft and sultry with a bit of an accent.

"Well, two children make only two bedrooms," I say, making a joke, "but then I was never good in math."

Omar doesn't smile. "Well, one for me too, of course... and a two-bathroom is a must."

I hastily write this down. "What else?" I ask, trying to hide my excitement at being face-to-face with my first real estate client. Omar puts his coffee cup down slowly. "A good school district."

I want him to think I have been doing this my whole life. "All the schools in Laguna are pretty good. Anything else?" I ask.

"I can't think of anything."

Boy, if it's this easy, I'm going to love this job! "So it seems a nice family house is what you're looking for?" I ask just to make sure.

"Yes. That's it. By the way, did Paul Newell tell you I'm a trial lawyer and don't have a lot of free time going around looking?" Omar stands up ready to bolt out the door. "I want to find a house as soon as possible."

"That's fine," I say. "I can preview all the houses which meet your criteria before we look."

A brief handshake and he's gone. I probably forgot to ask half the questions I was supposed to, but I am flying the sky, thrilled with how well it all went. I fantasize about being taken away on a white horse.. To expand on the fantasy, I remind myself that my boyfriend, Ted, is nothing more than a poorly paid professor who's difficult to live with. And I am definitely not in love with him. What could be more serendipitous than an encounter with such a divinely handsome man—and divorced too! When I pay for my groceries that evening, I face the grimmer facts of life. Nothing like a quick glance at my bank balance for a reality check. It is going to be a strict diet of peanut butter and jelly sandwiches for lunch until I sell something. I cannot afford to screw up this referral. Forget romance. There is only one thing on my mind now—survival. I will sell Omar a house even if romance doesn't come with the deal.

I preview several different neighborhoods and architectural styles— Spanish, Contemporary, Craftsman, Bungalow, Ranch—all suitable for families. The most popular family neighborhood is located on the top ridge of the Laguna Hills and appropriately called 'Top of the World.' These ranch homes were built in the sixties with large yards, two car garages and good square footage. Some even have ocean views. Another possibility for Omar is the more expensive, but smaller, re-modeled beach community in the center of town. These are my favorite—charming, well-kept homes with lovely manicured front lawns within walking distance of schools and shopping. Then there is Blue-bird Canyon which is a mixture of older homes with some newer avant-garde contemporary architecture although I'm a bit nervous to show these. Bette told me the area is known for landslides during heavy rains so I cross that neighborhood off my list. Then there are those few precious homes located right on the beach on the other side of Pacific Coast Highway. The zoning laws are much stronger now, but forty or fifty years ago these paradise homes were built within steps of the ocean. Equally prestigious are the newer gated communities of Emerald Bay, Irvine Cove and Three Arch Bay also on the ocean side of the Highway. But way out of his price range. Too bad. I'd love to show these, but I need to keep within Omar's financial qualifications. I've heard through the office that buyers get really frustrated if you show them something outside their price range. I also preview South Laguna, the adjoining township, but these homes have 'Mickey Mouse' floor plans. This refers to the numerous building additions constructed without any thought or reason. These fixer-uppers, as agents call them, are too funky for Omar and his family. I also tell Omar about Laguna Niguel, a new suburban development further south, but he decides it is too far from his practice in Irvine.

His reaction to all the houses I show him is one of polite disdain. Since he is so quiet, I am afraid to pry. I simply deal with his lack of interest by continuing to show him whatever new family home comes on the market. Days pass and the find a house as soon as possible plan turns from weeks into months. No sale in sight. I am slipping into negativity and half-believing the words I have overheard from my cynical office mates: Buyers are Liars and Sellers are Storytellers.

When I mention this to Sue Bates, one of the more successful agents in the office, she offers some sound advice. "Most clients don't know what it is they want. As their agent you have to continually ask questions and get their feedback."

"Well, we had a counseling session before I started showing properties," I say, confident that I had followed the correct protocol.

"How long ago was that?" Sue asked.

"About four months ago! Four months and he still hasn't bought anything! I thought he was a motivated buyer."

"Paula, four months is a long time. Remember, circumstances constantly change. Did you ask Omar his opinion while you were showing the properties—like, 'What do you think of the kitchen?' or 'Do you like the neighborhood?' Even a general question like 'How do you think today's house tour went?' can give you valuable information."

"No," I answer. Now I am beginning to doubt myself.

"Well, how did Omar react when you showed him houses? You know, his body language, facial expressions? Non-verbal cues are just as important as what clients say—sometimes more important, because they are more truthful."

Sue picks up the telephone to return one of the many stacked messages on her desk when I say, "Ah, so buyers *do* lie?"

She stops what she is doing and puts the phone down. "Not on purpose. Most people have no idea what it is they want. They have a hard time deciding what to order from a menu, so how can you expect them to make a decision when it comes to buying a house? That's why they need professionals, like us, to help guide them. You say your client is divorced? Perhaps Omar wants to be perceived as a 'Family Man,' but underneath he may really be a 'Bachelor Babe.' If that is the case, you could be showing him the wrong type of house."

> **RULE #2-1: CLARIFY WHAT YOUR CLIENT WANTS** Listen carefully to what your clients tell you. But do not stop there. During the sales process ask lots of questions. Observe reactions when you are showing a property, counseling a client and answering their objections. Remember, circumstances are always changing, so an agent's questions should never stop.

I decide to put Omar to Sue's test. On my next tour I include a bachelor pad located in Arch Beach Heights with a sweeping ocean view. A townhouse built in the early seventies; it is nothing like what he tells me he wants. It has paneling and lots of glass and the bedrooms are lofts. But Sue was right—as soon as Omar steps into the living room with the exposed rafter ceiling, wood-burning fireplace and wet bar, his facial expression softens. His eyes scan the full scope of the house. When he's done, a broad smile forms underneath his black moustache. He walks out onto the redwood deck and when he notices the sailboats with their colorful jibs dotting the waves, he clasps his hands together which says to me, "This is what I've been waiting for." Yep, my 'Family Man' really is a 'Bachelor Babe.'

It is late in the afternoon on a Friday and I have been planning a sailing trip to Catalina Island for weeks. Of course, Omar decides he wants to write an offer that night. This is the same guy I have been taking around for months without the least bit of interest in buying anything. I figure if he waited this long, he can wait another few days. "610 Barracuda Way has been listed for a month," I say. "I have plans this weekend, so why don't we wait till Monday to write the offer?"

Omar agrees and I leave for Catalina.

When I walk into the office Monday morning there is a hushed silence as I approach my desk. A sickening feeling grabs at my stomach. I attempt a feeble, "Good morning" but my mouth is dry from embarrassment. All eyes shift downward as people address whatever paperwork lies in front of them. I am hardly there five minutes when Paul Newell approaches my desk with short quick steps, motioning me to meet him in his office.

He shakes his index finger in my face. "Mr. Farad wanted that house and you left him in the lurch! How could you just go off for a weekend and not have anyone cover for you? Boy, are you lucky he is a loyal client and called me to write the offer."

I hang my head in shame, knowing I have made a colossal error in judgment. Paul Newell explains how important it is write an offer immediately. "Buying a home is emotional and spontaneous. A hot buyer can cool quickly and the opportunity to make the sale can be lost."

I feel bad I let a task that had been dragging on and on, fall to the bottom of my to-do list when it should have stayed priority number one. "No one told me this information before," I say, looking down at my hands which are beginning to tremble. "This is my first sales job, you know."

"Paula, it is just common sense. Do you expect to have your clients wait around until you are ready? Like doctors, salespeople have to be available 24/7."

"But he just didn't seem that motivated," I say in defense. "I've been taking him around for months and he hasn't liked anything."

"He liked what you showed him on Friday, didn't he? He did tell you he wanted to write an offer, right?"

"Well, he said he did, but he also told me he wanted a family home and that is certainly not what he bought."

"Paula, if you had asked Mr. Farad why he didn't like the houses you were showing him, you might have gotten some important clues to why he wasn't buying. But what I really want you to understand is this," he points to a clause in the real estate contract written and asks me to read it aloud.

My voice is shaky.

"Louder," he says.

I swallow hard and mumble, "Time is of the essence."

"What do you think that means?" Paul asks, lowering his voice.

"Act immediately—as soon as a buyer's ready," I say, still not willing to look up.

Paul continues slowly. "Okay. Important lesson learned. Next time a client says they want to buy, don't take the weekend off."

As I make my way back to my desk, I try to integrate the impact of Paul Newell's last comment—*that he would take half of my commission for all the work he did to keep the deal together.* I figure the math in my head—the whole commission is 6%. Since Lingo is representing the seller and Newell Associates is representing Mr. Farad, our office's portion is 3%. Since I am a new agent my split with Newell Associates is 50/50 or 1.5% of the sales price. But now Paul Newell is saying he is taking half of that so all I end up with is 0.75% on $150,000. How can I survive on $1,125? I haven't had any income for eight months! Ted expects me to pay my share of the rent, the groceries, the utilities and gas for the car. I feel like going back and telling Paul Newell this isn't fair. It just isn't. Maybe I'll quit. That's right—I don't have to put up with this. I'll go back to research and get paid a regular salary! Then I remember the lab with the furry little hamsters, the men getting all the promotions and the boss constantly leaning over my shoulder. I shudder.

I take a deep breath, grab my things and go for a walk. I need to think all this through. Maybe it is true what Paul Newell said. If he had not been available, Omar would have found someone else to write the offer. Then I would have ended up with nothing. At least I'm getting something. A few days ago I thought having a weekend holiday with Ted was more important. I now realize that what I really want is to be successful in my new job. From now on my plan is to focus on my career. Maybe I'm not a natural-born salesperson, but I still graduated with honors despite the fact that I was not a natural-born student either. I can make this career work.

I know I am ambitious, independent, eager to learn and quick to get bored. From working in the medical field, I also know how important being of service to people is. Becoming a successful salesperson will require forfeiting my own personal plans occasionally, but this job offers me the lifestyle I want. I feel it is worth the sacrifice. I tell myself that gratification is not going to be instant in this line of work. I will just have to learn to be patient

> RULE #2-2: PRIORITIZE Be aware of what you need to do at work and in your personal life. List all the tasks that you are responsible for. Number them in importance. Do not put off important tasks because they are time consuming. When it is not possible for you to be there for your clients, ask a trusted colleague to help you.

Rachel Simmons sweeps into our office one day like a whirlwind. Wispy, shoulder length, strawberry hair frames her angelic heart-shaped face as she gives everyone a wide engaging smile. Her tall angular body and long legs remind me of one of those New York City runway models. She extends a gracious hand as she is introduced around the office and gives the impression that she is more some kind of VIP than a new agent. Whereas my self-esteem has been earned through hard work and accomplishments, hers is completely apparent by the way she moves. How nice it would be to be accepted by just being you and not having to prove anything.

I show her around, take her on tour, and help her with the basic questions any new agent has. We go to the title company parties together—not only to have fun as Paul Newell suggests—his belief being that, "a happy salesperson is a productive salesperson"—but also to start forming our team of professionals i.e., title officers, escrow coordinators, lenders and contractors whom we will rely on during the sales process. "The best way to choose who you wish to work with is to meet them in person," Paul advises. "Besides, networking with other agents is essential so you know your competition up close."

I should have suspected something was amiss when we attended our last office meeting. Paul Newell lauds my praises to everyone present for getting my first listing. Rachel does not sit with me at the meeting and purposely shuns me when I start talking to her. She had a pretty good month so I tell myself she'll get over it. It all seems so high school. Then comes the inevitable day when we both have clients for one of our office's "hot" new listings.

Rachel plans to show the house first, promising she will leave the key underneath the mat. (The listing is so new that the lock box has not even been installed.) I arrive shortly thereafter with my client, James Wallace, a fellow I met at an open house the week before. He was thrilled when I called him. This is the neighborhood—it's close to his family, his friends and his job and is in the price range he wants. Since this will be his starter home, he does not mind that it is small and needs work. He is ready to move. "I've overstayed my welcome with my parents," he says. He has been diligent in saving his money for the down payment. I have a willing and able buyer who has already been pre-approved by a bank. Besides having saved 20% for the downpayment, he also has another 3% saved for closing costs, such as title and escrow fees and building insurance. He also has a 30% debt to income ratio, a good 760 credit score and has been pre-qualified by a bank.

As I fumble for the key underneath the mat, James tells me how appreciative he is that I found something for him so quickly. He steps around to the side of the house, rubbing his hands together. Eagerly anticipating what's inside perhaps? "It needs a little work like I told you, but it's really charming," I say brightly, hiding the disgust I am feeling as gritty dirt is now underneath my newly polished fingernails. I remind myself to remain upbeat, calm and collected. This is a great house and I have the perfect buyer. So what if I have to get a manicure after this? I look up from my awkward pose with a happy face. "You will not be disappointed, I assure you. Just give me a moment." Where is that damn key? Throwing polite decorum to the wind, I toss the welcome mat onto the grass, intensifying my search. "It's got to be here somewhere," I say.

"Paula, are you sure she said the mat? Let's look under the plant boxes," James says. The key is not there either.

Next we try the back door mat and above both doors. The key is just not here. Then we get the smart idea of trying to break inside. We check all the windows, hoping to find one unlocked. There isn't. James tries to pry one open, but I am afraid he will break the glass and tell him to stop. Looking for a solution, I point to the small dog door in the back. "Do you think either of us can fit through that?" I laugh, trying to see the humor in a situation which is making me more uncomfortable by the minute. I glance over at James who is not laughing.

"Paula, I'm really disappointed. I had to call in sick today and left my boss short-handed. It is really difficult for me to get off time from work. Can't you do something?"

"I am sure there's been some misunderstanding. Let's go back to the office. Perhaps Rachel left the key there," I say, making sure I remain positive. I hop in my car, praying that I misunderstood Rachel somehow. James follows in his as we drive back to the office.

No key there and no Rachel. I ask around the office checking if anyone has seen her. No one has. I leave a message for her at the front desk and one at home. I shrug my shoulders as James gives me a reproachful look and heads out the office door. "Call me as soon as you find out," he says.

"I promise," I say as I wave farewell and put on a happy face, wondering if this is the last time I will ever see him.

Rachel never calls me back. The next day I ask about the key when I see her scurrying around the office with paperwork flying here and there. My suspicions are confirmed when she says, "My client wanted to write an offer so why should you bother showing it—it would have been just a waste of time!" I feel the blood rising to the top of my temples and turn away lest I say something I will regret later. That's it! I don't care how pretty she is—our friendship is nothing more than past tense.

With Paul Newell's permission I move my things to another desk and ask him to do something, hoping for some sort of compensation. "I cannot undue what is already done Paula. The house is sold. Money has already been placed in escrow. Remember, as agents we are not officially part of the contract—we are only the bridge between the buyer and the seller."

"But what if my buyer wanted to pay more," I say, exasperated over this unfair treatment of my client.

"That's unfortunate. But to tell a seller now might mean a lawsuit involving not only two of my agents, but also the listing agent. A law suit would be a black mark against our company and you wouldn't want that, would you Paula?"

"Of course not," I say. "I just feel like I've been screwed—especially after all the help I've given her." Maybe I should not be so explicit with my wording, but I'm upset and I want Tim to know that.

"Be more careful next time and call the listing agent directly. I will say something to Rachel, but keep in mind she is young and inexperienced. You have plenty of deals."

"That's not the point. What she did isn't ethical."

"That's conjecture only. She told me she was so excited that she just plain forgot about leaving the key." I look up, trying not to show my pain. Tim gets up from his chair and gives me a warm handshake and an encouraging wink. "Fine—it's all settled then."

James does not return my calls for several days. When I finally reach him he tells me he has found another real estate agent who is more reliable. I am back pounding the pavement, looking for business to replace the sale I lost. I walk my neighborhood, hold open houses, send out mailers and get as much floor time as I can. I do my best not to get discouraged—remembering the success of my newly acquired listing. I realize there are those agents who will do anything to make a deal—kind of like cheating in college—and management is reluctant to get involved with what they consider petty problems. So the sharks stay and the rest of us fish try to keep out of their way.

RULE #2-3: BE CAREFUL WHO YOU TRUST A pretty smile does not give a person character. There are unscrupulous people in all businesses. It is your job to discern who you can trust and you cannot.

CHAPTER THREE

TENACITY
Overcoming Obstacles

R EAL ESTATE SALES are based on a sink or swim mentality. Paul Newell is a competing manager and does not have the time or the inclination to teach me much. I have to learn by observing the other agents. I listen to how agents in the office talk on the phone, set up appointments and close deals. Once I understand the process, I will have to count on simple trial and error. To help take the guess out of the equation, I join the local MLS to take their introductory class. Now when I am introduced to a potential home buyer, I can search the MLS system and retrieve information about all homes for sale in a given area and price range. This entitles me to weekly updates on recent sales as well. This will help me suggest to my sellers a more accurate market sale price. I go on tour and learn the neighborhoods. I attend the weekly meetings and take notes. I go through the forms in the office and familiarize myself with all the different contracts. Still, it is not enough.

To be successful, I will need the help of an expert. When Sue Bates asks if anyone would like to accompany her to a sales seminar, I volunteer. The cost is two hundred dollars and, although it is beyond my budget, I know I need to get my business rolling. Sue tells me the speaker, Tommy Hopkins, is the best in the business—a multi-millionaire dollar producer, who truly shares his secrets. Like any motivated buyer, I am ready, willing and able to do whatever is necessary to get what I want—success as a top producing real estate agent.

I can still remember that stuffy auditorium in LA, bursting beyond capacity with over five hundred people. Certainly no fire marshals here. Just rows and rows of eager salespeople wanting to improve their game. Sue and I finally find two seats together in the middle of all this madness. We are forced to climb over people's legs to get seats, juggling our coffee containers like accomplished trapeze artists. We stretch our necks over peoples' heads to get a glance of Tommy, striding from one side of the stage to the other, bellowing out his sales techniques. But I don't care. I am mesmerized. Tommy Hopkins is so full of charisma, so confident, so arrogant, that I know if I follow what he says, I will be successful.

He tosses us a few nuggets of wisdom: We have to get clients to like us first. Only then will they consider doing business with us. We do that by building on whatever we have in common. Whether it is playing tennis, raising children or going to church. Next nugget of wisdom—sales is a numbers game. The more people you connect with, the better chance you have in getting a listing or landing a buyer. Listings are golden, Tommy says, because you have a signed agreement with the seller who is now tied to you. Buyers, however, are not so loyal. You can work with them for months, but they can jump ship and buy through someone else at the last minute. At the very least, Tommy explains, get your buyers to make a verbal commitment to you. A broker can obtain a Buyer Retainer Form from the local MLS and ask the buyer to sign it, but most buyers are too apprehensive to do so. Only the top-echelon agents can insist on a written commitment. His last and most precious nugget: Most of all remember—*Time is money.*

The whole new world of sales is opening up for me. Pumped up after the seminar, I request more floor time. This means I am spending time at the front desk where I get first dibs on all inquiries—people calling in or walking in off the street. These potential clients know to come to us, because they have seen our newspaper ads, a *For Sale* sign on a property or perhaps were referred to us through a previous, satisfied customer. With the sales skills I learn from Tommy Hopkins, I hope to make an appointment and turn potential buyers into paying clients. Tommy Hopkins says the statistics are one in eight of getting the first appointment and then one in four of turning this potential client into a sale.

Another way of landing new clients is the *Open House.* Again the statistics are discouraging—one in ten. Despite these numbers, this works to my benefit because I am more engaging face-to-face than over the phone. I tell everyone in the office that I am available to host open houses. The most lucrative way to get business, Tommy says, is cold calling on listings which never sold. The properties appear in the Multiple Listing Book as Expired. Few people take the time to do it, so the odds are more in my favor—one in seven.

This is how I find a three-bedroom house in *Top of the World*. I got to know this family neighborhood well during my intensive search with Omar, so I feel fairly knowledgeable in pricing. These rudimentary boxy tract houses are not the renovated beach homes I drool over, but for me—a beginner—it is a good place to start. The owner is a woman, so I figure she will be less threatening for my first call. I review the cold call sales script Tommy Hopkins suggested we use and dial the phone.

"Hello, Mrs. Burns. My name is Paula Pagano. I noticed that your property has expired. I wondered if I could stop by and tell you what Newell Associates has to offer."

"Who is this again?"

I find myself stumbling for words. "Can I come by and take a look at your house? No cost or obligation, of course," I say (I heard one of the other agents say that and it sounded good). She doesn't think a visit is necessary. I follow it up with another question. "Did your previous agent advertise on a regular basis? Did he hold open houses and Broker Tours?" Mrs. Burns is vague and noncommittal. "Well," I say, "I have a marketing plan which will knock your socks off!" (Again, a line I heard a senior agent use.) Mrs. Burns tells me to call her another time.

My call feels like a dismal failure. I am so unprepared for the rejection I feel, that I gather up my things and go home. I stay in bed for two days, watching reruns of *Dr. Kildare* and wondering if medical research might still be a possibility for me. I actually spend a day looking through the classified job opportunities for another career. Seeing nothing, I decide to give real estate another chance.

But I still need guidance. As inspiring as Tommy's seminar was, one seminar is not nearly enough. I ask Sue if she would be willing to share some of her marketing ideas. She shows me that she brings a full resume to her sales presentations. I follow suit, compiling a resume with my educational background, job experience and hobbies, slanting it as much as I can towards sales. Sue also advises me to ask the secretary for promotional material on our company that I can show to potential customers.

I stop by the MLS office and get some information on *Top of the World*—the school district, public transportation, neighborhood activities. It is the only subdivision in Laguna, so any home located outside of this area will not be a statistic I can use. I can hear the well-worn phrase *Location, Location, Location* echoing in my head. It is what Anthony School, Paul Newell and Tommy Hopkins all stress when determining what a property is worth. Only after a location has been valued do other factors come into play, such as the condition of the property, square footage, room count, architectural style and amenities—view, fireplace, updated systems, such as, air conditioning and thermal pane windows.

I compile the data of three-bedroom houses. My analysis has three parts: houses which have sold in the past six months, those currently on the market and the ones which, like Mrs. Burns's, have recently expired. The first figures give me the range of sale prices; the second, the competition we are up against and the third, homes which are overpriced and don't sell. Since there are so few houses for sale in *Top of the World,* I check out four-bedroom houses as well. I also include sales made in the last year. Once I have data on six to ten homes, I will be ready to talk to Mrs. Burns.

Mrs. Burns has said I can call another time. Maybe she was trying to get me off the phone when she said it—but maybe not. Tommy says you have to hear the word No at least five times before you give up on a sales prospect. Most agents give up after only three. Before I call Mrs. Burns, I go over my notes once again. My notes say: "Don't stay on the phone too long and don't give away all your expertise. You want them to need you." I remind myself I am just practicing with Mrs. Burns. I then tell myself no one ever died from hearing the word No. "Don't take everything so seriously," I say, all of a sudden realizing I am speaking out loud. I smooth out the script in front of me and notice my hands trembling. Still shaking, I pick up the phone and dial Mrs. Burns' telephone number. She answers.

"Good day, Mrs. Burns! It's Paula Pagano from Newell Associates. We talked last week. I want to share some interesting sale statistics with you and wondered if now would be a good time?"

"Oh, yes, Paula . I remember you. I've had quite a few calls from agents this past week. Everybody wants the listing, but I'm not sure if I want to sell now or not" (Tommy said this might happen). "What exactly is it you want to share with me?"

"Well, Mrs. Burns (I make sure I use her name a lot in the conversation), most of the homes in your neighborhood sold, but yours and one other did not. I think there may be a connection."

"Really? How so?"

Well, now I have her interest. "I'd like to meet in person so I can show you."

"You can't just tell me over the phone?"

"I'd prefer not to if that's okay with you. I promise I won't pressure you. I think you'll find this information helpful in making your decision."

"Really?"

"Mrs. Burns, it sounds to me like you have a bit of an accent. Where are you from originally?"

"Dorset. Dorset, Vermont. I'm surprised you noticed. I've lived in California over twenty-five years." Okay, now here's my connection.

"Well, I'm your close neighbor. I'm originally from upstate New York," I say, happy to find a common thread, no matter how slight. "Is it all right if I come by some time today to show you what I found?"

"Well, today doesn't work, but why don't you swing by later in the week? I'm home most days. Gotta go now, Paula."

Well, at least she remembered my name. Tommy Hopkins maintains rapport can only be established in person. I need to get a face-to-face meeting with her. I stop by her house several times and on my third attempt I find her there. She opens the door in jeans and a worn apron. She is older than I expected, her brown hair tinged with gray, her soft blue eyes surrounded with deep-set wrinkles. She remembers our phone call and invites me in. In the living room, she keeps glancing at my marketing packet. I'm glad I took the time to get a manicure to cover up the nail biting I've been doing the past week.

"So, Paula, what is it you wanted to share with me?"

I open my packet and hand her a copy of the comparable listing. "This house is the one that didn't sell," I say, handing over a sales sheet. "Like your house, it has only a bath and a half. The other properties which sold in your price range had two full baths."

"So? I can't change that," Mrs. Burns says.

"No, but maybe a buyer can." I take a breath and continue on. "That's why I wanted to stop by and take a look at your house."

"Oh, I see. Why don't I show you around then?" She ushers me inside.

Clients want to do business with people who they like and trust, echoes in my mind as I step across the threshold. "Mrs. Burns you certainly have a knack for decorating. I love the paint color you chose here in your living room." She gives me a wide smile. I make sure our eyes meet. I scan the room, looking for something else positive to say. I do my best not to focus on the floor where a mustard shag carpet offends my aesthetic senses. I don't want to lie, but need to say something. She'll know I'm being insincere if I praise the rugs or the drapes, so I point to some photos on an end table. "And who—may I ask—are these little people?"

"My children. Do you have any kids?"

"No, but my brother and his wife just had identical twin boys. What a joy children are." I remember to emphasize, not our differences, but what we have in common. Thank you, Tommy!

"Ummm," is all she says. She looks tired. This could be my segue into getting the listing. Relieve her of the stress of selling her house.

"So what are your children doing now?" I ask.

"They are long gone, living their own lives." She seems sad.

"Why do you think your agent wasn't able to sell your house?" I remember Tommy telling us to ask that question. I don't want to make the same mistakes the first agent made.

"I don't think he ever really liked my house. Besides, he was pretty busy. He has a lot of houses for sale in the neighborhood."

Well, at least I'm a woman. That has to be in my favor. "It sounds to me like you need a woman's touch," I say, and quickly add, "Plus, right now I'm in between listings. Your house will be the only house I'll be marketing."

"That's a relief," she says as she shows me the half-bath.

"A buyer could easily put a shower here," I say, as I point to the linen closet next to the bathroom. "In fact, I think there used to be a shower here. Look at this! " I show her the patched plaster.

"There was. It kept leaking, so when the kids moved out I thought it better to just take it out and put in a closet."

"Well," I say, "I think we've solved the main problem of why your house didn't sell. This is an easy fix. It is likely that the buyer for your home will have children, so they will welcome an additional full bath."

I let Mrs. Burns lead the pace of the conversation while she shows me the rest of the house. Although it doesn't show that well, she is immensely proud of her home. The drab earthy tones and oversized furniture are making me claustrophobic. She offers me a cup of tea and motions for me to sit down on her overstuffed (and over-worn) green couch. From the living room I can see the avocado appliances in the kitchen. Well, she certainly loves that pea green color. In spite of all the drawbacks of this home, I'm thinking what a nice lady Mrs. Burns is. She certainly likes my idea of restoring the bathroom. This sales job isn't as hard as I thought. In fact, I'm beginning to like being a Realtor. Noticing I'm beginning to drift, I give Mrs. Burns an engaging smile. I'm wondering when to ask the million dollar question—"How about signing with Newell Associates?"—when Mrs. Burns breaks the silence.

"Paula, I really like you, but both my sister and I are owners and she is away for the weekend. What shall we do?"

I say, "Why don't we wait until your sister gets back? I'll leave my marketing packet here for your review. You can show it to your sister and I'll call you Monday morning." My plan is to bring the Exclusive Right to Sell Agreement the next week for Mrs. Burns and her sister to sign. That contract would officially employ me and my agency to market the house.

Like a robot I get up and head to the door. Something doesn't feel right. I can't wait to get out of there. Surely that is not how Tommy Hopkins would have handled the situation, I tell myself as I drive home. I should have brought the agreement with me and had Mrs. Burns sign it. What happened to the assertive nature I take such pride in? I had the listing and threw it away. I might as well have tossed my commission into a garbage can!

When I confide to Paul Newell the details of the interview, he rolls his eyes in disbelief. "Paula, I want you to high tail it back up there and get the listing agreement signed—one signature's better than nothing." I call several times over the weekend, but Mrs. Burns's telephone just rings and rings. I stop by twice, but no one is home. On Monday morning, when I call, as promised, Mrs. Burns tells me how sorry she is, but her sister has another agent in mind.

I had a good chance of representing Mrs. Burns in the sale of her home, but I did not have the confidence to make the deal. Could it have been that I was afraid? Or did I feel I didn't deserve success? I was convinced that it was no coincidence that I did not get the opportunity to market Mrs. Burns's house. I promised myself I would never be that unprepared again.

RULE #3-1: BE PREPARED TO TAKE THE ORDER Plan ahead by bringing all the necessary paperwork with you to appointments. Most importantly, be emotionally prepared if clients are willing to move forward.

Ever since I requested more floor time from Paul Newell, I sometimes find myself alone in the office, manning the front desk, while everyone else is enjoying Laguna's gorgeous weather. It is another beautiful day at the beach. I agree to cover for the floor person who went home early because of a headache. Everyone else has other plans. I am sure they are all down at *Las Brisas* having piña coladas and feeling the soft tropical breeze of the ocean. Tired from a full week of touring houses and answering the endless phone calls, I am tempted to close early. In spite of my fatigue, another part of me is determined to make this job work.

A few minutes before five, a short balding man in his forties pushes through the door. He is muttering under his breath about all the real estate offices being closed this Friday afternoon. He introduces himself as Alan Davenport, and he is curious about the market. He and his wife are moving here with their three kids in six weeks. He is unsure whether to buy or rent. Luckily the rental agent isn't here—otherwise she would sweep him up like a whirlwind. Now, at least, I have a chance.

I sit Alan down for a quick counseling session, asking him about his new job, the size of his family and their basics requirements. (Tommy said to be sure you qualify your clients before you show them houses.) "What about your current home do you like? Anything you don't like? If money weren't a problem, what would your perfect home be?" While asking all these questions, I am taking copious notes. Once in a while I look up and nod for that personal connection.

My legwork for Mrs. Burns's house is going to pay off, I think to myself. Researching all those three and four bedroom family homes in *Top of the World* last month familiarized me with the houses Alan Davenport would want to see. *You can't sell something you don't know.* I zero in on two possibilities which we can see today. "They are both located on the flat part of the ridge overlooking the ocean. It is a perfect family neighborhood called *Top of the World,* and each has four bedrooms, three baths and a large yard. Plus, the best school district we have here in Laguna."

Alan talks slowly, rolling his vowels as he speaks. "Well, you see my wife's not with me."

I'm not giving up quite yet. He still seems like a real buyer. I show him the photo of the less expensive house. "It just came on this week. I hear the seller has been transferred and needs to sell quickly. A house priced this well does not last long." When he does not respond, I ask, "What's the harm in looking?" I flash him my best smile. He goes for it.

We tour the one house while I make sure that I point out all its positive features while asking his opinion, just as Tommy told us to do. "What do you think about the floor plan? The living room with fireplace? How do you like the large country kitchen with all the newly appointed appliances?" When I get a sense that this house may be a match for Alan, I can precede to the *Tie-Down* questions.

Alan tells me the floor plan works for his three kids, the closets are big enough and the eat-in kitchen is great for family breakfasts and Sunday brunches. His wife is a cook so would love definitely love the kitchen. He takes his time and examines the stove, dishwasher and trash compactor. I can tell he's interested.

The next set of questions will get Alan more committed to the property every time he answers Yes.

"Wouldn't your kids love this yard with the swing set? It's a lovely view of the canyon, don't you think? Can't you imagine having great barbecues on this deck?" I ask, anticipating a positive response from each question, I am "tying him down."

He takes the bait and answers *yes*. Yep, I am on my way to selling him this house. On the way back to the office I decide a direct, open-ended question is the best close. "So, Mr. Davenport, what do you think about the house?" He does not answer right away. I start to speak and stop myself. A salesperson's biggest mistake is talking too much.

"I'm concerned that my wife isn't here with me. I think she'd like it, but I'm not sure. Buying a home is a big decision."

This is a valid objection and may be the stumbling block for me in making this sale. I try the *Alternative Close* by asking, "Which would be worse—to have no home at all, or one that is not quite perfect?" (When using "or" in a question it gives the client a feeling he has a choice. It really is a bit of a set up, because I only give him two choices—this is an *Alternative Close*. In real life there are usually more than two possibilities.)

"No home at all," is his answer.

"We can't have that, can we?" I say, using another *Tie-Down* question. As we walk up the steps to the office, my mind is working hard on how to get his signature on the contract. I know he is vacillating between buying and renting so I need to emphasize the advantages of owning:

1) *Paying a mortgage is better than a savings account, because you can't withdraw it easily.*

2) *Rent money is money down the toilet—you will never see any of it again.*

3) *You will save additional money by getting significant tax breaks.*

4) *You can modify and decorate the home to meet your needs.*

5) *Because of inflation and a limited supply of good beach property, chances are you will get good appreciation on your investment.*

6) *Unlike stock, 80 % of your investment is being financed by a bank.*

"With your permission, I am going to borrow Ben Franklin's method for just a moment. (As one of the founders of our country he often made tough decisions by listing the pros and cons of an argument. Franklin was such a good negotiator that he was able to convince the government of France to join us against the English in the Revolutionary War. Without them we would never have won our independence and would not be where we are today. No wonder sales classes teach his technique!) I list the above six points then continue adding the positive features of the home:

7) *The good school district*

8) *The sundeck*

9) *The four bedrooms and two and a half baths*

I stop mid-way through my long list, remembering that Tommy said it is even more powerful when you let the prospect list the items themselves. Whatever they write down will obviously be the pivotal points to what is important to them. What I think is important may be not be the same as what a client thinks is important. I hand Alan Davenport the pen. "Here, why don't you write down specifically what you liked about the house." He takes the pen from my hand and writes down the following:

10) The updated kitchen

11) The safe neighborhood

12) The two car garage

13) The large yard with jungle gym

14) The view

"Anything you want to add in the negative column?" I ask, offering no suggestions this time. Tommy Hopkins said clients do not need any help with this part. They will have enough of their own reasons not to buy. So when Alan tells me he thinks the master bedroom is a bit small, I say nothing as he writes this down. Alan then says he does not like the carpet.

"Well, changing the carpet is easy," I say. "We can either ask the Seller to replace it or ask for a credit." My voice is casual and light— I am feeling positive. In fact, Alan voicing an objection or two is a good sign, because now I know he is actively considering buying. If he is looking so closely to notice this small detail, he is serious.

RULE #3-2: LISTEN CLOSELY TO OBJECTIONS When a client starts voicing objections to a property that means s/he is seriously considering buying. Listen to what they are saying. Respond if there is a simple solution and remain calm and objective while they process the fact that the house may not be perfect.

When he is finished writing, I ask for the paper and go back to emphasizing the positives of what he just told me. "Let's not forget the family friendly yard you can enjoy all year round. And the ocean view—I bet you don't have views like this in Minnesota, do you?"

Alan had to admit he did not. I am hoping he is thinking that the size of the bedroom and shade of the carpet are not so important. Who wouldn't love it here? It was ten below last week where he's from. "This is typical weather for us," I say as I point outside to the swaying palm trees. "It is almost eight o'clock in the evening and still balmy warm weather. You don't even need a sweater and since we're by the beach, it hardly ever gets too hot. A real paradise, don't you think?" Those *Tie-Down* questions are invaluable!

He nods.

It is time for me to ask for the order. "So as far as an investment you couldn't do better—strong demand and a limited supply. I would hate to see you lose an opportunity here".

He nods again.

"Plus, by owning your home, you will have complete control of your destiny. You won't be at the mercy of some landlord who gives you and your family a thirty day notice to move out and find someplace else to live."

"I get only thirty days?" His calm demeanor suddenly shifts to serious concern. "I travel a lot—what if I'm away on business?"

"Only thirty days. That's it. Who wants to be at the mercy of some fickle landlord? Personally, I don't think it is worth the risk—with a family and all." I open my briefcase and start filling out a purchase contract.

"What are you doing?" Alan asks.

"Just filling out some paperwork." I am doing exactly what Tommy Hopkins told me to do. Never say contract, signature or anything technical. Keep it light and simple. "I'll need your approval, of course. Why don't you help yourself to a cup of coffee while I finish? It will only take a minute or two."

Price is the biggest objection for most sellers. I show Alan some comparable sales with higher asking prices. He is still hesitant. I try a contingency close. "If you could get this house for $10,000 less, would you be willing to give him a bid today?"

"Okay, but I won't pay a penny more."

"Mr. Davenport, please don't tell me what you will or won't take. During the negotiating process, anything can happen. Let's just take it step by step, okay?" I smile as I say this. I don't want him fixated on any particular price. We can close this sale, if I can keep him open to the negotiating process.

He agrees. A little back and forth with the seller over the weekend, and Alan Davenport is the proud owner of a new home in *Top of the World*, Laguna Beach. His wife couldn't be more pleased.

Rule #3-3: Keep Asking For C4ommitment You need to be willing to hear the word No at least five times before you make the sale. If clients say No when you ask for a commitment, rephrase the question. If they continue to say No, find an excuse to meet with them again. Most agents can hear the word No only two or three times. Be the exceptional salesperson.

Alan Davenport was my first independent sale, which gave me lots of confidence. As a result, I doubled my efforts. Imagine my excitement when I got a call from Rex Whitworth, asking me to help him find a home on the recommendation of Grace Elliot, a fellow Realtor from Bakersfield. I had met her at a Relocation Seminar and given her my business card, following it up with a short note a few weeks later. Rex and his boyfriend, Sandy Quinn, are both good looking, charming and financially approved by a bank. If they were straight, I would be happy to date either of them. Rex, a city urban planner, looks a bit like Michael J. Fox, but more fit because he gets up early every morning to row with his crew. Sandy is older, probably in his mid-forties, dark complexioned, well-built and bearded. I can hear my girlfriends saying, "What a waste—too bad they're gay!" Being from a straight-laced Catholic upbringing, I am forced to learn about the gay lifestyle on the job, because so many of the professional men drawn to California are homosexual. When I meet Rex and Sandy for our counseling session, they tell me they want a two-unit building.

"Looking at your combined incomes, I don't see that you have to limit yourself to a multi-family building. You can also afford a single family home," I say.

"It is not because we need the income," Sandy says in his sexy baritone voice.

"What is the reason then?" I ask.

They both shift uncomfortably in their seats and share an intimate glance. I realize I have asked a question that has intruded on their privacy. I am perceptive enough not to intrude further. Finally, Rex pipes up. "We don't want our families to know we are living together."

"Oh, well in that case… " I mumble, "Let's only look at duplex units then." I open up the MLS listing book and forge ahead, now that I have important information to help them locate their dream home. We identify some possibilities and start looking at units. I find a two-unit on the periphery of the gay district that meets all their criteria. Thinking they are ready to write an offer, I call Liz McEvoy, the listing agent, to find out all the particulars: How much action the property has had, why the seller is moving, any pertinent disclosures/inspections and length of the escrow period. Liz answers all my questions, letting me know that she will be presenting an offer later this afternoon. Lucky I called. When there are multiple offers, closing a deal can be a foot race—the first agent who produces the signed acceptance wins. If I hadn't checked with the listing agent ahead of time, we might have written an offer on a property that already had sold. I didn't want to make that mistake!

Knowing that someone else also wants this property gives Rex and Sandy the confidence to move forward. I take out the contract (which I now always carry with me) and write it on the roof of my car. When Rex asks if they have to go to full asking price, I ask, "How badly do you want this?"

His response—"We want it."

"Then we have to show the seller we are serious," I say.

"So that means we meet their asking price?" he asks.

"We meet their asking price and we offer good terms," I tell him. I ask Sandy and Rex to come with me as I drive to Liz's office. I have them wait in the car while I present the offer. This is a precaution in case I need their signatures on a counteroffer. Liz and I talk briefly about my clients and discuss the terms of their offer. The closing has all happened so quickly that I have been unable to obtain a pre-qualifying letter from a lender, but assure Liz she will have it tomorrow (Darn! Next time I will have this detail done before I start showing property). Since Liz has already presented one offer to her clients that afternoon, they respond to our offer immediately. They decide to take the first offer. Liz explains that the first set of buyers had lost a few properties and wrote a seamless offer with no loan condition. Plus, they wrote a hand written letter to the owners with snapshots of their family, assuring them that they would take good care of their new home. I had never thought of doing that! With slumped shoulders and head down I leave the house to meet my clients.

Rex and Sandy stumble out of the car, wanting to know what happened.

"The other party got the house," I say.

"Really? We didn't know we had to go over the asking price to get it." Rex, as usual, is his calm low-key self in spite of the disappointing news.

Sandy starts to get indignant. "They wouldn't even counter us? That's downright rude!"

"Sellers can choose how they want to respond," I say. "They had an offer already. They can counter both offers or accept one on the spot."

"But we offered their asking price and good terms!" Sandy shakes his head in disbelief. Rex talks to him in a low soothing voice.

"Our price just wasn't good enough." Rex then turns to me. "Why didn't you advise us to give the seller more money?"

"I guess I should have asked Liz more pointed questions," I say, still amazed that we were knocked out so fast. "We came into this listing late, and the other buyers had time to prepare." I share with them what Liz had told me. "The truth is even if we came in higher I don't think we would have gotten it. These buyers got all the inspections done ahead of time and wrote a letter to the sellers, telling them how much they loved their property. They even included snapshots."

"Snapshots? Snapshots of what?"

"Of them, their kid and their dog."

"You're kidding! Why would they do that?" Sandy exclaims, still in shock over losing the property.

"To get the sellers to connect with them, I guess." Because I liked Rex and Sandy so much, I decided to impart the valuable lessons in this dismal turn of events. "Sometimes a sale is not always about the most money. If sellers have sentimental memories of the house they are leaving, they often want to sell to someone who they like. Someone who loves the house the way they did."

"Well, next time we'll do things differently," Rex says. He smiles broadly. "The next time we'll be so well prepared that we'll come out the winner! Keep looking, Paula. We are more interested than ever." Sandy shrugs his shoulders, so it seems I am still their real estate agent. Doesn't Tommy Hopkins say, *Learn to fail effectively?*

The next home they choose is a Spanish style, solidly built in the 1930's, with several subsequent additions. This particular property has been on the market for months. In the real estate business, this is called a sleeper, because it has been on the market so long. So it is either overpriced or seriously flawed. At least, I hope, it is unlikely that Rex and Sandy will be outbid on this one. Lesson learned, Rex and Sandy of course write a personal letter to the seller. We make a contingent offer–one that is subject to an inspection of the property's condition before the buyer proceeds with the loan. I bring a bottle of champagne along to the inspection, figuring Rex and Sandy will be celebrating the sale with me before I head east for vacation.

All the galvanized plumbing has been replaced with copper. The wiring has been updated to circuit breakers with 220-volt service in the kitchen and laundry room. The foundation of the house is sturdy. The pan-and-cover barrel roof with its dark crimson clay tiles passes with flying colors. So far so good. We get to the kitchen which has been extensively remodeled. The listing agent had assured me that although the seller did not get permits for some of the work, it was not important. Now I want the opinion of an independent expert.

"You don't need permits for these simple renovations, do you?" I ask, feeling a little nervous.

"Sure do," Ed Stephens, the contractor, answers matter-of-factly.

"It's my understanding that if appliances are just replaced you don't need a permit," I persist, wondering where Rex and Sandy are. Probably placing their furniture in the living room.

"That's true. But in this case there's been extensive remodeling."

"Really?" I say. "How can you tell?"

"All you have to do is trace the old electrical and plumbing routes." Ed taps the end of his pencil on his temple a few times.

"Oh," I say, happy Rex and Sandy aren't around to see this exchange.

Ed proceeds downstairs to the second unit, which is now becoming a looming concern for me. If the seller didn't get permits for the kitchen, would he have gotten the permits for the two-bedroom garden apartment? I wonder. I follow Ed down the creaky back stairs. I call to Rex and Sandy to follow. As awful as the outcome may be, they need to hear all this for themselves. The good and the bad. Looking at the second unit this time around, it does feel like an impromptu addition. Ed does not say anything, but scribbles unintelligible notes on his pad. I am too intimidated to ask what he is noting. Besides, I tell myself, I will surely find out soon enough. I shift my attention to Rex and Sandy who are still smiling ear to ear. I joke about what a great Christmas present they are getting for each other.

Then Ed asks for the permit history. I hand him a copy of the building record. Now I wish I had taken the time to review the material with my manager. Then I'd understand more what the permit history revealed about the legality of the unit. He takes his time to read it thoroughly. My suspicions are confirmed when Ed announces in his brisk non personal style, "It is not just the kitchen and bathrooms that don't have permits, but the whole second unit. I hope the city doesn't get wind of this." Ed hands the paperwork back to me as he prepares to make his exit.

I turn to Rex and Sandy. "Maybe we should talk to one of the city inspectors directly?" Rex gives me a disgruntled look which I take seriously, because he is usually so agreeable.

"I don't need a second opinion," he says.

But asking questions is the name of the game. I may be uncomfortable, but it won't pay my rent or my vacation which I have been planning for four months. "You're not going to let the fact that the unit is illegal get in the way of buying this property, are you?" I ask, making sure I smile. "We can always ask for a credit from the seller." As soon as I say this I am sorry. Again I realize I asked an inappropriate question. I need to back off and soften my approach.

Rex's jaw is tight and his voice deliberate as he turns to face me. "Paula , I do not want to buy a property which may require us to correct for possible code violations. Not only would it be a hassle for us logistically and financially, but it could jeopardize my standing with the City Council. It is just not worth the risk."

Then Sandy pipes up. "I am so sick of living in my small apartment—can't we make some sort of deal with the city?"

I look to Rex. This is not a time for me to put pressure on. Rex must come to his own decision whether to buy or not. His voice is low and his demeanor steadfast. "This is not the property for us, Paula. We are not approving the contractor's inspection. Draw up the necessary paperwork."

"I guess that's our answer then," Sandy says as he gets in the car.

Another transaction down the tube! I do my best not to let it get me down as I cancel our escrow, postpone my trip back east and continue my search for another property. It is close to the holidays, so there is little inventory. Finally, I have motivated clients, who are ready to go, but no property to show them. I don't want them getting so discouraged they end up going to another agent. I have to keep moving this process forward. Desperate, I need to look beyond what is currently listed in the MLS.

> RULE #3-4: DEVELOP PATIENT PERSISTENCE Do not let a few failed transactions obstruct your success. Keep on looking for a solution while you model the qualities of positivity, patience and persistence for your clients.

With the help of a title company and the reverse directory, I get the names and telephone numbers of owners of two-unit buildings which have been up for sale in the last year, but never sold. Some are *For Sale by Owners* (FSBO's) and some are *Expired* (like Mrs. Burns's home). I spend the next two days making cold calls. It is worth all the effort when I finally find an owner who wants to sell his three bedroom Victorian home with a separate carriage house. Richard Benson and his family have already moved to an inland suburb for a better school district. Although he just found some tenants to rent his property, he had not signed the lease yet. "Let me talk to my client before you sign anything," I tell him.

Barely able to contain my excitement, I call Rex and Sandy with news of this property that is perfect for them. The only other caveat, I explain, is that Mr. Benson wants full price. "So?" Rex says. "If it is a good property, we are ready, willing and able to buy." Rex and Sandy are perfect buyers to have, like ripe apples ready to be picked off a tree. They are so anxious to move that they make room in their schedules to see the property the very next day. We are not disappointed. Understanding the importance of time, we meet at a nearby coffee shop to write up the offer. (Traveling with all my forms has proven to be a great boon to my business.) Wanting both parties to sign on the dotted line as soon as possible, I drive to Mr. Benson's house. It is almost a two hour drive away in some nondescript sleepy bedroom community, safe for his young children, but too boring for me to even remember its name.

Richard Benson is a classic anal retentive personality, who finds six tiny changes he must make in the pre-printed contract. I make all the necessary changes. He also insists on having the changes initialed by tomorrow because, as he says, "I can't put my tenant off any longer." It is close to midnight when I call Rex and Sandy.

They pick up immediately. "We've been waiting for your call."

"Mr. Benson made a few small changes—shortening our inspection time frames and stating you are to take the property in *As Is* condition."

"What does that mean?" asks Rex.

"If the contractor finds any defects, Mr. Benson is not willing to pay for any of the work."

"Well, what if we find something major wrong with the building like last time?" Rex asks.

"We still have the option of getting a contractor's inspection," I say. "However, with an *As Is* clause we cannot ask for a credit from the seller." I notice I use *we* a lot. I feel protective over my clients, like a Mother Hen with her chicks, and want them to feel fully taken care of. "By the way," I add, "I already checked with the Planning and Zoning Department. The property is a legal two-unit building and all the permits appear to be in order. Just be aware that no building is perfect—the contractor may find a few things here and there."

Rex says, "Well, we really like the property and will be reasonable, so don't worry. Minor fix-up items don't bother us."

"I'm feeling confident that all this is going to work out," I chirp. "You know what they say—third time's the charm."

"Okay, then. Let's move ahead. Both of us have busy schedules tomorrow. Can you come over now? We'll sign those changes."

"Of course," I say, trying not to gush. "I'm only a few blocks away." I turn up the stereo in my car on the way as Sly and the Family Stone belts out—*I want to take you higher! Higher! Higher!* I sing along. One more sales success story—a double end sale representing both the Buyer and the Seller at a full 6% fee!

CHAPTER FOUR

PASSION
Loving What You Do

IT IS 1961 IN THE DEAD COLD OF WINTER in upstate New York on one of those dark and gloomy overcast days—more toward the end of winter than the beginning. Groundhog's Day has passed and I am sick of tobogganing and making angels in the snow. Most of all, I have come to despise putting on my galoshes, winter coat and mittens whenever I have to go outside. In our fifth grade class, as I sit shivering against the cold coming in from the classroom's drafty paned window, Miss Langley poses a question. I still remember her graying white hair, big bosom and booming voice which echoed off the walls decorated with last week's homework.

She jolts me out of my faraway daydreaming. "Who of you here wants to be happy?"

I am wide awake, sitting upright in the hard backed wooden chair looking straight ahead. It is a peculiar question and I don't know why she asks it. We aren't discussing anything relating to that topic, but she is serious and asks the question again. We all look at each other like deer in headlights. (A common sight in upstate New York.) Not waiting for anyone else, I shoot up my hand. For me, life at home was not that joyful. Mother yells most of time and Daddy—although I adore him—is hardly ever home. When he is, he doesn't want to be bothered by his pesky young daughter. I want my life to be more than it is, so I raise my hand.

"Well, that's too bad, because you will be sorely disappointed," Miss Langley announces, looking directly in my direction. My mouth, I am sure, hangs wide open from surprise. Sorely disappointed?!!

The hope that happiness is just around the corner—that is what keeps me going day after day. Miss Langley, a cranky, no nonsense teacher, who never leaves much room for discussion, continues on about how happiness is some lofty, idealistic impossible goal. I expect some classmate to object. Maybe Kay Rogers? I have always admired her bold confidence in challenging the teachers. I turn around to see if there are any hands in the air, hoping to see Kay's. I wait for her to say something, but she sits empty eyed with her hands on her desk, fiddling with a pencil. Other hands, which I thought went up, are now down. Is mine the only hand that had gone up? I pull it down quickly, going back to the study of obtuse triangles, hexagons and octagons, promising myself I will never let go of my secret dream to be happy—no matter what Miss Langley, Mother or Daddy says.

I think of Mrs. Langley fifteen years later as I feel the soft crystallized sand shifting between my toes, the warm tropical breeze against my face and the taste of the ocean's salt between my lips. I look above, noticing the mesmerizing blue sky with its fluffy marshmallow clouds—It's as if I can almost touch them. And yet somehow... I am so unhappy. What is wrong with me?

I handpicked this charming beach town, because I thought it was the closet thing to paradise. Then when we got here it was me who decided that we should settle in Laguna, not Irvine, the new industrial planned community, where Ted worked. Ted has to commute twenty miles back and forth everyday to work and never complains. But I do.

I put on my sundress over my lavender crocheted bikini and gather up my pink and purple towel. I bought them for their bright, joyful colors, but the new purchases, the beautiful setting around me and my closed escrows are not making me feel satisfied. It is not as if I am some short, fat, dimply gal, who is uncomfortable at seaside resorts either. I can easily compete with the stunningly slim bodies that this consistently gorgeous beach weather attracts. I am a beauty contest winner with a tiny waist, knockout figure and luxurious shoulder length hair. My blue eyes sparkle and my olive complexion takes a tan like no other. I don't like to brag, but I am a healthy twenty-six year old woman with good genes in the prime of my life. Even though most of the Laguna Beach beauties are blonde with twig-like bodies in teeny-weenie bikinis, I don't care. I've got qualities that the anorexics don't have—tons of energy, an inquisitive mind, an adventuresome spirit and big ambitions. Their sole purpose in life is to be a model or marry some rich toad. Sometimes they look at me as if I just stepped off the plane from Mars with my over-the-top excitement, loud voice and Italian-style hand gestures.

Laguna certainly is not anything like where I grew up, but it has a movie theater, a bunch of fun beach bars and a dozen upscale restaurants. Plus, in the summer, it hosts the Festival of the Arts which displays the most exquisite avant-garde art work (all of it good, most of it expensive) and the renowned 'Pageant of the Masters' in which local residents pose in life size picture frames simulating famous paintings. And last but not least, Laguna offers lots of gift shops. Expensive gift shops filled with things I can't afford. But everything has its pluses and minuses, I tell myself—whether it is a town, a career or a relationship.

If Ted and I had not broken up months before, maybe I would be feeling differently about Laguna. But when I was with him, I also was not satisfied. Being ten years older, he was my mentor and had supported me in my decision to get into real estate. This I sincerely appreciated. Unfortunately, Ted did not know how to share. Our car was a constant fight. He always wanted to use it in his commute to the University at Irvine, but I needed it sometimes to show properties. He was a handsome 6' 2" blonde with blue-eyes and, the truth is, if it had not been for Ted, I would not be in California. I owed him. I certainly did not want to be one of those clawing, back-biting women who use men to get to the top, but I did not want to be a wilted wallflower either. But when he forgot our anniversary, I blew my top. I probably overreacted, but that is all history now. I packed up my things, called him at work and told him to come home quick. When he arrived I grabbed the car key—I had bought the car myself in New York before I left and loaded it with my personal belongings and moved out. Maybe Ted and I just are not a match. Like Laguna and me.

> RULE #4-1: FIND YOUR NICHE To be the best you can be, your surroundings should be congruent with your personality strengths, goals and what's most important to you. Take the time to find an environment which will support you on your journey.

I need a boost. I decide a short vacation would help. I remember Maria Gonzales, whom I had met at a party at the University of California at Irvine six months back. She was dark-haired and vivacious (like me) and a nurse by profession. She also had a boyfriend, Lew Brannan, who, like Ted, was an older, successful professional. When Lew and Ted became engrossed in a far corner, discussing some theory of earth-shattering importance, I had Maria all to myself. Looking like Sleeping Beauty with her brunette ringlets, rosy cheeks and voluptuous figure, she told me about her home town, San Francisco, the flower capital of the world, and its diverse culture and people. She spoke of the great places to eat (popular Californian-cuisine restaurants, charming Italian outdoor cafes, authentic French bistros and inexpensive Asian take-outs), the many things to do (plays, stand-up comedy, history walks, wind surfing, poetry readings) and exciting classes (on everything from holistic health to ballroom dancing). She was thinking of leaving Lew and the superficial Los Angeles area and returning to the bustling activity of San Francisco, which she considered a cultured city. She told me of her extravagant evenings at the opera, ballet and symphony, making me envious of those who had the extra money to spend.

"But anyone can go," Maria told me excitedly. "The city made it purposely affordable for everyone. Get there the same day and prices are half-off."

"I don't think I can even afford that," I admitted. "I'm in the midst of changing careers from being a scientist to a salesperson. I am making it, but just barely. I still have a lot to learn in this business before I am successful."

"Well, they have Standing Room tickets too and those cost even less. Just being in that old-world Opera House with its vaulted coffered ceiling and sweeping balconies gives me goose bumps! And if that formality doesn't suit you, there is always free Opera in the Park, free rock concerts at Stern Grove, and tons of free art shows. And the art's reasonable. I have two original watercolors I bought there for under $100!"

I gasped. "That would never happen here."

"Oh, I absolutely agree. It is all about money in L.A. San Francisco is different. It is a city filled with artists, intellectuals and entrepreneurs. Of course, they still have the high society crowd and business people, but they all mix together with the gays, the poets, and other minorities. It has been an open liberal city from its beginnings in the heyday of the Gold Rush."

I remembered the song, *Be Sure to Wear Flowers In Your Hair*, and ask Maria about Haight-Ashbury. "Have you ever been there? What's it like? I still have my bell bottom jeans from college," I said, starting to laugh.

"You know it's funny, but more people know about the Summer of

Love in 1967 San Francisco than know that the United Nations was founded there. I guess the hippies have had more impact on our culture than the older generation would want to give them credit for." Maria suddenly lowered her voice to a quiet whisper when she noticed Ted and Lew approaching. "I have to be careful. Lew doesn't know of my plans just yet. I don't plan to tell him till everything's all arranged. No muss. No fuss. That's the best way."

"Promise me you'll keep in touch," I said as we turned our attention back to our dates.

True to her word, Maria gave me her address when she moved. She had called me several times from San Francisco telling me she made the right decision and how happy she is. Now I hope she will let me stay with her for a week or so. I need to get out of this monotonous town which feels like it is closing in on me. I check the plane fares and there is a special next week. Then I give Maria a call. We arrange for me to stay in her apartment.

The first thing I notice as I get off the plane in San Francisco is the cool moist breeze against my face—a refreshing change from the dry, sun burnt weather to which I am accustomed. I let myself give in to the relaxed frame of mind of being on vacation. Pulling my suitcase behind me, I follow the person in front of me. He gets on a shuttle headed downtown. I do the same, handing the driver a crumbled piece of paper with Maria's address, where I'll be staying. I won't be seeing much of Maria, though. She is in the midst of a hot romance. I am happy for her and don't mind she won't be around. I like exploring on my own anyway. I find the key underneath the mat, let myself in and grab a sweater, some money and good walking shoes. With travel guide in hand, I hop on a bus to a favorite tourist stop—Fisherman's Wharf.

I see the huge sign for Ghirardelli, and recognizing the name of this premium chocolate shop, get off with a gang of other tourists. Fascinated, I watch as a thick and sticky, dark brown concoction is being stirred in a huge metal vat. San Francisco is the place that Domingo Ghirardelli chose to open his first chocolate factory with cocoa beans he imported from South America. I say yes to the sample the sales lady hands me. While I munch away, I ogle the sundaes dripping with hot fudge as they are being delivered to the nearby tables. I check out the rest of the store, displaying chocolate of all shapes and sizes, filled with raspberry, caramel, mint, almonds and more—perfect gifts for my friends in Laguna. Even the vintage photos lining the walls interest me. The short descriptions underneath tell me the history of how an Italian immigrant makes it rich in the confectionary business after failing at gold mining and the exporting business. I'm relating. Perhaps there is hope for me in real estate after all!

Next I take a long walk through the old red brick Cannery which has been converted into a score of gift shops and small restaurants. A man with long hair wearing a purple psychedelic shirt and blue jeans approaches me. A guitar is slung over his shoulder. Under his breath he says, "Smoke. Wanna smoke?" as he passes by me. I can barely hear him.

"I'm sorry," I say. "I don't have any cigarettes."

"I mean—do you wanna buy some? I have some good quality Guava Gold from Mexico." His demeanor is surprisingly gentle.

"Oh, no," I say, startled that someone is selling drugs right on the street.

He gives me the peace sign and a big smile. "Have a nice day," he says and escapes back into the crowd.

A mime is performing on a makeshift stage in the center of the courtyard. He is dressed all in black. He has painted his face and hands stark white and around his mouth, black. He is standing perfectly still, but it has been several minutes and he has not moved an inch. I move closer to get at better look, glancing at the people's reaction around me. Still no movement. Is this it? He is only going to stand there motionless? A young woman with neon bright, orange and blue streaked hair is dressed in a leotard, white petticoat, tights and ballet slippers and is sitting directly in front of me. She is not the *earth momma hippie* I have been looking for, but perhaps something better—a punk rocker? The mime makes a stiff bow to her and tilts his top hat. She giggles. The mime grimaces. The frown is extenuated because of his black colored mouth. He bows again and points to the inside of his hat. An embarrassing silence permeates the audience. Someone finally yells, "He wants you to put some money in the hat." Instead the gal gets on the stage and does several pirouettes to the audience's loud applause. The two then do an impromptu act as people shuffle up and donate money. A few other daring spectators join the two performers, improvising their own personal dances. The feeling of spontaneous creativity is freeing. When there is a half-dozen people on stage, I find the courage to climb up and do my version of the Peppermint Twist, knowing I can't embarrass myself too badly if I don't know anyone.

After several minutes of the pump and grind, I move on to my next adventure. I find myself surrounded on all sides with street vendors displaying their wares: stained glass windows, macramé wall hangings, antique photographs, landscape watercolors, caricature etchings done on the spot, T-shirts, and an assortment of low-end handmade costume jewelry, including puka shell necklaces. This last is the most popular. This guy has two helpers and he can't keep up with the demand. A long line is beginning to form in front of his kiosk. I stop for a moment, trying to figure out why. Even though I am in a touristy mood, I cannot get excited about a string of cheap beads. I ask the couple next to me, "What's the big deal?" The man's bulky frame, cowboy boots and hat and the woman's bouffant hairstyle, pancake makeup and stretch pants tell me they may be from Texas.

"Weren't these beads popular during the Swinging Sixties?" he asks, giving me a wink. He then grabs this woman's amply endowed buttocks, brings her closer to him and plants a big kiss on her lips. They burst into uncontrollable laughter and I join in. Well, San Francisco seems to attract all kinds, I say to myself.

And that is what this city is showing me—all kinds. Besides the assorted artists and musicians, the street people and the punk rockers, the blue collar workers and the business men, there are the wealthy couples flaunting fourteen carat gold pendant necklaces (more the men than the women), the infatuated gays walking hand in hand (again, more the men than the women), and the typical wide-eyed tourist like me. A real melting pot—this is what America is supposed to be like. Feeling the stomach pangs of not having eaten, I buy a circular loaf of sourdough filled with creamy white clam chowder at Alioto's Grotto. I take it to go and plop myself down on a nearby wooden bench, making sure I am not too close to the strong-smelling fishing boats, but close enough where I can watch the seals. I take a taste of the bread which is soft and chewy. It practically melts in my mouth, and combined with the slightly salty soup, it is an epicurean delight. I am in heaven, for, as I eat, I hear a seal barking, taxi horns and conversations humming around me. I notice a majestic red-gold bridge across the water, which I surmise is the famous Golden Gate Bridge, named for its distinctive color. I remember reading about its innovative suspension design and its construction in the thirties— ahead of schedule and under budget. I strain to see the affluent tourist towns across the Bay—Sausalito, Tiburon and Belvedere. Maria has told me that they are quaint, like Laguna, and I might want to take a ferry over to visit. But I don't want to—I love it here! So many things to look at and do. Quaintness just is not on my agenda. I have had enough of quaintness after living in a beach town for two years. I find myself dawdling, vainly hoping to hear San Francisco's foghorns—though today is unlikely because a clear, crystal blue sky hangs overhead.

It is time for another walk. I continue on along the pier. Getting a bit lonesome, I stop and chat with a street artist as he makes jewelry out of gold wire. He tells me his name is Brian Rinsom. I have him make me a name pin in order to prolong our conversation. I am not into this tacky type of jewelry, but Brian's friendliness, easy- going manner and soft gaze of his grayish blue eyes make me want to linger. I show him a postcard I just bought of a row of restored Victorians against the backdrop of the San Francisco skyline. It is one of the classic images of San Francisco. The postcard describes them as the *Painted Ladies,* a small remnant of the 48,000 houses built in the Gold Rush era and still existing after the Great Fire that followed the 1906 earthquake. "Where can I find these?" I ask.

Brian refers to my map, explaining that this now famous row of Victorians is on the other side of town—at least a two bus ride away. I notice he is pointing close to the Haight-Ashbury district. I am excited. I tell him about my experience with the long haired guitar toting street druggist I met an hour before. "Well, now you can tell your friends down South you had an encounter with a real live hippie." He starts to laugh, then adds, "There's really not that much to see in the Haight these days. Sure, you can walk by the Victorian mansions where Janis Joplin, Grace Slick and Jerry Garcia lived, but you can't get inside. You'll see a few old hippies wandering the streets preaching love, peace and social justice while they eke out a living by panhandling, playing music or selling drugs, but that's about it."

"What do you suggest I do now?" I ask, knowing there are plenty of sights around here to see. Brian points to a tall circular tower on a steep hill which has funny shaped windows up top. "Have you climbed up to Coit Tower yet?" he asks.

"What is it?" I ask, never having seen a building shaped like that before.

"It was built in the shape of a fire hose nozzle as a memorial to the San Francisco firefighters after the 1906 earthquake. The funds were provided by a woman of the name of Coit—so—a point for you feminists."

"I never said I was a feminist," I say.

"Well, it seems the rage these days," Brian says. "My last girlfriend was. We just broke up three weeks ago. It got tiring when she wouldn't let me open doors or pay for anything."

"That's interesting." I thought a moment. "My ex and I split partially because he insisted I be a feminist. I wanted flowers, candy and dinner out once in a while, but he thought I was compromising women's rights and so he wouldn't."

"That's his loss." Brian gave me an acknowledging smile. "So you like a man who is chivalrous?" he asks, moving a bit closer.

I nod my head enthusiastically. I notice a hint of twinkle in Brian's eyes. Maybe he's going to ask me out for a date.

"Well, if you like the hippie culture, I'm sure you're into music. How about being a little adventuresome and coming with me tomorrow night to a hip San Francisco night club?"

"That sounds like fun," I say without thinking.

"Have you ever seen a punk rock band?"

I shake my head no.

"It may not be the rock style you are used to, but it has raw energy, a good beat and a lot of feeling. Plus, like the sixties, a lot of intellectual integrity goes into the lyrics, you know, criticizing the establishment—power—authority."

I agree. I figure if Brian is here day after day selling jewelry, he is not some common criminal. I give him Maria's telephone number.

As Brian suggests, I walk the European-flavored neighborhood with its narrow streets, hillside gardens, pedestrian alleys and secluded staircases through Russian Hill to the top of Telegraph Hill. Here, the architecture is more a blend of old-fashioned flats, Edwardians, Art Deco fifties and Contemporary style—some boring and some cutting-edge modern. Most, I imagine, with superb views of the bay and beyond. It feels like I am walking in a living museum.

Occasionally, I spot a Victorian, but there are not too many survivors in this area. Finding a city bench, I pause, opening my guide book, wondering why. I read how Van Ness Avenue was dynamited to prevent the Great Fire from spreading so the majority of the *Painted Ladies* are in the western districts of Haight-Ashbury, Pacific and Presidio Heights. Because the owners of these properties have recognized that their architecture is a commodity, they have gussied up these homes with prefabricated molding, harmonious color schemes, elaborate door frames and leaded and stained glass windows. I glance through the pages, noting the many types of Victorian architecture—Stick, Eastlake, Queen Anne, Tudor and even one called Italianate! These were the most favored style, because they could be constructed with many different building materials, were more affordable and more stylish. New technologies made it possible to produce cast iron decorations for the hooded door and window moldings, the elaborate roof brackets and cornices as well as for the balustrades, balconies and cupolas. The Italians, once again, influence the day-to-day life of people with their aesthetic appreciation—even as far west as San Francisco! I feel a special bond with the architecture of this city. Perhaps, it is because both Dad and my great grandfather were architects; my two uncles real estate developers. My great grandfather I never met, and I hardly knew my uncles, but I conclude that the love of buildings must be in my genes.

Once I reach the top of the tower, I am in for a special treat. Not only do I see an aerial panorama of diverse San Francisco architecture, but I also have a good view of the Bay Bridge with the cities of Oakland and Berkeley clustered at its foot. Mount Diablo looms in the distance. The bay is busy with small tour boats going back and forth. I notice three islands: The one in the foreground, the prison island, the home of Al Capone and the Birdman of Alcatraz, I know. Then there is Angel Island, a state park, and man-made Treasure Island, with its prominent 1939 World's Fair Exposition building. Next I position myself so I can see the Financial District and the distinctive tower of the Pyramid Building, San Francisco's tallest. I take one more lingering look before I start the hike down to my next destination—North Beach. I read how this Italian neighborhood with its assortment of outdoor cafes, restaurants and nightclubs has a very cosmopolitan feel. On the winding streets approaching the Italian commercial district, I notice small spots of greenery with borders of colorful flowers in front of all the houses.

It brings me back to my early memories of the joy Dad got from gardening. Not only did we have a huge vegetable garden on our acre spread in suburbia with rows of corn, squash, cucumbers, peppers, lettuce and tomatoes, but Dad also loved flowers. Our yard had an assortment of irises, tulips, daffodils and gladiolas along the long flagstone walkway and retaining wall surrounding our house (Dad, having that builder gene, constructed those structures himself, along with our modern Frank Lloyd Wright inspired house).

All of a sudden I am on the corner of Columbus and Broadway. I spot a huge four story neon sign which seems like it should be in Las Vegas. It is the Condor Club with a naked silhouette of Carol Doda, famous for her large silicon-implanted bosoms and burlesque 'naughty, but nice' act which she has been performing since the early sixties. During the mid-1800's miners, sailors, and travelers hungry for female companionship sought out the prostitutes and outlandish entertainment along Broadway. The streets are still loaded with girly topless bars, as well as Finocchio's, another famous hot spot, which features fabled female impersonators. These beautiful looking women are men? I move closer. Some of them have long hair—is it their own, I wonder, or a wig? It is hard to imagine with their impeccable makeup, sexy clothes and feminine bodies. A broad shoulder man outside one of the establishments asks if I want to come in and take a look, assuring me I have never seen anything like this before. I assume I have not either and, like a shot out of cannon, head back to safer ground.

Glancing diagonally across the street, I notice the City Lights Bookstore. Recognizing the name, I duck inside to pore over the book selection. I read a blurb on the wall declaring itself as the best independent bookstore in the United States. Browsing through the titles, I find books on poetry, philosophy and politics. Founded in the fifties by the poet, Lawrence Ferlinghetti (another Italian!) the store exemplifies the beatnik's legacy of non-conformity, spontaneous creativity and revolutionary spirit. Although I am curious, I cannot really grasp this alternate intellect culture so I leave. Who the heck is Allen

Ginsberg anyway? The only beatnik I ever knew was Maynard from watching reruns of the TV show *Dobie Gillis.*

I amble down Columbus Avenue, noting the menus posted outside its many Italian restaurants. I wonder if their pasta is as good as what I enjoyed in my childhood—Spaghetti Bolognese, Fettuccini Alfredo, Manicotti, Cannelloni and Lasagna. Mother might have been Irish, but her Italian dishes were unparalleled. To this day no restaurant comes close to Mother's special red sauce, made from our freshly picked garden tomatoes. Observing my surroundings I realize how rich my heritage is—not only are the Italians great planners and builders, but great landscapers and chefs as well. My Italian pride kicks into high gear as I observe the influence of my heritage upon this city.

Suddenly aware that my legs feel like heavy cement blocks, I need to find a place to sit down. I settle into a cozy café called Café Roma with operettas playing in the background and waiters speaking lilting Italian accented English. When I cannot understand what they are saying, the black suited waiters motion in big dramatic hand movements. I walk up to the refrigerated deli case and point to the object of my desire—a thick square of custard cake dusted with dark chocolate called tiramisu. It looks so delicious on my plate I take a photo before I take a bite. Ummmm… reminiscent of the rum-soaked cake Mother served during special religious holidays. A steamy cappuccino with thick milk foam arrives at my table a few minutes later. I reminisce of the few days I spent in Rome before college. Life just does not get any better than this! I daydream further. *What if I could surround myself with this everyday? And work here? What if…*

After a delicious respite, I nose my way into Molinari's Delicatessen, another San Francisco landmark, rich in aromas, tastes and visual delights. Huge bins of olives stand in front of the store. A refrigerated deli case has a wide selection of hard cheeses, cold cuts and ready made salads. A variety of salamis hang from the ceiling. Pasta, most of which they make themselves, come in a variety of shapes and sizes— fusilli, shell, spaghetti, bow tie. Jars of Italian specialties line the tightly-packed shelves. I look for pickled lamb's tongue, Dad's favorite. Wouldn't he just love this place? I buy some strong smelling cheese, pistachio mortadella and a hard-crusted roll for breakfast.

Stepping outside, I notice that the sunny autumn-like weather has changed. The sky has turned grey and a sharp piercing wind is whipping through my sweater. I hug my chest to conserve energy, bend my head against the wind and make my way to the closest bus stop. My next destination before home is the Buena Vista Café for an Irish coffee. Maria said it is a tourist haven and not to be missed. An established San Francisco tradition, the owners had perfected an old Irish recipe—the perfect remedy for the bitter damp air coming off the Bay. Besides, I need to even the score for the other half of my heritage. (My mother's grandparents were from Urlingford, Ireland and had immigrated to New York during one of the potato famines.)

The bar is hopping busy, being a popular stopover for the longshoremen, fishermen and tourists. I push myself past the filled tables, feeling the press of the crowd around me. I spot a solo stool and sit down. I watch three bartenders line up half a dozen glass tumblers, filling them first with hot water and then emptying them. Next they add black coffee, two sugar cubes, a jigger of whisky and a dollop of coagulated cream to each. It is a fascinating ritual. Waiting for my order, I scan the room, trying not to stare at the diversity of the faces engaged in lively conversation. I notice how the blue collar workers mingle easily with the sophisticated city dwellers and naïve travelers. No class distinction in this city. I feel my heart warming to the humanity of it all. The handsome barman with shockingly iridescent green eyes and thin black moustache hands me an Irish Whiskey. His hand brushes against mine. Is it on purpose? The glass mug is hot to the touch. "I'm assuming you want one of these," he says.

His intoxicatingly good looks make me wonder if his roots are Black Irish, like my mother's. I am tempted to ask, but thinking that too forward, I say, "Don't you serve any other drinks?"

"Beer, sometimes." Then he is on to the next customer. I am not much of a hard liquor drinker, but, hey, I'm into the experience of San Francisco. I take a sip, wanting to find out what the fuss is all about. I make sure I get a good amount of sweetened cream. It actually tastes good! However, after the initial tastes, the cream has dwindled so I add two more packets of sugar. Nothing like a good adrenalin rush to ensure I will make it back home. I take out the map and study it like an exam. In between taking orders, the man with the mustache helps me plan my route, starting with the cable car across the street. Cable cars are slow, but their open air views are, he assures me, something I want to experience. As an enthused visitor, I agree. I shake his hand, thanking him, still hoping he will ask for my phone number. He does not.

Out in the damp cold, the bellowing sound of the fog horn I had been hoping to hear comforts me as I stamp my feet and rub my hands together to keep warm. An amateur guitarist strums the Otis Redding's hit of San Francscoo's bay, hoping for a tip. He is off key, but I give him a dollar anyway. I figure he is adding to the whole ambience I am experiencing. I sing along in my head, changing a few words: "I left my home in Upstate, cause I had nothing to live for. It's been three thousand miles I've roamed."

Can I make this city my home? San Francisco has been pulling on my heart strings all day. Could it be Southern California, like Upstate New York, is not a suitable match for me? Could not being in the right town be one of the reasons my business has not been humming along? Perhaps courage, clarity and tenacity are not the only traits necessary to be successful. San Francisco stimulates me, motivates me, inspires me. I feel more in touch with who I am and what I want more than any other place I've ever been. I am confident that if I lived here I could accomplish anything.

RULE #4-2: ALIGN YOUR PASSION WITH YOUR GOALS Passion—the feeling of joy, excitement and inspiration—is the fuel which enables us to pursue our dreams. Setting goals, the necessary component of success, is then a source of pleasure and not hard work.

It is my turn to board. A uniformed man takes my money as the conductor has his hand on a long lever. Whether it is to make us stop or go, I am not clear, so I stay up front to watch this huge machine lunge forward. As we make our way up and down the hills of the city, I take in all the lights, admiring San Francisco at night. I put myself into a self imposed trance, feeling like Peter Pan in Never Never Land. I pinch myself back to reality, knowing I need to pay close attention to where I need to transfer. I ask just to make sure. Without too much trouble, I am back at Maria's apartment before midnight.

Invigorated by the city, I wake up early, ready to embark on new adventures. Maria's apartment is located in a neighborhood called the Sunset, consisting of Mediterranean-style stucco homes built primarily in the thirties and forties. I read in my tour book that it was once an expanse of sand dunes in the late 1800's and is now the largest district in San Francisco, stretching from the southern border of Golden Gate Park to the Pacific Ocean. Maria's apartment is located in the Inner Sunset, which is more centrally located and a bit warmer than the Outer Sunset, but it still gets some of the fog San Francisco is famous for. As I step outside, I immediately feel the cold brisk wind. Luckily, I took Maria's advice and brought warm clothes. I button up my coat and tighten the scarf around my neck. Wanting to find a hot cup of coffee, I remind myself to pay close attention to where I roam. Maria said I probably will not find her neighborhood on the map, because it is more residential than touristy (She chose the Sunset to live because of its excellent schools—she has a twelve year old daughter—the low crime rate, affordable housing prices and proximity to Golden Gate Park). It is easy to get around without a map, however, because the streets running north to south are alphabetical—Hugo, Irving, Judah, Kirkham and the east to west are numbered avenues. Even I would have a hard time getting lost here. I find a café on Irving Street, an animated and attractive commercial area, bustling with a diversity of small businesses. I note the influence of two distinct cultures—the Irish (lots of drinking establishments) and the Asians (lots of local Chinese markets, eateries and laundromats).

My main destination though is Golden Gate Park. With solid walking shoes and a firm step, I make my way there sipping on the steamy coffee warming in my hands. The park reminds me of New York's Central Park, but not nearly as crowded, and by the map, larger. So although this is a city, there are lots of trees and grass and plants its citizens can enjoy. What good planning! I can have my cake (the many things to see and do) and eat it too (enjoying nature in the process). It would take months to enjoy every feature Golden Gate Park has to offer. It houses several museums—the art-filled de Young, the California Academy of Sciences and the Flower Conservatory. The park also offers an array of physical activities—boating, archery, handball, skating, golf, horseback riding, lawn bowling, and even fly fishing.

I think about Dad's love of fishing. Not only would we have trout every other Friday (breaded and pan-fried in olive oil with the tail on and the head off), but our front yard was supplemented with wild flowers, ferns and tree saplings Dad acquired during his fishing excursions. Unfortunately, that stopped when a forester caught him red-handed taking a pink lady slipper. This type of orchid rarely survives transplanting, but Dad had done it several times. Of course, he did not tell the forest ranger that. Being a builder and nurturer of plants was just who my dad was. What can I say? It's the Italian!

Because Golden Gate Park offers so much, Haight-Ashbury will just have to wait. Biology major, Nature lover and Italian that I am, I choose to walk the Botanical Garden at Strybing Arboretum. The fragrance from all the plants is exhilarating. This is a perfect way to spend a crisp early morning. I keep looking for the bison, which Maria told me roam free here, but don't see any. What I do find, though, is an ornate archway with an Oriental inscription. I enter an intricate complex of paths, ponds, sculptures and bridges. I notice that the subtle anxiety which has been my constant companion since childhood is gone. I am actually feeling peaceful. In the center of these serene gardens is a tea house. When I am done wandering, I stop inside and order some jasmine tea. The tea is served by a young Japanese girl in an exquisitely painted kimono of birds and flowers. She takes an inordinate amount of time serving me. Even though I have planned a full day I feel calm and centered and find myself enjoying the serenity of the moment. I like watching her. Every movement of her pouring is delicately subtle and ceremoniously planned. I sip my tea slowly, tasting the hinted flavor of flowers, while breathing in the flowery scents around me. When I am finished, I open my map to plan my next destination.

I find the closest bus stop. After a twenty-minute ride, I get off when I see the Giant Dragon Gateway leading into Chinatown at the corner of Bush and Grant Streets. I want to experience more Asian culture which, like the Italian culture, has a predominant influence in San Francisco. Scores of shops line the streets, selling everything from flimsily made house slippers and fake satin robes to single or double handled woks to expensive jewelry of the finest grade gold, fresh water pearls and varied colored jades. A great place to buy a few mementos and gifts for friends, but not exactly what I am looking for. I meander around some more, searching for the more authentic roots of this culture. I find it on Stockton Street. Whereas the Italians in North Beach speak lilting bits of English, here the language includes few words I can recognize. I look at the crowded buildings around me—so unlike the fancy gingerbread Victorians with their prim and proper gardens. These multi-unit houses have a haphazard, slipshod appearance, from being added on to numerous times without much planning. The sidewalks are crowded, bustling with activity as hordes of small people push this way and that. Old wrinkled women with young children dart in and out of small dark alleys—places I would not dare venture. Recently butchered chickens, with head and feet still intact, hang upside down in meat markets. In the windows of restaurants fish swim in large water tanks—ready to be cooked and placed fresh on your table. Great idea, but the pungent smell makes me want to hold my nose. I move on to the produce markets. I only vaguely recognize many of the vegetables—bok choy, snow peas, mustard greens—others I don't have the faintest clue as to what they are, but I can handle and choose the object of my desire. I grab some oranges for a snack later.

I want to sample some true Chinese fare and choose Sam Wo's from my guidebook. I make my way up a narrow winding staircase—similar to the barely navigable curvy streets outside—certainly not made for us robust Caucasians. Being petite and agile, I have no trouble managing. Noticing the kitchen was on the first floor, I wonder how the waiters manage to get the food up three flights. Ah-ha! Along the far wall is a dumbwaiter! Dingy plasticized menus cover the tiny tables. A fan works overtime to give a slight breeze to the tiny stifling room. I double check my guidebook to make sure I got the name of the restaurant right. Yep, that's the right address. I read the description over: "… the perfect place to enjoy tasty authentic Chinese fare. Ed Wong is a charismatic waiter, who entertains his customers by making them set their own table, telling them how to sit, and what to order. Do not go if you're thin-skinned and can't take hardy, sometimes rude, humor." I put on my meekest face to blend in and giggle as Ed pokes fun at the people sitting next to me. The food is a long time coming, yet fragrant and delicious, cooked with plenty of oil and onions. The rest of the ingredients I'm not so sure of, but don't want to ask. Since I have a hot date with Brian tonight, I'm careful with my onion intake. I wonder what the evening will be like. What will Brian be like? Well, it really doesn't matter, I tell myself. I am only here on vacation. Or am I? I open the fortune cookie, hoping for some guidance. Opportunities await you. What opportunities? Career opportunities? Romance? Money? I take the fortune and put it in my wallet. This is a definite keeper.

For a change of pace, I decide to catch a bus to Union Square and window shop with the upscale shoppers. On the way, I notice the electric street cars, bursting at their seams as they transport just about every race, religion, and color—the seemingly meek Asians, the flashy Blacks, the proud Latinos, and the joy filled Italians like me. And let us not forget the gays—their prominence is felt everywhere in every neighborhood. On the buses, in the streets, in the stores and in the restaurants. Here gays come in every variety of height, weight and skin color. I find it refreshing that no one is trying to pretend to be something they're not. Here in San Francisco you can flaunt whoever you are and you are accepted—no matter what! How happy it makes the shy, self-doubting part of me smile.

When I get off the bus, I scan the four blocks of boutique stores sandwiched in between the famous department stores of I. Magnin, Macy's and Saks Fifth Avenue surrounding the green square. It feels a bit like bustling Madison Avenue in New York City, but not so daunting. And certainly not like the blind, "keeping up with the Joneses" mentality of Rodeo Drive. Why is that? All three cities have basically the same designers—Armani, Gucci, Versace, Cartier, Ferragamo. Is it because now I appreciate the European sense of style and beauty more in San Francisco? I glance up at the palm trees in the park. Or is it because San Francisco blends commercialism with nature so beautifully? I look at the open faced people around me. Or perhaps it is these friendly culturally diverse city dwellers which make a difference? I stroll around, feeling San Francisco pulling me closer to her like the Sirens luring Ulysses in The Odyssey. I wake up from my dream by checking the time on my watch. Astonished that it is already late afternoon, I decide to hail a cab rather than figure out the maze of bus lines, schedules and transfers. Besides, I need a quick nap before my night out on the town with Brian.

Startled, I wake up and look at the time. It is already half past eight. I jump out of bed to get ready. A quick shower, fresh makeup and a change of clothes revitalize me. Putting on the finishing touches, I hear the doorbell buzz. I fling the door wide, still breathless, but beaming, hoping my skirt isn't too short.

Brian gives me a quick once over then says, "It's a bit nippy outside tonight, you might want to wear jeans instead."

"That's okay," I say brightly. "I have a coat."

"Well, Paula, where we are going is not a 'dress up' sort of place. Remember we are going to see a punk rock band. It isn't exactly Carnegie Hall."

"Describe more in detail where we are going then," I say, wondering if I should leave the safety of my room.

"Polk Gulch is kind of a college-esque commercial area with lots of trendy bars, low cost restaurants and a few drifters here and there. Where we are going is not really a dive bar, but certainly not chi-chi— more like a converted warehouse. It's safe as long as you are careful, but you don't want to be walking around in a pretty dress with heels. You asked for some local San Francisco flavor instead of the routine touristy stuff so… "

"That's fine," I say, interrupting him mid sentence. "I'll go change." I head back into the bedroom.

Brian yells through the closed door, "Oh, I should tell you there probably will be some hardcore gays walking the streets—dressed in black leather, chains, and steel studded boots, but don't let them scare you—it's more for show than anything else. Besides, they'd be more interested in me than you anyway." He laughs. I bring enough money for a cab fare home—just in case.

At the local club, the punk music is loud with a lot of jumping up and down by the band. The audience members follow like pogo sticks. Punk Rock really is not my preference—I can't hear the words and the music is not all that good, but I am enjoying myself. It is creative in a dark, liberating sort of way and I am getting what I wanted— freedom from my claustrophobic depression of the last few months. Brian and I sing along to The Car's new song, *You're Just What I Needed!* I feel foolish, but jump up and down with everyone else, recognizing that San Francisco may be the solution to my problem. I have been seeking a place where the inner core of me can blossom and grow like the plants Dad took such good care to nurture. Everywhere I turn there is something fun to experience, something new to learn or get excited about. Waking up in San Francisco every day would be like opening presents on Christmas morning. Every day would be a gift.

When the band takes a break, I tell Brian I cannot remember when I have had this much fun. I pummel him with every question I can think of about San Francisco: Job opportunities, neighborhoods, weather, cost of living. I smile at what a real estate agent I am becoming. First I do an analysis of Ted as though he was an investment opportunity and now I am interviewing Brian as though he is a first-time home-buyer.

RULE #4-3: TAKE ACTION When you want something, go for it. Do not settle for familiar routine. Instead, think outside the box, taking advantage of opportunities to make your dreams a reality.

That night I give in to my dreams, imagining myself living here; stopping by the local market on my way home from work, buying flowers, wine and a take home pasta dinner for two. Then I open a bottle of red, let it breathe, smell the bouquet and sip on it slowly while I discuss the events of the day with my delightful date. We'll take our shoes off and put on a pair of those inexpensive Chinese slippers we picked up in Chinatown so as not to scratch the oak flooring of my Victorian apartment (We won't be living together yet, because my business hours would be too demanding and I would need my own space). I will put on an Italian opera to set the mood as I make the salad, not using the bland and boring pre-packaged iceberg so predominant in New York. Nor will I use the low cal, celebrity crazed, tastes like nothing Laguna sprouts either. I will choose the varied ingredients from a San Francisco grocery—romaine, watercress, arugula and the tangy and zesty radicchio—so common in Italian cooking.

I notice how I keep going back to my Italian roots—their love of food and wine, art and architecture, beauty and design; their connection to nature and the robust engaging way they live their lives. I feel like I belong here—like I have found a long lost love. Is that why after just a few days I feel a lift in my spirit, a heightened sense of aliveness and an appreciation of life I have never felt before? It is becoming much clearer that if I choose San Francisco as my home, I could be the independent, financially secure and personally fulfilled business woman I have always wanted to be. I know no one here except Brian and Maria, but I have made up my mind. Yes, San Francisco... you are just what I needed!

CHAPTER FIVE

CONFIDENCE
Developing a Strong Sense of Self

IT IS A WEEK BEFORE THANKSGIVING when I get in my car with a small collection of personal belongings to make the nine hour drive from Laguna to San Francisco. I am a bundle of anxieties when I arrive. I am not sure what I will be doing to make a living. I was not as successful as a Realtor as I had hoped to be in Laguna. The Tommy Hopkins one day seminar helped, but it was not nearly enough. I know only two people in this entire city. I know I need a better support system. I will need friends to talk to, so when a sale falls through I won't fall apart. I also know I need to learn my way around San Francisco. Maybe I will get a temp job as a store clerk or waitress while I get my bearings.

Maria Gonzales, who introduced me to San Francisco, realizes it is not easy to find affordable rentals and offers to help. An old beau of hers, Danny Donnelly, agrees to rent me the converted attic in his parent's house. He uses it whenever he's in town, but told Maria he could use the extra spending money. (The truth is—I think Danny was still in love with Maria and would do just about anything to please her.) The apartment is small, but located in a hot San Francisco neighborhood, right on bustling Union Street in the Cow Hollow neighborhood. Weird name, but as people explain to me, this area was a dairy farm land in the late 1800's. An octagon farmhouse a few blocks away is concrete evidence of that historical fact. On the downhill block toward the scenic Marina district is another historical landmark. Previously a Russian Orthodox Church, the Vedanta Meditation Center is a peacock blue building with three turrets. Beneath the apartment is a small coffee shop if I ever get hungry; next door, a bar called Tar and Feathers if I get thirsty; on the corner is a grocery store if I need light bulbs or toilet paper. I am in the perfect neighborhood to experience San Francisco—interesting architecture, a rich mix of history and culture and total convenience.

As soon as I arrive I call Brian Rinsom, my street artist friend. Since

Maria is always busy with her daughter or her latest boyfriend, Brian is really the only person I can count on here. During the last few months he has supported my decision to leave Laguna and come to San Francisco. A decision, he promises, I will never regret. He also offers to help me in my move.

Brian picks up the phone on the first ring. He has been waiting for my call. He lives in Eureka Valley on the other side of the city, but it is a straight shot down Divisadero Street to my apartment. He is there in less than twelve minutes. Moving like the Energizer Bunny, he runs up and down the wrought iron fire escape—the only entrance to the apartment—handing me boxes from the car over the handrail. My Chevette is unloaded in record time. I lean on Brian, because I do not know the city and he is fun to be around. In return he gets to feel needed. The arrangement is convenient for both of us.

The first week in San Francisco is an eventful one. The mayor, George Moscone, and a city supervisor, Harvey Milk, are assassinated. A few days before a local minister, Jim Jones, leads his flock to mass suicide. Leo Ryan, a California congressman, and three reporters who investigate the cult are also murdered. Growing up in a safe, sleepy suburb, attending an insulated college in upstate New York, and then living in an affluent California beach town, I am wondering if this is typical city news.

I find a job as a cocktail waitress at a fern bar, a type of lounge popular in the eighties. It is furnished with sturdy oak tables, gaudy stained glass chandeliers and, of course, lush ferns hanging from every conceivable place. The owner, Willie Mac, is a tough, hairy and burly, grim-faced man in his early forties, who dresses in leather and rides a Harley. The cocktail girls tell me to stay away from him, because they say he is into s&m. The reticent bar manager agrees Willie Mac is a misogynist, but claims he is hardly ever there. Despite Willie's extracurricular activities I take the job, conscious of the fact that this is one of the hottest bar scenes in town. I am guaranteed to make contacts here.

The work is grueling, holding the heavy cocktail trays above people's heads and pushing through the crowd for the eight hour shift. I was promised two official breaks a night, but the first is a half hour dinner break I take the minute I arrive and when I try to take the second the bartenders throw a fit. I am sure this goes against all labor laws but no one complains. At the end of the night my ears ring from the deafening noise of loud conversation; my hair reeks of smoke and my legs ache from the hard concrete floors. While it is true many young professionals frequent the place, the pace is so hectic I don't ever have time to take their cards, much less exchange a few words with them. There must be a better way to make contacts.

One evening when Brian calls, I am in full blown victim mode—I had just gotten fired. "How could this happen? I've been such a good employee. How can I go in if I'm sick?" Etc., etc., etc. Ad nauseum.

Brian's optimistic stance makes me listen. "You have got to read this book I've been reading called *Psycho-cybernetics*. It's all about improving your self-image. Your boss may be doing you a huge favor. Paula, you don't want to be pushing drinks for a living, do you?"

"Of course not!" I say.

"You keep telling me how you miss real estate. Well, you've been here three months now."

"But it's so hard to meet people. I thought I'd be better connected by now."

"What happened to the woman who came up to me on the street last year and flirted with me?" Brian asked.

"She's worn out, Brian. When I met you I was on vacation. I was seeing San Francisco for the first time—I was full of hope and energy. Now I'm just too tired to reach out to anyone new."

"So you have to do something about that," Brian said.

"What am I supposed to do? Go to Hawaii for a week and come back refreshed and rested?" Brian is beginning to piss me off.

"Well, that might not be in your budget this month, but there is a book you can read."

"A book that can help me meet people?" I ask incredulously.

"Yeah. This one can. Why don't you try it?" Brian continues. "You just need a boost of self-confidence. I think this book will help."

The next day I go to the bookstore, find the paperback and read the blurb on the back. The author is a doctor. Well, that's good news—at least it is written by an educated professional. I read further. He is a cosmetic surgeon. Not a likely book for a young woman who wants to break into the real estate business. What could this guy possibly teach me about sales success? But everybody in San Francisco reads self-help books. They are all discovering their human potential. There is Alan Watts to improve your sex life and Abraham Maslow to help you stop smoking and Wayne Dyer to guide you to your personal destiny and Carl Rogers to discover your identity through interaction with others. I take one last look at the cover before thinking, "When in Rome, do as the Romans do." I decide to buy the book and am on my way.

> RULE #5-1: KNOW THYSELF Always concentrate on your (and others') strengths, but also recognize your limitations so that they don't impede your success. Good friends can give you key insights to start the process of self-examination.

I am very glad I read the book. Dr. Maxwell Maltz wondered why, after successful surgeries in which he improved people's appearances, many of his patients returned unsatisfied, complaining they still felt ugly. If only he did one more small adjustment, they asked—a lift here, a tuck there, a slightly smaller nose, a fuller chin—all would be well. But doing more surgeries did not change how they saw themselves. Even when Dr. Maltz took before and after pictures and had concrete evidence of improvement, patients still couldn't see a difference. Hundreds of case studies later, Dr. Maltz concluded that improving people's exterior appearance is not enough. In order for people to feel better about themselves, they need to be repaired from the inside out. They needed to build a stronger self-image.

Self-image is a mental picture that each of us has about ourselves—a summation of strengths and weaknesses. These beliefs may be completely inaccurate, but what matters is that we believe them to be true. Once I read *Psycho-cybernetics* I begin to realize that, like Dr. Maltz's patients, my success and happiness are dependent on some erroneous perceptions. Coming from a critical unsupportive family, I often feel like I am not good enough. Now this negative thought pattern is getting in the way of my success. I am not focusing on what I really want to do—sell real estate. Instead I am slaving away as a miserable bar maid. It does not have to be that way. I can build up my self-image by changing how I view myself. I can focus on my strengths of tenacity, courage and passion.

> RULE #5-2: BUILD YOUR STRENGTHS Each snowflake, each starfish and each flower is unique—as it is with each one of us.

Take the time to determine what special strengths you have and concentrate on enhancing them.

Brian and I celebrate my newly found knowledge by going out to a romantic dinner on the north side of town. He chose this restaurant because he knew I had backpacked in the Greek Islands. I have already had a full glass of Merlot and am feeling pretty mellow. The moussaka, which just arrived, is how I like it—the eggplant fried a light golden brown with alternating layers of lumpy mozzarella, ground beef, béchamel sauce and a garlic laden tomato sauce—all topped with a sprinkling of freshly grated Parmesan. I am ready to take my first bite of this mouth watering delicacy when Brian says, "You know, you're not done yet—you've just begun."

"Begun what?"

"To get what it is you really want. Now you know that your self-image is directly linked to your success. It is an important step, but it's not everything."

I smile broadly. "I know. I need to be clear what it is I want."

"So what do you really want?"

"Maybe I'll try real estate again," I say, turning my attention to the meal which has been laid in front of me.

"Maybe?" Brian lays down his fork. "What's holding you back? I'm always hearing how you don't have any money, what hard work waitressing is and how you want to find a job that's fulfilling. So how are you going to start improving your self-esteem to go after what you want?" Brian looks deeply into my eyes for a moment, then says, "Paula, how about taking a personal awareness course to learn more about yourself? Maybe then you would have more confidence in choosing your career path."

I tell him about the one day seminar I had taken from Tommy Hopkins and how much it helped me in understanding how to relate to people.

"Well, what did you learn?" he asks as he leans closer to me.

"You know, the basic sales techniques—how to prospect, hold an open house, telephone etiquette."

"That's it? Nothing about YOU? Nothing about getting to know the wonderful, marvelous being who is you?"

"No," I say, wondering where he's headed.

"Well, that's certainly not enough. Sales are much more complicated than simple learned techniques and following a route script. It is a whole way of being. You can't expect people to trust you with one of the biggest investments they'll ever make if you don't have a strong self-image."

"So you don't think I'm confident?" I ask, trying not to be defensive.

"It is not important what I think, Paula. We are talking about self-image—about what you think about yourself. You might want to consider taking one of those human development courses offered here."

I had met a few San Franciscans who had taken Werner Erhard's training program, but was a bit leery of doing it myself. "From what I hear it is a bunch of mumbo jumbo California new age nonsense. No thanks. I'm not interested in getting brain washed."

"I understand you being skeptical, because it's a new model of how to live—a strange mixture of Eastern philosophy, existentialism and motivational psychology, but it worked for me. It gave me the confidence to start my own jewelry business."

"Really?" I say.

"I think you could gather some gems of wisdom there that you can't get anywhere else. Like in Laguna for instance. Or upstate New York. Take advantage of living in San Francisco—we're on the cutting edge of the human potential movement, after all." He gives me an all knowing wink. "I'd hate to see you miss an opportunity."

I take some time to think. I am not ready for Erhard Seminars Training (EST), but agree it is time to find a job where I do not have to carry twelve pound trays of smelly beer. I start looking for a real estate company which has a training program. I find one, not in my neighborhood with the imposing grand mansions of the super rich and famous, but one across town with a new young ambitious manager, Tim Brown, who helps new agents like me. I am not ready for the personal development class Brian thinks I need, but know I have to brush up on my sales technique—how to set goals, get clients and close the sale.

Saxe Realty is located in the Mission, a colorful fusion of Latino and American culture. The working class, the artists, the feminists and the freelancers live here because of the low rents. Its busy streets are lined with cheap burrito joints, Spanish tapa bars, makeshift flower stalls, prolific produce markets and thriving thrift stores. Every couple blocks or so I notice a bright mural painting on the side of some build-ing—not exactly the neighborhood I had in mind. I don't like the graffiti, litter strewn sidewalks and pick-up trucks in the driveways ei-ther, but the close-knit families with their adorable chubby cheeked children win me over. I figure that the Catholicism and the love of family, food and flowers is a big enough connection to my Italian her-itage. Besides, I tell myself , it is just a first step. I do not have to stay here forever. Also, since the homes are reasonably priced, the agents less formidable and the support system at Saxe Realty better estab-lished, there is a better chance of making it here than in the more affluent districts of town. I say yes when Tim Brown offers me a desk.

Eileen Maxwell, a studious, modish gal who dresses in tailored pin stripe suits, appears to me to be the whiz kid of the office. Her thick, dark hair is pulled back in a tight bun and is accentuated with large black framed glasses. She even looks like a genius. I learn she gradu-ated magna cum laude from Berkeley and is a frequent reader of *The Wall Street Journal, The Washington Post, The San Francisco Chronicle* and *The San Francisco Examiner.* At first I am impressed with all her knowl-edge. She knows all about the Consumer Price Index, Gross National Product, Unemployment Rate, and the Dow Jones Industrial Average and how it affects the real estate market. After a month or so, I real-ize she is not doing as much business as I thought. She knows a lot, that's for sure, but in the result department she coming up short. She is spending all her time analyzing economic trends instead of closing real estate deals.

On any particular day I'll hear her saying something like: "Did you notice that San Francisco passed a rent control initiative, so now we can't sell income units—it's just way to risky—we could get sued." Or, "Did you read that Alan Greenspan is raising the prime rate again so interest rates will climb to the worst it's ever been—18%! He claims inflation is still too high so he has to take action. What is he think-ing?" Or, "Look at our high unemployment rate—we're surely in a full blown recession now and maybe even headed for a depression. Who will be able to buy homes?"

Confused, I ask Tim Brown, the ultimate pragmatist, his opinion. He believes real estate is the best investment one can make—in any economic climate: "People have to live somewhere. When you rent, all that money goes down the toilet. You can't recoup any of it. At least when you own a home there's substantial tax savings and the possibility of appreciation. Remember, so-called experts are not in the trenches like we are and each one has his/her own view on what's happening. I suggest you stay away from the news and their predictions of doom and gloom—it will only bring you down. Remember, if you are not upbeat, positive and enthusiastic, you can't sell."

I go home that day and cancel my newspaper subscription. I switch the television channel if anything negative comes across the screen, including Ted Koppel's *Night Line* covering the Iranian hostage crisis. I also no longer accompany Eileen on house caravans. I continue my search for a mentor—someone who can help me to make it in this business. I come across three possibilities—all top producers exhibiting maternal instincts which could work in my favor: Mary Francesca Moeller, a heavy-set Italian woman who carries herself with a subtle panache, Nettie Dieves, a confident spectacled slip of a woman and finally, Heidi Carter, a very blonde Swede with a thick accent and midriff to match. When I learn Heidi has been the number one agent for the last two years, I decide to approach her first.

Heidi must be from a small town in Europe, because she dresses like a country bumpkin with huge fluffy hats in varying shades of red, orange and purple. She is also a bit full of herself—in spite of her dress attire—so I learn quickly she is not well liked in the office. I ignore what other people think and purposely stay away from gossiping colleagues. I am not going to let their negativity get in the way of my success. She is getting results and I want to know why. I compliment her when she gets a new listing or a new hat. Occasionally—so I am not too much of a nuisance—I ask her advice. I notice that she has a monthly newsletter and I manage to squeeze a copy out of her. She is flattered with all the attention and tells me that she personally delivers the newsletter every six weeks to her surrounding neighborhood. Saturday and Sunday afternoons are best, she claims, because people are home. Not only does she give her neighbors timely real estate news but she also includes a recipe and a discount coupon to a local establishment.

Heidi helps me choose a neighborhood to canvass. Now that I am clear that I want to be a successful real estate agent, I use my special strengths of courage, passion and tenacity to help me achieve my goal. I improve on Heidi's ideas by choosing a more professional layout and better quality paper with my own personal flair. Even when I don't feel like it I walk the neighborhood. I remember Tom Hopkins saying it can take anywhere from six months up to a year for the first sale. I also remember him saying that sales are purely a numbers game. Most of all I remember him yelling over the loudspeaker— "Just do it!" So I do.

> **RULE #5-3: SURROUND YOURSELF WITH SUPPORTIVE PEOPLE**
> Start making friends with people who are more knowledgeable, powerful and established than yourself. Just being around these experienced people will teach you aspects of business that you cannot learn from a book and will greatly shorten your learning curve.

I really did not know Mary Moeller all that well, but I must have made some sort of impression, because she asks me to cover for her during her annual two month trip to Italy to visit her relatives. Maybe it is just a maternal instinct to help a new fledgling. She, like Bette, is my mother's age. (Is this a subconscious need or what?!) Mary is personable, fun-loving and a smart dresser. She wears jewel colored co-ordinated suits which compliment her Mediterranean olive skin and, what looks to me, professionally applied makeup. I welcome the help—Maria, who gave me my first taste of San Francisco, had moved to Russian River with her new boyfriend and Heidi, in spite of her best intentions, was difficult to be around.

I already have a few sales under my belt and am establishing my own real estate business pretty rapidly, being consistent at working my 'farm' (neighborhood) and doing plenty of floor time and open houses. Her connections, though, are with a higher echelon clientele who can afford more. A few days before her vacation she takes me out to lunch at a family owned Mexican restaurant with the Christmas decorations brightly lit and still hanging—although the holiday is long past. As we munch away on chips and salsa, she hands me the list of clients she wants me to contact.

"Thank you," I say and take the piece of paper in my hand. I am careful not to look disgusted at the lumpy pea green concoction the waiter just put on our table

"Haven't you ever had guacamole?" Mary asks as she takes a huge helping.

"I guess I've heard of it before," I say, "but I never imagined it would be so green or so... eh... mushy looking."

"Give it a try—you may like it. It's kind of like sales," she says with a laugh, "it seems kind of strange at first, but then you acquire a taste for it and you can't imagine living without it."

I take a chip and dip it in, opening my mind for another new experience. "You know," I say, as I take another taste, "I think you're right. It has a bit of fullness and zing to it." I give Mary a wink, "Just like real estate!" We both start to giggle. I am giddy with delight at having a new friend. I gathered some courage and then ask the question I have been pondering for the last few days, "Why did you choose me over the other sales people in the office to cover for you?"

"Paula, you know what you want and go after it. Plus, you have a gusto for life which I find refreshing. Sure, most of the other people in the office have more experience, but they take their business for granted or are too busy to really enjoy what they're doing, so guess what? They are not going to connect to my clients as well as someone like you who is enthusiastic. Your follow through will be much better."

I am grateful for the kind words and tell her so. "Any advice you want to give me as a new salesperson starting out?" I ask.

"Before selling real estate I worked for Sarah Coventry Cosmetics. I learned the importance of making a good first impression, establishing rapport with your clients and how to close a sale, but that's not enough to last in this business. We are dealing with people who are making the most important investment in their lives—both emotionally and financially. To deal with them you have to have a strong sense of self."

I remember Bette Mae's similar advice, but am curious of what she means.

Mary takes a moment to answer. "I would say a truly self confident person is a person who embodies a balanced blend of giving and receiving. Being an ingratiating people pleaser won't work in sales. By giving without constraint your clients won't respect you and the other sales people will walk all over you. Of course, the polar opposite is the self absorbed narcissist, who can't give at all. When you are truly confident you do not need to brag, put people down or act high and mighty. It is interesting to watch when these people's external accomplishments are taken away. They deflate like pin-pricked balloons—their self-esteem blowing off into thin air."

Mary continues. "When you come up against an obstacle, rely on your strong inner core of confidence to get you through it. And, of course, surround yourself with upbeat, positive people who appreciate you." She lifts her glass to me.

I follow, clinking my glass against hers. "Here's to our new business partnership," I say. Noticing that the guacamole bowl is empty, I motion the waiter to come over. "Could we have some more please?"

Mary gives me a wide smile. "I know you're going to be a big success—just wait and see."

The first of a series of well qualified buyers she refers to me is a couple who lives in Berkeley. Mary gives me the tantalizing scoop before she leaves: Justin, a long standing tenure professor at Cal-Berkeley in his mid-forties, is a client who has just left his wife for Diane—an attractive, will-go-far graduate student in her late twenties. Mary blushes as she tells me, "How shall I say it... they need to get out of town and fast!" Then quickly adds, "They want a Victorian with a view and garage." Doesn't everybody?

It is with this knowledge that I get ready to meet my first reasonably affluent clients. I already know that they are real buyers and since they are a referral they probably have not talked to anyone else. If I can show them that I am professional, knowledgeable and honest, they will be loyal. I have only driven across the Bay Bridge once or twice before and have no sense of direction. I plan ahead by getting an early start. I go over the instructions on how to get to their place one more time, put on my newly purchased red power suit and a touch of lipstick. I make sure I bring my listing book and calculator to help pre-qualify them. I stop at the local car wash and request "the works"—inside and out—just in case they want to start looking today. I double check my map one more time and, taking deep, long breaths, I prepare the nerve racking drive across the expansive five lane bridge. All the while I am on a constant lookout for the merging traffic while I do my best to locate the exit. After a few wrong turns I finally find the correct address off University Avenue and ring the doorbell—full of optimistic enthusiasm.

RULE #5-4: PROJECT CONFIDENCE What you think about yourself will project outward and influence how others treat you. If you emit confidence, people will want to work with you.

Justin and Diane are pretty much what I expect—academic well-off hippies. They offer me some herbal tea and rice crackers while I lead them through a property qualifying process which I learned from my sales training class. I give them each a blank piece of paper and have them individually describe the home of their dreams. Next they are to rank the characteristics they want most. Once they prioritize their wants I have them compare their lists. There is usually some negotiation between partners at this point. It is here I act as a facilitator by asking open ended questions. Justin and Diane are pretty much in agreement. They want a three bedroom, two bath Victorian with a two car garage, a small yard (Diane says she likes to garden), a fireplace and a view of downtown. Since we seem to have established a good rapport, I ask them to sign an agency disclosure form. This form describes the fiduciary duties of a buyer's agent, seller's agent, and a dual agent, opening up the discussion of how real estate agents get paid (If the potential buyers fail to sign the form, then they become a B client—someone I will work with only when I have no other business).

During the counseling session I also ask lots of questions to translate the features (the physical characteristics of a property, such as the number of bedrooms and baths, yard, garage, neighborhood,) into *benefits* (pride of ownership, prestige, convenience, safety, investment). Once I understand what is important to them, I can serve them better. For instance, Justin and Diane may say they want three bedrooms, two baths, a view and a two car garage, but I need to find out Why.

"Diane, you said that you want three bedrooms—do you mind me asking what you plan to use them for?" My pen is ready... (Being young and single, I make sure I pay most attention to the woman to eliminate any jealousy. Besides, it will be her making the final decision—whether she contributes financially or not).

"As you probably know, it is just Justin and me. We don't plan on having any children, but we both do a lot of work at home and want our own separate offices."

From asking that one question I find out a lot of information. I continue. "If I am able to find a house which has two bedrooms and a study, would that work for you?"

Diane gives a quick glance to Justin who nods. "And how about bathrooms? If I find a great house which has only a bath and a half, would you be willing to add a shower later?" Since I don't want them to feel like they are being interrogated, I add, "The reason I am asking you all this is because if you are flexible on your criteria, you'll have a larger selection of houses to choose from." (I am also establishing a realistic expectation level for them. No one ever gets 100% of what it is they want—not even multi-millionaires.) I then explain that a two car garage in San Francisco is practically unattainable in their price range. They decide it is an unnecessary luxury, but do need additional space for storage.

"So do you think an attic, basement or even a large laundry room could work?" I open my listing book which has descriptions of the current houses available to show them the possibilities. Since price is always important, I can now give them a wider range of possibilities— some which are only two bedrooms with a bath and a half. Others have no garage. The view is a whole other issue. Almost every client who initially looks in San Francisco says they want a view, but views of the bridges and downtown are pricey. There are, however, other views which they may find appealing so my job is to pin them down to what benefit they are seeking—whether it be aesthetics, prestige or a brighter open environment.

I am also fortunate in being able to gauge what Justin and Diane may want from a visual perspective by observing their current surroundings. Their rental is an Arts and Crafts turn of the century bungalow amidst a yard full of blooming plants. Putting them in an unimaginative sixties box, for instance, would never do (The flower generation had great imagination and style, but the people building houses at that time did not. Coming from the Depression era, they hold values around saving money so it is no surprise that the fifties and sixties homes are known for their practical simplicity). To get a clearer sense of Justin and Diane's taste, I ask them to give me a quick tour. Their interaction with their home will tell me a lot. I make sure I mention that they will be lucky to get the top five items on their wish list (If they are particularly frugal buyers, they may only get the top three. Again, I am doing my best to keep their expectations realistic. If they aim too high, they'll get disappointed and maybe blame me, which may cost me a sale).

The counseling session takes almost two hours. We are all emotionally spent. We decide to wait until the following week to start looking. As I wave goodbye from the walkway, I know the meeting has been a success. The next step in the sales process is a good follow through by sending them a hand written thank you note for choosing me as their Realtor (I want to keep that cozy warm emotional connection). Keep in mind that most clients will describe what they want in terms of the physical characteristics of a house, such as the number of bedroom and baths, yard, view, etc. As a sales professional you need to translate what they say into the value they want by owning, such as, pride of ownership, prestige, convenience.

Although Justin and Diane have a busy schedule, I make sure I call them to keep them abreast of the houses I am previewing. Since this is the beginning of our relationship, I need to be in constant communication. When they mention they can look on their own that Sunday, I insist that we set up private appointments instead. I don't want any high pressured salesperson to lure them away from me.

After three visits to San Francisco, Justin and Diane put an offer on a sprawling three bedroom Craftsman style home in Liberty Heights. The house has a sweeping view of surrounding vintage homes, trees and the hills—not a view of downtown as they originally hoped—but all wishes don't come to pass. On the plus side, it does have more space than they thought they could afford. At close to $350,000 ($ 2.5 million today) this is the highest sale I have made. No need for peanut butter sandwiches or having to decline theater and dinner invitations any longer. Success is so sweet!

CHAPTER SIX

POWER
Disciplining the Mind

I AM GETTING SMARTER ABOUT SALES, so when I receive a call from a 'For Sale' sign one Saturday I am fully prepared. The man on the other end of the line identifies himself as Joe Phelps. He explains that he and his partner, Mark, (Business partner? Lover? I am experienced enough now not to ask until we know one another better) have found a property they may want to buy, a property with my company on the sign. He is calling the number on the sign to find out how much the house costs. Even though he is eager to give me the address of the house, I pause. I ask him to get a pen and paper. I spell out my name and give him my telephone number, in case we get disconnected. Only then are we ready to do business.

"What is it about this property that you like?" I ask. Joe tells me that this small bungalow is close to his work, public transportation and shopping. He then asks me for the price again.

"Four hundred and seventy-nine thousand," I answer, quickly following it up with another question—the person asking the questions is always in charge. Plus, I need this information to help Joe and his partner. "Is that the price range you had in mind?"

"Yes," Joe answers, sparking my excitement. I explain that there are other houses in the same neighborhood which also meet his criteria. I stay in control of the conversation by doling out information sparingly. I am careful not to give him the exact addresses of similar properties. My vagueness will keep him intrigued and in need of my expertise.

I next ask if he knows what they want to pay a month, because that will tell me whether they have given serious thought to buying. When a prospective buyer says it does not matter and they are open to all possibilities, they are not far along on their decision making process. Seriously motivated buyers know exactly how much they can pay. When Joe tells me that they would like to pay no more than $1800 a month, I use my Hewlett Packard amortization calculator to figure out the amount they will need to borrow by putting in the current interest rate for a period of thirty years. When I meet them I will also need to make sure that they have the full 20% to put down as well as the closing costs. I wait because that is too delicate question to ask now. Instead, I have information now to go for the close—to get the appointment with them as soon as possible. "How about tomorrow? I think I might have an opening." I tell Joe to hold while I look at my calendar. I have nothing planned, but I make it sound like I am fitting them into a packed schedule. My delivery—which I practiced ad infinitum in the sales training course—is calm. It convinces Joe to make an appointment with me.

We agree to meet at the property after work. I would prefer to meet them at my office, but sense their reluctance when I suggest it. This is common—they have not met me yet so they are more comfortable on neutral ground. Although they seem like serious buyers, I do not want to take anything for granted so the next day I call Joe to confirm. His partner, Mark Kropensky, answers. They're on.

Even so, I am nervous as on a first date—wondering if I will be stood up. When they arrive fifteen minutes late, I feign confidence as I shake their hands and introduce myself. I make sure I do not point out the obvious in the house, like saying, "Here's the kitchen and this is the dining room." Instead I say, "This breakfast nook is really charming, don't you think?" and "Take a look at this cabinet—perfect for spices—although it was originally a built-in ironing board."

"We don't iron or do much cooking. It's dry cleaners and take-out for us." They start to laugh and I join in. I feel myself relaxing, knowing I am making a connection with these young men. Joe is a speech pathologist and Mark is a hairdresser. They are a great pair.

After a quick tour, I can tell from their demeanor that they are disappointed in the interior of the house. Their polite comments reflect no enthusiasm. I was prepared for this, even if they were not, since typically the property a client calls on is not the one they buy. I give them a sunny smile and usher them into my car. "Why don't we go back to my office and let's see what else is available? We'll drive back here later to collect your car." Before they know what is happening, Joe and Mark are listening to me chatting away about neighborhoods and possible loan options.

Before opening up the Multiple Listing Service book, I help them figure out what they can afford. "Most lenders will want your monthly payments covering principal, interest, taxes and insurance (PITI) to be approximately a third of your monthly income. However, with good credit, banks may go as high as 40%." I give them names of three lenders to call to get the loan process started. "It is good to get the pre-qualifying done now, because once you find a house you really like you do not want to be wasting any time putting in an offer," I advise.

Knowing that most people are sensitive about revealing the specifics of their financing, I tell them 20% of the purchase price is the typical down payment. I also remember to explain the 3% closing fees (Alan Davenport's jaw had practically dropped to the floor when he learned he had to pay me an additional $7,000 at close).

"What are closing fees?" they ask in unison.

"Well, the bulk is for lender's charges, because interest does not cover the bank's cost of lending money. Plus there is the credit check, appraisal report and loan setup costs. Finally, there are the title insurance, escrow fees and property insurance."

"Tell me more about escrow and title. What's all that about?" Joe asks.

"An escrow agent is a neutral party, like a mortgage officer at a bank, who disperses all monies during the sale of the house. For instance, the bank establishes an escrow account to pay property tax and insurance during the term of the mortgage. The escrow agent also transfers the deed of the property from the seller to the buyer. This involves recording all the necessary documents at City Hall. In addition, the escrow agent will research the history of the property and give you a report which lists any existing liens, easements or encroachments attached to the property."

Mark interrupts, "I don't mean to sound ignorant, but what are liens, easements and encroachments?"

"There's no such thing as a dumb question," I say, pleased that I am no longer afraid of questions. No longer ashamed I do not know an answer. I have learned to simply say, "I don't know, but I'll find out." In this particular case, I do know the answer. "A lien is any money which the sellers owe associated to their property—loans, taxes, unpaid utilities and, in some rare cases, unpaid bills to contractors. All these bills must be paid off once the property is transferred to you."

I let all that information sink in and when I notice their eyes upon me, I continue.

"An easement is the right of another to use your land for a special purpose. For instance, access to an adjoining property by using a path through your property is an easement. In contrast, an encroachment is when a person uses your property and does not have the right to do so. Think of it as trespassing. It does not happen often, but it is a situation which a title company can correct when they do a survey. The most common notations on a preliminary title report, besides liens are utility easements, such as telephone poles or power lines on your property. Those types of easements one usually just accepts—it is part of living in an urban area. An easement that might be more of a concern would be when a private party has the right to cut across your property to get to his parking space. In this case the easement is for the benefit of someone else and a detriment to you. You might want to think twice before you purchase that particular house, because you don't want people traipsing across your yard. That is why a title search is so important—to guarantee that the rights of the people on title are protected. Should a problem arise, the title insurer—not the owner—pays to protect your right of ownership."

"That's a lot to understand," Mark says.

"One more thing," I say, "Since you are only making a down payment of 20% and your bank, has invested 80% of their money for the purchase of the property, they will require that you purchase title insurance for them as well."

I then pull out my title company rate sheet. I show them the figures for the title fees they will have to pay and the rest of the closing fees: the escrow fee, fire insurance policy and the varied loan costs. I make sure I explain that these are estimates only. I do not want them disappointed at closing if the actual expenses are a bit higher.

Joe is scribbling notes as fast as he can. I assume he is figuring out what they can afford. He looks up briefly, admitting they may be a bit short of cash to cover the 20% down payment in addition to all these closing costs.

"Sometimes," I say, "a seller will agree to pay your closing costs or give you a small second loan to help make the deal. I can negotiate all this for you, of course." I pause. "That is, if you decide to choose me as your agent." This is the perfect opportunity for me to explain

that real estate agents work only on commission. "Not only will I negotiate on your behalf for the house of your choosing, but I will also
preview houses beforehand—which will save you a lot of time. Plus,
through my network of real estate connections, I can find properties
fast to help get you a better deal. Sometimes," I lower my voice, "who
knows—I may even find a house that is not available on the open market." I hesitate once again, noting their reaction. Their faces are
open, their shoulders relaxed and they both appear to be listening in-
tently. Gaining confidence, I say, "I will do all this groundwork for
you—provided that you work exclusively with me." I look them
squarely in the eye as I say this.

Joe glances at Mark, who nods.

I shake their hands and tell them if they see an ad in the paper or
a sign on a property they like, they are to call me directly and I will
find out all the particulars for them. "Finding a home is stressful
enough, so let me take some of the pressure off," I say, smiling
broadly. By being more involved in their research process, I can reduce the risk of them talking to other agents. I want them to remain
loyal to me.

I have a committed buyer! Now my job is to preview houses in their
desired neighborhood and price range. A short three weeks later, we
are ratified—meaning our offer was accepted—on a two bedroom
Victorian row house in the Ingleside District. It is a small transaction,
but it gives me a boost of confidence. We are just about to close when
Nettie Dieves, one of my previous mentor hopefuls in the office, approaches my desk. She had been widowed for three years now. I
haven't gotten to know her well because she seems as bitter as she is
fiercely territorial. "That really should be my deal. I know Mark Ka-
plan. He works where I get my hair done. He never told me he was
buying a house."

I give her a weak smile but say and do nothing else. I have only
been working here six months. I certainly do not want bad blood between us.

"So what are you going to do about it?" Nettie gives me a menacing
look. When I don't come up with a quick answer, she says, "You can
get back to me tomorrow."

I am so new I do not have any firm allies in the office yet. Nettie can
mess my wonderful new job up for me. I like my office, love my man-

ager and feel I am close to success. So after a sleepless night, I wake up wanting some of Bette Mae's matzo ball soup. This is weird, because it had taken me months to acquire a taste for this Jewish specialty. I now yearn for that dish, along with Bette's soothing voice and some motherly advice. I pick up the phone and call Laguna.

"Hi, kid!" Bette answers as she always does when I call. "When are you coming home? We miss you."

"Bette, you know I love San Francisco." Bette had urged me to sublet my apartment in case I did not like living in San Francisco. I did not have the heart to tell her I would never be back. I laugh before I spill my problems with Nettie. "What if she's gossiping about me in the office?" I ask, trying to hide the anxiousness in my voice.

Bette's first question is— "Did you ever hear Nettie speak of this man?"

"No, of course not."

"Well, then, you have not done anything wrong. See if you can't work it out with Nettie." She pauses. "You're such a skinny little thing—are you eating enough and getting lots of protein? None of that fast food, I hope."

I tell her I miss her homemade soup. I can almost feel her smile over the other end of the phone.

Bette tells me once more how much she misses me. She says, "I know you can work this one out with Nettie, Paula. But promise me that you won't go crying to management about this thing. They hate in-fighting."

I promise and thank her for the sound advice. Off the phone, I change into my jogging shorts. Whenever I start to get anxious about Nettie, I push the thought away and run harder, concentrating on my breath. If I want to stay in this business, exercise will have to be part of my routine. No more excuses. After a good sweaty run I am feeling better, but still am unclear what to do next. I call my street artist friend, Brian.

"I notice that ever since Nettie confronted me, painful memories of my childhood keep popping up: Being punished for getting a "C" on my report card; being scolded for not smiling when we had our class picture taken and being grounded when I lost a library book. I start reliving all these past negative experiences. Remembering all this agonizing stuff makes the whole situation with Nettie even harder." I want to sob, but catch myself.

"Paula, you seem to be wallowing in a field of negativity. Why not clear your mind of these depressing thoughts?"

"Huh?" I say.

"You are always talking about how you love nature and all. Why not think of thoughts as growing plants in the soil of your mind. Wouldn't you rather have pretty flowers growing than ugly weeds?"

"Hmm," I say, "I would if I could. I just don't know how. Besides, they are just thoughts."

"Just thoughts?" Brian asks. "Thoughts are powerful things. I think a bit of self-discipline in controlling your thoughts might make a big difference in dealing with Nettie."

"So you think my negative thoughts are part of the problem?"

"Yes, I do. Past memories, their attached belief systems and accompanying fears don't just go away. They lie dormant in our subconscious. Nettie knows you are new and naïve. She may even have observed that you are susceptible to criticism. She probably has a belief system that people owe her, so you have two belief systems–yours and hers—colliding with each other."

"Great!" I say, upset that my thoughts have played a part in this whole drama. "So what do you think my belief system is?"

"That people take advantage of you."

I feel like I have just been hit by a two ton truck. "What did you say?" I ask.

"I said that you think people take advantage of you."

I certainly felt my parents did. And the kids in high school. And Ted. And … all of a sudden I get a visual flash of a gigantic puzzle floating in space with some pieces coming together. The image is startling. How did Brian know this about me?

"Now that you know that you have a thought system that believes people take advantage of you, you can recognize it when it crops up again. That's the first and biggest step."

"And then what?" I ask. "I'm feeling a bit helpless that my subconscious has such a hold on me."

"Your subconscious merely connected some past experiences with Nettie's assault on you. Your subconscious may be powerful, but it is not time sensitive. The truth is you are no longer a five year old child—you are a smart, savvy business woman. Don't let negative, past images affect you now."

"So how do I get my subconscious to help me instead of hurt me?" I ask, thinking I should be able to reason my way out of this.

"Imagine yourself as a driver of a chariot. Your powerful subconscious thoughts are the horses. The harness is your conscious mind which can direct the thousand horse powered subconscious to where you want it to go."

I gasp, getting the full picture in my head. First, an image of an uncharted chariot running amok and causing chaos; then, a second impression of me, using the reins to direct fast moving horses galloping to their destination. I now say aloud what I am thinking—"In order for me to be the successful agent I want to be, I am going to have to control how I think."

"Exactly! Nettie is merely an obstacle in the road."

RULE #6-1: MONITOR YOUR THOUGHTS The mind creates a reality by aligning the external universe with internal beliefs. Think of thoughts as images being projected onto a big movie screen. The motion picture show is our life drama in which we are the writer, director and star actor—a reality show in which we can change the course of events at any time.

Brian starts talking again. I do my best to bring myself back to what he is saying. "I have the afternoon off. Why don't we go to that French restaurant, Le Central, you've been talking about. We can discuss how you can use the power of your mind in handling Nettie."

I immediately accept, remembering that I have not eaten since yesterday at noon. I hang up the phone. Then I focus on the positive: appreciating the good things in my life—the support of my friends, an affordable apartment on chic Union Street and a job that I like. I dress in a snap and take the quick bus ride downtown. I know exactly where the four star French bistro Brian suggested is located because I have been salivating to go there for months. I enter the restaurant with its crowded tables, fresh flower centerpieces, starched white linen tablecloths and impeccably dressed French waiters. Brian is already there, sipping on a Chardonnay. I turn my attention to the menu, recalling the wonderful meals I had in Paris—the delicate sauces, the crispy pommes frites and the melt-in-your mouth crème brûlée. Of course, I will have to have the escargot smothered in garlic. I wonder what Dad would think if I told him I eat snails. He would be proud of me. Being Italian, he was a true food aficionado. I scour the menu one more time—should I have the Beef Bourgogne or the Filet Mignon au Poivre? The Beef Bourgogne is more affordable, but I feel like a splurge. I am into abundance after all.

Brian starts to explain how he thinks the subconscious works. "Paula, picture an iceberg with only 10% of it showing above water. This is the conscious mind—it is analytical, logical and rational. It handles our every day tasks by coordinating our intentions with actions. The 90% submerged part is our subconscious—a huge data base which gathers information with no discerning abilities. The subconscious mind does not know the difference between a dream, the present or years back, and understands only images and emotions. It is impressionable and indiscriminate."

I savor my snails while he talks. Brian may be a street peddler, but he is one bright guy. I am lucky to know him. He is able to focus on my problem as though it were his own.

Brian takes a hunk of French bread and reaches across the table to dunk it in the garlicky oil left over from the escargots. "There are four states of brain activity: Beta, Alpha, Theta, and Delta." I push the plate closer so he doesn't drip anything on the starched white tablecloth. "In order to access the subconscious, we need to either be in Theta, characterized by dreaming, or in Alpha, when we are in a very relaxed, meditative-like state. Albert Einstein, Thomas Edison and Alexander Graham Bell developed their cutting edge theories when they were walking in nature, taking cat naps or being alone and quiet. It was from their subconscious that they received their inspiration, creativity and innovative ideas. In these states you can also let go of old, limiting thought patterns and substitute new, healthy ways of thinking."

I have an 'Aha!' moment. "So instead of just working hard to become successful, people also need to relax so they can get through to the subconscious?"

"Yes, yes!" Brian clasps his hands together, excited that I am grasping what he is telling me. "Being an entrepreneur, as you are learning, is not that simple—you have to live on the edge, constantly adapting to changing circumstances and constantly being placed in challenging situations. You need the power of both your rational, conscious mind and the creative subconscious."

I remembered Tommy Hopkins's suggestion of using the Subconscious to solve problems that the analytical mind cannot explain. Tommy said when you combine feeling with visualization, you can start creating the reality you want. He suggested we put all of our positive feelings into our thumb by recalling any past accomplishments like acing a test, excelling in a sport or winning a card game. Tommy said it does not matter how small the accomplishment—what matters is how we feel about the accomplishment, because it is the feeling behind the action that is most important. Before an appointment, he suggested, press your thumb and forefinger together and—voilà!—you feel confident, positive and ready to handle any situation.

> RULE #6-2: COMBINE VISUALIZATION WITH DESIRE Before you begin a task, define the goal you want to achieve. Place all your energy, all your will power, all your desire and all your passion behind that goal. Do you see it clearly? Now visualize the goal accomplished.

I am taking no chances in the matter of Nettie, so I do this subconscious ritual right before I go to the office the next day. I visualize Nettie approaching me. I imagine me smiling, being calm and collected as I tell her that her claim is bogus. I visualize her walking away, never to bring up the subject of Mark again. Sure enough, after my visualization, I walk by Nettie projecting a self-assurance I didn't know I had. "Hello," I say.

With her hands on her hips, Nettie approaches. "Well, have you thought about what percentage you plan to give me out of your commission since you stole my client?" she asks.

I shrug my shoulders say, "I didn't steal your client, Nettie. I had no idea you knew Mark until you told me on Friday."

"Well, I do."

"Just because you know Mark does not mean you are entitled to a commission," I say, astounded at my matter of fact composure. "I showed him and his partner property, found a house they liked and got them a loan. This was a two month long process. Mark never once mentioned your name. Are you sure he even knows you work here? He's been to the office many times, but you never came up in the conversation."

"Really? How did you get them as a client?" she asks, moving closer.

I feel it is none of her business, but answer anyway. "They called inquiring about a property."

"Well, maybe they first asked for me."

I pause a moment and think well before I answer. I make sure I speak slowly, enunciating each word with emphasis. "Nettie, Mark did not ask for you. In fact, it was his partner, Joe, who made that first call. He told me that he was looking for a Realtor to help him."

"I bet that's not how it happened," Nettie says, hissing through her teeth.

"Nettie, if they wanted to work with you, why would they make an appointment with a Realtor they never met?" I am putting the onus on Joe and Mark now.

Nettie gasps at my response. "You are just trying to weasel out of this," she says, narrowing her eyes. "And I am not going to let you get away with this. I am going to straight to Tim Brown and tell him what you've done."

Bette Mae's voice echoes in my head: Do not go whining to management. Let Nettie be the one who is the complainer. Not me. I turn to face Nettie directly. "Fine," I say, finally believing in my heart of hearts that I have done nothing wrong. My visualization that I will keep my full commission has sustained me through this uncomfortable encounter.

Tim never calls me into his office. I collect my full commission when escrow closes. I stay at Saxe Reality for another three years and make sure I say hello to Nettie when I see her, but I never say anything else.

I go on to work in the same office as Nettie without any problem. This transaction teaches me to stop assuming that others are always right and I am always wrong. I have learned to respect myself, and my knowledge of the intricacies of the marketplace. I have also learned there are people out there who can push my particular buttons and make me nuts. I identify them early and take steps to protect myself—whether they are co-workers or clients.

Getting along with clients is sticky. I have to learn to draw the line with Dr. John De Palma and his wife, Alicia, a pair of difficult clients, when they buy a Victorian in a *crème de la crème* location near Alta Plaza Park. It is in the midst of the quaint Fillmore District of Pacific Heights with trendy shops and restaurants. Even though it does not have a garage, it is on a major bus line and there is plenty of street parking along the park. The high ceilings, crown and picture moldings, rounded arched windows and large chandeliers hanging from cherub adorned rosettes capture their imaginations. As soon as the De Palmas see the sheltered walk-out English garden deeded exclusively to their unit, they are smitten. I lead them through several rounds of negotiations to win this house of their dreams. A short year later, John is transferred to Boston and has to sell. Disappointing for them. Fortunate for me.

The house, which was beautiful to begin with, is even lovelier now that Alicia has lavishly decorated it with custom finishes and priceless Eastlake furniture. John is eager to set a price so that he can sell and move on, but Alicia is insistent on listing way over market, because of all the money and time she has invested. I appeal to her reason by showing her comparable sales in the neighborhood. She tosses them in the trash, believing those houses are not near as special as hers.

I suggest we lower the asking price she has set so that we will increase our chances of a bidding auction. "Then you will be able to get above your listed price," I advise.

Alicia is not convinced. I push her to make her decision quickly, to get the property on the market before April. I emphasize that there are plenty of buyers looking then, being driven by their accountants' recommendations to get tax breaks. "Most sellers mistakenly wait until the better weather to sell. Historically, in the early spring, we have a limited supply of inventory with lots of pent-up buyer demand. Selling in March will put us in the perfect position of getting the best price with the best terms."

Alicia takes a long time making her decision. It is not until mid-June that she agrees to list, begrudgingly, at my recommended lower price. By now, the market has shifted. There are plenty of beautiful condos for buyers to choose from and the demand is not as strong.

We get an offer, but only one. The good news is that the buyers, a middle-aged couple living in Japan, are highly motivated. Their son will be attending college in San Francisco so they have only a week to find a place for him to live. Renting is out of the question for this financially savvy couple. They want a prestige neighborhood good enough for their only son. They have the money to invest in a prime unit that will appreciate. I am hopeful that they will be able to accept

Alicia's inflated asking price, because they just lost a bid on another house. Alicia, still convinced her house is worth more, insists on countering their offer for over the list price. The Japanese couple counters to a price slightly over, but not near the price Alicia had in mind.

"If we had listed at the higher price I originally wanted, we would have gotten my price!" Alicia's voice is brittle as it hits my ears. "Why couldn't we have done it my way?"

What is most aggravating to me is not Alicia being angry at me, but what is going on inside my head: *I should have—I'm wrong—I didn't do it right!* It feels like I have a gigantic searchlight coming out of my forehead, reviewing all my mistakes—with Alicia, with past clients, with my ex-boyfriends. This is not quite the throwback to childhood that Nettie's attacks inspired, but I am very uncomfortable and unsure of myself. My mind is like one of those airport scanners going back and forth—looking, looking, looking. It will not let me off the hook: I could have agreed to Alicia's higher listing price. Maybe Alicia was right: *If we asked for more, maybe we would have gotten more.* I swallow hard. In the sweetest voice I can muster say, "Alicia, your condo has been on the market for almost two months. You know yourself that we have advertised in all the top journals and magazines. I have had it open every weekend and on numerous brokers' tours—everyone in San Francisco knows it is for sale. If we were going to get a better offer, we would have gotten it by now. Look at the comparable sales," I say, doing my best to win her over with logic. "You are getting the highest price of any home without a garage in the Fillmore District."

"That doesn't mean anything and you know it! I don't care what other people got—I just care what I get." She starts to sob. "You just don't care about how I feel. I put my heart and soul into that house to make it special and you don't give a damn. It is just another sale to you."

Alicia agrees to sign the counteroffer, but that evening I am still haunted by what she said. Why couldn't I have been more empathetic? Why hadn't I thought to say something like: "I understand your disappointment, especially when you were expecting a much higher price." Or, "It must be very difficult to move from a home you love."

As I go over what happened, the scathingly critical part of my subconscious emerges like an army drill sergeant, yelling and screaming at me about how I did not handle Alicia's concerns well enough. I understand now that these pictures are brought to my consciousness for a reason, but also know that the army sergeant image is in part because of my highly critical parents. I count on my rational conscious mind to sort through all this, knowing that the submerged part of my brain is trying to teach me something.

Alicia probably does not want to leave San Francisco. It is likely that she resents anyone who represents the move. My listening more and talking less would have yielded a better outcome. Yes, next time, I will be more empathetic to clients who are attached to their homes. At the same time, I accept the fact that I make mistakes once in a while and plan to do better next time.

> RULE #6-3: LEARN TO FAIL EFFECTIVELY The critical 'Inner Voice' can be your friend, providing that it is not so critical that it hurts your self-esteem. Acknowledge that this 'Inner Critic' is trying to help. Learn the lesson and then move on.

If my mind continues to beat me up, I keep bringing it back to what it is I want—a good connection with my clients—all the time being patient with myself as one would when disciplining a small child. Each real estate situation is unique, so I will always be learning on the job. No matter what problem I am facing I can use the power of my mind to solve it. Sometimes the conscious mind comes to the rescue of the unconscious mind. Sometimes it is the other way around. But there is always an answer, even ones I think are impossible, like the situation with Leeza O'Reilly.

Leeza comes to me through her friend, Roy Jackson, a mortgage broker in San Jose. I had met Roy at a real estate conference and we exchanged business cards. I was delighted when Leeza calls a few months later to ask me for help in finding a loft in the up and coming South of Market District. From the moment I meet Leeza I am stuck by her exotic beauty. She is not what I would call movie star beautiful, for she has a prominent nose and a figure too curvaceous by current Hollywood standards. Yet Leeza has femininity about her which I find appealing. When she opens her door, she flings it open wide and in her lilting Irish voice welcomes me inside as if I were one of her dearest friends. I think it is the combination of her deep-set green eyes and the lusciousness of her wavy shoulder-length auburn hair which reminds me of a mermaid. My first impression is confirmed when I notice the many aquatic wildlife photos lining her hallway walls. When I ask her about them, she tells me they were taken during her various scuba diving adventures in Bali, Fiji and the Great Barrier Reef.

She switches gears to the business at hand, confessing she does not have a lot of money to spend, but thinks a one bedroom loft would suit her perfectly. "Just give me a basic amount of living space and I can do the rest," she assures me.

As I look around, I believe her. She has turned an unimaginative sixties box into a warm luxuriant home. Right now I have a full schedule. I really don't have time to work with another client, but I am enchanted by Leeza—her charm, her lifestyle and her beauty. I decide I can take her on.

Soon we are in escrow on a loft with an interesting urban view of a red and white neon lighted Coca-Cola sign which gives the unit the uniqueness Leeza is seeking. Leeza has only ten percent for the down payment, so Roy Jackson, her old friend, has to obtain the typical 80% loan. Then he has to find a 10% bank loan for the balance. Sometimes the seller is willing to loan to the new buyer the 10% balance in order to make the sale, but in the case of Leeza's loft, the seller is not. Because the additional loan for the balance of the down payment will be recorded behind the first loan, it is riskier. As a result the interest rate will be higher. Roy assures me that Leeza's income to debt ratio is still sufficient to qualify.

We get approval for the 80% loan early so we are halfway there, but it is not a home run—we still need to get loan approval on the 10% second loan to bring the down payment up to twenty percent. I stay on top of my game by inquiring about the status of the second loan every time I talk to Roy. Each time Roy tells me, "No problem." I worry nonetheless.

By this time I am getting emotionally close to Leeza—she is as beautiful inside as she is out—and I want her to get 'The American Dream' of owning a home. Close of escrow is only a few days away when I get the disastrous news. Leeza did not qualify for the second loan. All of Roy's declarations of No Problem were false. I call Roy to ask for an explanation. He sounds weary. "I submitted the loan to every conceivable lender out there, Paula. There are just no takers."

"Have you told Leeza yet?" I ask.

"I just told her before I called you. She was pretty upset," Roy says.

I give Leeza a call. She picks up. "Leeza, I heard the news."

"Paula, how… how could this happen?" She is choking on her words. I can tell she has been crying.

"Can you borrow from your family?" I ask.

"You mean my mother? She can hardly make it financially herself. I have been on my own since I was sixteen. She can't help me. My brother has two little kids and can barely make ends meet. What am I going to do? I already gave notice to my landlord. I am all packed up with no place to go. I'm essentially homeless."

"How about any distant relatives—an aunt or uncle? Grandparents?"

"No one," she says, starting to sob.

"How about a good friend? A work colleague? Someone who trusts you. Someone who has some extra money to invest. You can give them a good interest rate—a good return on their investment. We'll make it all official and record the loan against the property. Isn't there anyone in your circle of friends who might be able to do this?" I ask, desperate to come up with a solution.

"None of my friends have any money—they're worse off than me."

"A work colleague then?"

"No one," Leeza is in full crying mode now and again asks the question: "How could this happen?"

I know why but cannot say that Roy wasn't doing his job. Roy is her friend. *Go for the solution,* I think, reminding myself to use the power of my subconscious mind. By thinking outside the box, I might be able to come up with a way to make this right.

I call Roy back. "Say Roy, would you be willing to kick in your mortgage fees and the referral fee I am giving you to give Leeza the down payment she needs?"

"That's a lot to ask, Paula," He is subdued, but not sorry enough to help Leeza out.

"I was thinking that I would put in my commission to make this work. If you do the same, the combined amount would be enough to cover the ten percent Leeza needs.

He is silent.

"I rarely do this," I add. "But you know Leeza will pay us back as soon as she can. Besides—she's given notice to her landlord and has no place to live.

"I just can't," he says.

"Even if it means you won't get anything at all out of this sale?" I'm surprised at his answer. I take a few deep breaths, knowing I have to proceed carefully—Roy is one of Leeza's closest friends.

"I'm a little overextended financially myself, Paula. I took on a lot of debt to buy my mortgage company. Hey, why doesn't your company lend Leeza the money she needs?"

"That is an impossible request," I tell him. "Hill and Company is not in the business of lending money. The only way it would work is if we all pooled our money."

"Like I said before—I can't." Or won't is what I feel..

We are due to close in three days. I need to think of something else. When I check in on Leeza to see how she is doing, she keeps asking the same question over and over: "How did this happen?"

"Don't give up," I tell her. "Keep picturing yourself inside that new loft. Meanwhile, I will think of something, I promise."

I try to get myself past the stress of this sale with my dance classes, Advil and the worry dolls Maria Gonzales gave me for my birthday. I find the small patterned pouch where I keep them in my dresser beneath my gold hoop earrings. There is a legend among the highland villages of Guatemala that if you have a problem, you can share it with these dolls. You put them under your pillow and they solve your problems while you sleep. Again—I use another ritual to access the powerful subconscious. I take one doll out from the quilted pouch, and closing my eyes I place all my concern for Leeza into this tiny object. After I'm done I lay this doll underneath my pillow and ask God, the Universe, and my subconscious for help.

> RULE #6-4: ACCESS THE POWER OF YOUR SUBCONSCIOUS Rituals, being in nature, meditating, writing in a journal or taking up a relaxing hobby, such as painting, gardening or cooking, can help you still your mind and access your subconscious. The creative, subconscious mind can give you solutions which your rational, conscious mind has not considered.

The next morning my headache is gone. I take my meditation pillow and go sit outside on the deck amidst my potted plants. I luxuriate in the briskness of morning air and delight in the occasional red-throated hummingbird buzzing around. Maybe nature in its divine wisdom can help. I sit for twenty minutes before the face of a gal in my office flashes through my mind. Stephanie Ahlberg, like me, is one of the top ten producers, and has had an incredibly good year. Maybe she would be willing to lend Leeza enough money for a second loan. I make the call. No dice. All her money is tied up in other investments.

Before I hang up the phone, I ask, "By any chance, do you know anybody else in the office that might be willing to lend some money to my client? Leeza O'Reilly is really trustworthy and will pay back the loan no problem—I can assure you of that. Plus, she'll agree to a good interest rate. If you know anyone who might be interested, Leeza and I would be willing to meet with them today." I was acutely aware of how little time we had.

Stephanie says she doesn't and wishes me good luck. As she starts to hang up the phone she stops short and says, "Wait a minute—maybe my mother would be willing to invest some of the money Father left her. Of course, the property would have to appraise so she would be secure in her investment, but I could check it out for her. Let me find out if she would be willing to do this."

"Great," I say. "When do you think you can get back to me?" I hate to put the pressure on, because Stephanie is doing me a huge favor, but want her to know the parameters of the situation. "We're supposed to close in three days."

"Today—I'll call her today. When can I see the property?"

"Whenever you say—this is top priority."

"This afternoon?"

"This afternoon—just tell me what time works for you."

When Stephanie sees the property that afternoon, she admits South of Market is a bit marginal for her taste. I bring the comparable sales and convince her it is a good investment. With Stephanie's stamp of approval, her mother agrees to lend Leeza the money. Then I ask for a two day extension to complete the paperwork. The seller is happy to work with us and we close the following Tuesday. Leeza is there with two beautifully arranged flower bouquets—one for me and one for Stephanie. I still remember the vibrant orange color of the tiger lilies as if it were yesterday. I so appreciated Stephanie for helping that I made a donation to her theatre company (she had been an actress be-fore she started in real estate) and still attend her fundraisers.

I had worked my magic! But was it really? I think about what has happened. Stephanie Alhberg is one of the top agents in the office. It made perfect sense for me to call her and ask if she or someone she knew would have some money to lend. And if she did not, I could have asked other top producers in the office. But what was it that caused her face to appear in my consciousness? Who knows exactly how our creative subconscious and rational conscious mind commu-nicate with each other, but I know if I still my mind long enough, I can achieve phenomenal results.

CHAPTER SEVEN

OPTIMISM
Looking at the Bright Side

I AM BACK IN TIM'S OFFICE doing my best to be positive while being surrounded by negativity. No, it isn't Nettie this time—I stay away from her—it is one of my clients. Henry Clemens is upset because the house I listed a few months ago is not selling. Henry has been calling all hours of the day to complain.

"He is even swearing at me," I tell Tim, trying to hide the hurt I am feeling inside.

"Paula, there is no reason you have to put up with that abuse," Tim replies as I start to cry. "You have enough business without Henry. Dealing with his sort of personality is only going to be draining. Did you show him all the ads we've been running and everything you've done to promote his home?"

"Of course, I've done all that," I say, taking a deep breath. "But the house is a pig sty and he won't clean it up. I guess he doesn't understand the importance of 'showing a home.'"

"Well, I'll be happy to talk to him if you want. I want to tell you, though, I won't let him push me around. If there's any verbal abuse on his part, I'm prepared to give him back the listing. Look at how it is affecting you. How can you be productive in this frame of mind?"

"You mean you may tell him we don't want to work with him anymore?" I am feeling so out of sorts that such an approach had not even occurred to me.

Tim is surprised that I have not considered this alternative. "Personally I feel your time will be much better spent promoting your other listings rather than working with a nutcase. It is great to be tenacious, Paula, but there is a point at which you have to set boundaries." When I don't respond, he asks if I have ever heard of making lemonade out of lemons. "Why not look at this whole situation as a learning experience? Work only with those clients who understand that selling a home is a team effort and avoid these soapy dramas." Tim pauses then adds, "—which you seem to be involved in on a frequent basis."

"Well, isn't that the nature of real estate?" I ask, wondering if I am the only one with problem clients.

"It is, to some extent, but you seem to thrive on turmoil." Tim gives me a smile, but I can see the edges of his mouth beginning to quiver. He is losing patience with me.

It is hard to sell when feeling down in the dumps. I need to do something to regain a sunnier outlook. Before I went to Tim, I had complained to Jed Johnson, a colleague, of my difficulty in dealing with the ups and downs of real estate. Jed, like Brian, suggests I take the Erhard Seminars Training (EST), which is all the rage in San Francisco at this time. As an experience centered workshop, the purpose of 'the Training' was to show participants how to achieve a sense of personal power in their lives—to be the best they can be.

"But aren't EST and all those human potential movements, like 'Lifespring' and 'Actualizations' just cults?" I ask.

"Some people call these trainings *Fast Food Enlightenment,*" Jed laughs. "But Paula, you can make it into whatever you want it to be. The experience of improving your psychological outlook belongs to you. Just take the EST teachings that you relate to and leave the rest behind."

I know that EST has enabled both Jed and Brian to leave tedious nine to five jobs and get into sales. That, coupled with Tim's disappointment, is enough to catapult me into action. I sign up for a two-weekend seminar. If EST can help change my dismal view of what's happening, I figure it will be worth the time and energy I spend.

Sure enough, as soon as I arrive, a middle-aged man with slicked back hair introduces himself as William Reese and gives us a long list of rules to follow: no eating, drinking, chewing gum, cross talking or unauthorized breaks. This may mean sitting in the same chair for four hours at a time. Anyone who disagrees with these rules is allowed to voice their case. Several do. Some people resist being told what to do. Some have issues with trust. Some have medical problems and are asked to see the support people in the back of the room. The whole process seems to be going along at a snail's pace.

I check my watch and notice it is already past noon. We are still dealing with logistics and, getting restless, I wonder when this seminar will ever get started. I am thrilled when a gray haired gent asks if we could please move on, because we're wasting valuable time. Mr. Reese, the seminar leader, explains we all need to be in agreement for this process to work. "But I'm getting bored," the man says.

"So?" Mr. Reese says. "Boredom is just a passing emotion. Stay with it and you will notice it changes into something else."

The man continues, "I was promised this seminar would change my life and nothing's happening."

"That's an interesting perspective," Mr. Reese says. "From up here it seems a lot of stuff is happening out there." He points to the audience. "Are any of you feeling bored?" About a third of us raise our hands. "Who is feeling angry?" Another third. "Sad?" A few hands go up. "Resentful?" More hands. "Joyful?" Amazingly, a few more hands go up. Who could be happy, I wonder, when we've all been sitting here since nine in the morning in rigid metal-backed folding chairs talking about dumb logistics?

It is another hour before all of us agree on the arrangements. We finally break for lunch in small groups. We are sent to neighborhood places to get to know one another. Our only instruction is that we are to speak honestly.

I end up with a couple who whisper together all through lunch about scoring some marijuana. Not being a toker myself, I smile and nod now and again, but feel left out. As we leave the restaurant, I tell them how ignored I feel.

"I made several attempts of including you in the conversation," the woman said, "but, Nooooo, you just sat there."

This is not the first time I have felt excluded. I wonder—Why can't I belong? All I wanted was to be included in the conversation. An endless tape of how I'm not good enough begins, playing over and over in my mind. I remember Henry Clemens and how badly I allowed him to treat me. I felt like a doormat. I am feeling uncomfortable and want to get up and leave. Instead I remind myself about why I am here—to be more positive as a sales person and as an individual. I turn my attention back to Mr. Reese at the front of the room.

"Just be aware that thoughts and feelings are going in and out of our consciousness all the time, but it is not who we are." Mr. Reese says.

A girl in the front in a bright yellow top says, "You instructed us to feel our feelings. Now you are telling us feelings are not important. It doesn't make any sense."

My sentiment exactly. I took time from my hectic schedule to listen to this nonsense?

"I never said to ignore your feelings, because if you do, they will surface one way or another—usually at the most inappropriate times. What I said is: Your feelings are not all you are. For instance, if you have a feeling that people are out to get you, that is all it is, a feeling. If you feel you don't belong, that is all it is—a feeling of not belonging. I repeat—a feeling is NOT all you are. You are bigger than that. Change your feelings and, voilà, your reality changes. It is really that simple."

Hmmmm. I lean forward in my chair now, my ears perked, ready to listen.

A short muscular man with tattooed arms asks for the microphone. "What about all the bad things that happen to us? Are you saying all we have to do is change our feelings about what has happened to us?"

"Yes. Once you are able to change your feelings about your experiences, your reality will change."

The man interrupts and is beginning to sound angry, "What about poverty, war and injustice? We're just supposed to feel okay about these things?"

"What I am saying is that we all see the world through our own filters—and whatever we focus on becomes our reality." Mr. Reese casts a long lingering look outward to include everyone in the room, "Focus on what you want. Let go of everything else."

So we just accept the bad things in life? That doesn't make any sense.

"Let me explain this concept another way. Don't imagine a pink elephant in a white tutu with purple polka dots doing a belly dance. What do you see?"

"A pink elephant in a white tutu with purple polka dots doing a belly dance," the audience yells back.

"Exactly. The mind cannot decipher the negative. It ignores the "don't" and hones in on the elephant in the tutu. So focus on what you want to feel, not on what you don't want."

"But I don't know what it is I want," the girl in the yellow top says.

"Well, you better figure it out. You only have one life and you're at the rudder of your ship. Only you can change your life."

I decide to concentrate on all the people who appreciate me, such as Brian, Tim, Jed, Bette Mae and Mary Moeller. I decide not to waste energy on people like my whining client, Henry Clemens, or the woman at lunch, who couldn't bother getting to know me. With this new attitude, I feel more in control of my life. My emotion of despair changes almost instantly to one of hope, excitement and anticipation to find new, more cooperative clients.

> RULE #7-1: CHOOSE A NEW PERSPECTIVE The way we look at things affects our reality. If you are excited, hopeful and motivated, that is a perspective which will bring good results. Recognize you can change the way you view an event at any time.

Because of my EST transformation I decide to be captain of my ship and focus on remaining positive. One night a handful of us are working late when Tim Brown emerges from his office waving a piece of paper in the air. "I just got a call from a couple in Nebraska who read *The Real Estate Times* and say they want to buy this house they saw advertised. Since they haven't even seen the property, they could be some sort of nut, but does anyone want this lead?"

Since I had let Harry Clemens go, my schedule has freed up. I am ready for a 'hot now' buyer. I am not the same pessimistic person I was a few weeks ago and think I can handle the most difficult of clients. My hand is up in a flash, reminding me of the time in Miss Lanley's class almost twenty years ago. Before I know it I am taking Tim's paper out of his hand and walking back to my desk. Surprisingly, none of the other agents are the least bit interested.

Dan and Kathy Plunket arrive in San Francisco five days later. I pick them up at the airport. They are a middle-aged couple with a middle-age spread, dressed in polyester with a sunny, but naïve disposition. They have booked rooms at the YMCA in the Tenderloin District of downtown and want me to take them there.

"Are you sure that's where you want to be?" I ask. The Tenderloin is the dregs of San Francisco filled with drug pushers, prostitutes, pawn shops, girly topless bars and beggars. "I don't think it's that safe there," I add.

"Listen Pauline—your name's Pauline right? You seem like a nice young lady, but my lovely wife and I have traveled to lots of cities. We always stay at the YMCA. It's affordable, they have good facilities and are helpful to new people in town."

"The name is Paula, actually." I pause. I am proud of my city, but not all parts of it. The Tenderloin, in spite of it being in the theatre district, is the ugly underbelly. "I'm afraid you'll be disappointed with our YMCA's location."

"Don't worry we're savvy travelers, Pauline... er... Paula. Don't worry about us."

"Fine," I say, dropping a subject, I know I can't win. "So when do you want to see this property you called in on?"

"You mean the property we are going to buy?"

"Well, you haven't even seen it."

Kathy, the lovely wife, pipes up. "Dan has an uncanny sense of intuition. He is confident that this is the home for us."

"Really?" I say. "How long have you lived in Nebraska?" I ask.

"Our whole life. We are ready for a change."

"Hmmm," I say.

"Why don't we take a look at it tomorrow? Today we want to get situated and do some sightseeing."

"Fine," I say. "I'll call you tomorrow morning at nine."

"Why don't you make it eleven? We like to sleep in."

"No problem," I say, wondering if these people are real or what. Be positive, I tell myself. Give them a chance.

It is still dark outside when my alarm goes off the following morning. Damn! I must have set it by mistake. I shake the sleepiness out of my eyes and reach for my clock, realizing it is the telephone—not my alarm. I answer. "Hello?"

"Pauline. It's Dan Plunket."

"Good morning, Dan," I say, muffling a yawn. "What can I do for you? I thought you said you like to sleep in? What time is it anyway?"

"It's six in the morning and the place has bed bugs."

"What?!" I say. Now I am fully upright, sitting in bed.

"You need to find us another hotel, Pauline, and fast!"

"Oh, sure. Okay."

"And we don't want to pay more than $70 a night."

"Okay, yeah. I'll see what I can do." I hang up the phone, take a shower and start planning. Too early to call anyone for recommendations. I'll scour the yellow pages instead. Several frustrating calls later I find a hotel which is bare bones and clean and located in a better neighborhood.

"You'll have to cough up another $15 a night," I say when I call them back. Dan and Kathy agree. That is a hopeful sign. Maybe they have more money than it appears. Maybe they are just frugal people. I pick them up and get them situated at their new hotel. They are hungry and want to stop for breakfast.

"My treat, Pauline," Dan says. I don't correct him, figuring with these clients I'll just have to accept my new name. After breakfast we go take a look at the 'deal of the century'—the property they called on. I do not have much hope that this property is the one for them, but that is something for them to determine, not me. I do want to prepare them, however, so I say, "For this price it must be a tear down."

"Don't worry," the lovely wife says, "Dan is real handy." The house needs a new foundation, smells of mold and is in Visitation Valley, a less than desirable location bordering foggy Daly City. Not a place I would ever consider selling in. But I hold my tongue. This is something for Dan to figure out.

"This isn't it," Dan says firmly. "What else can you show us?"

"How high are you willing to go?" I ask, assuming they have been financially qualified. They have not, so we head back to my office where I am back on the phone again looking for a lender to counsel them. It is also a way where I can determine if they are sincere buyers. Blake Roberts agrees to meet with them, but at his office as he has a busy day packed with appointments. Fortunately, it is just a short drive away. We hop back in the car again. Meanwhile, Dan is perusing a copy of *Homes and Land* magazine and has circled several properties he wants to see. I notice one of the homes he has circled is in Crocker Amazon—again in the south part of San Francisco. However, unlike Visitation Valley, which has some hard-core projects, it is a close-knit community-oriented neighborhood with decent weather, good views and low crime statistics. Most of the locals don't even know it exists, so it is more affordable than most districts in San Francisco.

"The Plunkets qualify, no problem," Blake says after going over the numbers. "Plus, they can go up another $50,000 to $80,000."

"That is great news," I say and we are off—back in the car again, heading to the house Dan circled in the magazine. The mission style stucco house is a two bedroom, one bath home with a basement room behind the garage. It has not been lived in for several years and has lots of deferred maintenance—loose door knobs, a leaky roof and windows and cracked plaster. But the house gets great light, has a big backyard, a huge lower level which can be developed and is on a great pride-of-ownership street.

"Okay, then," Dan says. "Let's put in an offer."

"Are you sure? You just got here and saw only two properties."

The lovely wife smiles. "When Dan says 'Go for it' he means it. I trust his judgment completely."

We write an offer $15,000 under asking and it is accepted by the heirs without a counter. We close in a record fifteen days. I would not call the Plunkets difficult clients, but they certainly were quirky. My ability to not judge them in spite of all their weird behavior made this a smooth and rewarding transaction.

> RULE #7-2: ACCEPT CLIENTS' IDIOSYNCRACIES Remember that buying a home is a very personal, stressful and life changing event in people's lives and you may be witness to a lot of weird behavior styles. Remain positive, gracious and accepting while focusing on doing your job.

Because the Plunkets bought so quickly it was easy for me to remain upbeat and positive. However, real estate gets much more challenging when you have to hold onto a cheerful attitude with a difficult client for months. Like the time Tosca Giorgi and I represented Jack Krimpton in the sale of his beloved Victorian in Haight-Ashbury.

Tosca works in my office and, as luck would have it, we both were referred to Jack. I could have looked at this situation as a glass half empty, but after EST I saw this situation as an opportunity. Instead of competing for the listing we joined forces. Tosca lived in the Haight-Ashbury neighborhood and knew intricacies about the area that I did not know. She was also much more laid back in style than I was. I found her softness to be complementary to my high energy. Because of our balanced partnership, Jack chose us out of all the agents he interviewed.

Jack Krimpton is a jolly, rotund sort of fellow, almost as wide as he is tall, with full cheeks and a large jowl which jiggles when he laughs. After several months without any offers, Dania Bellington, a buyer's agent, tells me her clients are considering writing an offer. Dania cautions me that it will be a low offer since the house needs some cosmetics. I encourage Dania, thinking a low offer is better than none. I am taken by surprise when my jovial seller reacts so negatively.

I show Jack the MLS statistics on the houses which have sold over the last six months as well as the printouts of similar houses currently listed in the neighborhood. "Look here at the house you mentioned on Ashbury Street which sold for one million five hundred and fifty thousand. It had been remodeled with a new custom kitchen and double paned windows, refinished hardwood floors… "

"Are you saying that the house on Ashbury is a better house than mine?"

Knowing that Tosca has a hard time with confrontation, I continue. "No, what we're saying is," I say as tell-tale sweat begins to collect on my forehead, "most buyers want something that is more in style right now… like granite countertop kitchens with Viking stoves and Sub-zero refrigerators and marble baths with Grohe fixtures… "

"So you're saying my tiled kitchen is passé?"

"That isn't exactly what we're saying… what we're saying is… " My mind is working in high gear to rephrase the facts in such a way to not offend Jack. "… people's tastes change. Right now buyers want a more modern, sleek look than what you have here."

"All that may be true, but my house is much bigger than theirs," Jack says.

"So you think your house is much bigger?" Tosca asks.

"Yes," is his firm reply.

"The tax assessor lists your property as the same square footage of the house that sold," I say, looking up from our file, which states the number of rooms, year built and the square footage of Jack's house.

Jack still insists his house is bigger.

"During your ownership did you add on?" I ask. I did not think he had for this was a typical Victorian floor plan with a double parlor, dining room and kitchen on the main floor with the bedrooms and baths on the second floor.

"No," Jack answers. "Why do you ask?"

"That could be the reason for the discrepancy," I answer.

"Well, perhaps, the tax assessor information is just incorrect," Tosca says, adding fuel to Jack's argument.

Not saying anything would have been a better approach. Like I learned years back—do not automatically agree with clients, because then it will be hard for them to see the whole picture. As a seller, Jack has his perspective, but to come to an agreement, he will need to see the buyer's point of view as well. But Tosca and I have a partnership and I cannot go against what she just said. I gather my composure and try another approach. "Six months ago, the interest rate was also 1% less than it is now," I say.

"That should have nothing to do with it," Jack responds, his cheeks flushing a bright red.

"But to a buyer it makes a difference in their monthly payment." I pull out my Hewlett Packard calculator and using the amortization formula show him the difference. Right now the payment on $1,200,000 at 8.5% is $9,583. Six months ago it was only $8,338 which is a difference of $1245 a month." I now multiply the last figure by twelve and then by thirty. "So a buyer will have to pay almost $15,000 more a year and over thirty years that amount is $450,000!"

Jack shakes his head, claiming his property is worth every cent of the asking price.

Tosca, playing the good cop, asks, "So what do you want us to do?"

"I think I've heard enough for today." Jack answers. "Let's talk tomorrow."

I make my way to the door and say something light and funny. Jack does not respond nor does he shake my hand which is our custom. Out of the corner of my eye I notice him offer his hand to Tosca. On my way back to the office I review how things went—certainly not as well as I had hoped. Giving Jack facts and figures will help him make a sound decision, but it is not enough. Facts do not address the emotional turmoil he is feeling on leaving a home he has lived in for almost thirty years. Jack just can't see all the deferred maintenance his house needs and wants to believe that his house is every bit as good as the house which sold for a million and a half. Not feeling in the mood to talk to anybody, I turn the car around and head home. I need some down time. Once home, I make a long list of everything I have accomplished this year. I post it on my refrigerator door:

- Closed Escrows:
  1. 222 STATES
  2. 345 LOCUST
  3. 601 VAN NESS #1130
  4. 924 CHURCH STREET
  5. 260 RIPLEY

6. 25 MEDAU
7. 1220 JONES #601
8. 2077 JACKSON #107
9. 831 MASON

- Bought 3 Series Convertible BMW with leather seats

- Came in First in Tango, Waltz, Foxtrot and Second In Quicktep and West Coast Swing in Winter Ballroom Dance Festival

- Landscaped my backyard

- Dating Wayne Russell, my sexy dance teacher

Whenever my mind starts acting up, I look at the list, reminding myself that overall things are pretty good. Later that evening Tosca calls. "I noticed you weren't in the office this afternoon. Is everything okay?" she asks.

I tell her I'm fine—just a bit tired.

"Is it okay if I offer a suggestion?" she asks. Her voice is tentative.

"Of course," I say, preparing myself not to become defensive.

"You looked hurt today when Jack didn't shake your hand. You didn't take it personally, did you?"

"I tried my best not to, but it did hurt my feelings," I say.

#7-3: DO NOT TAKE THINGS PERSONALLY People view events from their own belief systems so what they think and say and how they react is much more about them than it is about you. Talk about your hurt, disappointment, resentment or whatever other feelings you may have with a supportive person in your life to let go of the negative and focus on the positive.

"Paula, you know it has nothing to do with you. Jack is upset because he knows he is not going to get the price he wanted. Since you were the one who presented the offer, he is trying to find fault with you."

"I know, I know," I say. And I do know. I think about other instances when I have taken a professional situation personally. Just last spring I was working with a couple who put an offer on a house which everyone else was vying for. We did not win the bid and the wife was broken hearted. I sat with her for over an hour, and remembering EST, suggested she envision a new house that was just as nice—or better—

than the one she lost out on. The couple eventually moved past their disappointment. Five weeks later, they were out looking at property with me. But when we lost out on the second house as well, the couple told me they wanted to start fresh with someone else. It did not matter that I explained it was a fast moving market and that it might take several attempts before we consummated a deal. They still blamed me. After all my hard work, I was devastated. But then I did what all good salespeople do—I focused on the next client.

After the phone call with Tosca, I realize that telling the truth to clients is necessary but, at the same time, clients want you to be hopeful, positive and optimistic. Sure Jack is disappointed, but I will not let his attitude affect me. The following morning I am prepared to jump back into the real estate melee. It is a good thing, too, because my day is packed with appointments. When I get stuck in traffic, I call Jack. Hopefully, a relaxing evening and a good night's rest will have given him a chance to process the offer. "Have you thought about what price you'd like the buyer to come up to?" I ask, assuming he wants to negotiate.

Jack ignores my question. "Paula, this buyer has no idea how special my house is," Jack says, sliding into his usual diatribe.

I don't want to make the same mistake I made yesterday, of giving Jack reason to feel I am not on his side. But Jack also needs to know the truth. Perhaps a more subtle approach may work. I decide to use a trick I learned from Mary Moeller years back—paraphrasing what clients tell you. So I say, "What I hear you saying is that you feel your house is just as special as the homes which sold for a million and a half—is that correct?"

"Yes," is Jack's response.

He is not being specific enough and I want to get to the root of his thinking so I need to ask why. "Because?"

"My house has more square footage, lots of intricate detailing and is on a corner lot."

"I see. You think your house has lots of space and detailing and because it is on a corner, it is worth just as much as the houses that sold?"

"Yes," he says.

"Even though some of those houses had a backyard, a view and were recently remodeled?" I ask.

"Yes," he says testily.

> **RULE 7-4: PARAPHRASE WHAT CLIENTS SAY** When you repeat what people say back to them it will do two things: 1) show them you are listening carefully and 2) force them to re-think what they just told you.

At this point I need to agree with him on something. "Well, your house certainly has the original detailing intact. And it has great light, because it is on the corner," I say. "What I think would be helpful is if we take a look at our competition. Why don't I set up some appointments for tomorrow and we can look at them together?"

"That isn't necessary," he says. "I've decided not to counter—the price is way too low."

"Really?" I remind myself that to get Jack's cooperation he needs to feel like he has been heard. I rephrase what he just said into a question. "So you think the price is too low?"

"Yes."

"Jack, what makes you think the price is too low?" I ask, hoping he will re-examine his reasoning.

He does not answer and I do not answer for him. Silence is golden. An old, but very useful negotiating tool. I remember what Tosca told me once—the reason we have two ears and one mouth is because we are supposed to listen twice as much as talking.

"The price is just too low," he says.

"Hmmm," I say. There is a long pause. Jack says he has to go. Even though he refused to answer my question, I am hoping that he will start rethinking his position.

Once at the office I call Dania, the buyer's agent. "Jack's considering your offer, but still digesting the low price."

"When is he planning to counter us?" she asks.

"He's just not ready to respond to you yet," I reply, knowing this is what happens when buyers' offers are too low. She asks me if Jack is upset with them. I don't like to set up either party as 'Bad' or the 'Enemy' so I explain that Jack is hoping for a better price than what they offered, adding, "Dania, realize that he is having a hard time letting go. This may take some time. Let's give him a few more days and I'll do my best to get him to respond."

"Truthfully, Paula, I don't know if my buyers will wait that long. They may start to cool."

Time is of the essence, as it says in the contract, and Jack was stalling. However, I also knew these buyers were desperate for a home, having just had a baby. On the off chance that these buyers simply had to have this house, I suggest to Dania that they put in another offer.

"Why should we do that? The seller is supposed to respond to us!"

"You're right, that is how it's usually done, but Jack is being a bit slow in reacting. I don't want your buyers to get discouraged. If we could just keep the communication lines open—even if you come up only ten thousand dollars—maybe it will be the push Jack needs. Just because his ego is getting in the way of this sale, doesn't mean you can't do something."

"I don't think we'll do that," Dania answers curtly. "My buyers don't want the property that bad."

It bothers me when agents answer for their clients without consulting with them first. One never knows what clients will do. "It doesn't hurt to ask," I say, hoping she'll reconsider.

She refuses. Her unwillingness to explore other options gives me only one choice. Go back to Jack and beg for a counter. In spite of all my pleading and sound arguments, Jack will not respond—even with no other potential offers on the horizon. "I've moved on," he says. "You should too."

I break the disappointing news to Dania and she delivers a fait complète—the buyers are putting an offer on their second choice. Tosca and I still have six weeks left on the listing. We make an appointment with Jack to discuss what's next. I am not afraid to ask the direct question—which both Tosca and I want to know—"Are you sure you want to sell?" If Jack continues to be unreasonable, we need to focus on other clients who will use our help and expertise to bring a sale to fruition.

> RULE #7-5: DETACH FROM THE OUTCOME Present your clients with the facts and then let them make their decision. You cannot force anyone to do anything they do not want to do. They may not be ready to sell (or buy) and need to lose a few sales first.

Jack assures both of us he does indeed want to sell. We meet with him and brainstorm on how to get more agents and their clients to come take another look. We've already had Sunday open houses, broker tours, and plenty of ads in local newspapers and magazines. We decide to host an afternoon twilight tour with wine and cheese. "We'll put up plenty of signs to get people driving home from work, and send out invitations to all the top agents," is my suggestion.

Jack is caught up in our optimism and has forgotten all about the past few days. "Now you're talking! I have a magnificent watercolor of the exterior, why don't we use that for the invitations?"

Tosca suggests that the attendees sign in a guest book. There will be a place for them to put comments about whether they think the house is a possibility. "That way, any negative feedback will be coming directly from the prospective purchasers so Jack can't get mad at us," Tosca whispers to me while we're alone.

"It's a great idea," I whisper back. Now it will be hard for Jack to deny the truth of what we have been telling him all along. The wine and cheese preview does not bring a buyer, but it does show Jack that we are on his side. We leave the clients' remarks with him, deciding it is best for him to review their comments in private. In that way, he can absorb what the buyers are really thinking, save face and not put the blame on us.

What to do next? We have done extensive marketing for four months with only one low offer. Anyone who is looking in the million-and-a-half price range has already seen the home. "We have given Jack the reasons why his house isn't selling," I say to Tosca, "but he has trouble hearing the truth. Both of us have been patient and listened to his concerns, but wishing and hoping won't change the facts. The market has spoken. We need for him to agree to a significant price reduction."

We have had the listing with Jack for four months now and it is about to expire. We ask for a three month extension with a ten percent price reduction. Anything less will have no effect. MLS statistics show buyers feel comfortable offering no more than five percent lower than the asking price. It is extremely rare that they will come in with less. We have no expectation of whether Jack will agree, but we remain positive, knowing if this transaction does not come to pass, another one will fill its place.

Jack is tired of keeping his house spotless, annoyed that he has to be gone every Tuesday and Sunday afternoon for open houses. He is just plain anxious to move on with his life. "Maybe I should have taken the first offer," he says when we tell him our plan to reduce.

"First offers are often the best," I say, "but we understand your reluctance. You wanted to be absolutely sure that we had fully marketed the house. The best scenario now would be if we reduce the price significantly so that the Brokers' community will take notice. Then hopefully we'll get multiple showings and maybe even multiple offers."

"Meaning," Tosca adds, "We may get you a higher price when two people start bidding on your home. To just continue on like we've been doing won't accomplish much."

"But maybe if I listed with another Realtor they would bring in more buyers," Jack says. He gives us an encouraging wink.

I bet he's just testing us. "Is there anything you want us to add to our marketing plan?" I ask, making sure my voice is soft. "You must know we want to sell this house as badly as you do and will do whatever it takes."

Jack smiles. "You gals have done a great job and I can't think of anything else you could have done differently. You really hung in there with me even when I was discouraged. I appreciate your thoroughness, upbeat attitude and optimism throughout this whole process."

"I have an idea!" I say. "Why don't we call all the agents who have toured the property about the price reduction and tell them you are really motivated to sell. That way maybe a previous buyer is still out there who saw the property, but felt he couldn't afford it."

"Will you also carry a small second loan?" Tosca asks. "That will also help some buyers who don't have the twenty percent down payment."

"Well, I don't need all my money right now," Jack says. "If it helps me sell, I'll do it."

I take out my Hewlett Packard calculator. "If we reduce to $1,350,000, a ten percent second loan at 9% with interest only payment would be $12,150 a year. Over ten years it would be a total of $121,500 in your pocket."

"Hmm," Jack says. "You are two smart gals. That would mean I would be getting just about what I wanted in the first place. Okay, sign me up for the extension and the full ten percent price reduction. Just promise me you'll call all the agents and let them know we reduced."

Both Tosca and I answer at once, "We promise!"

That week we get several showings. An agent who had shown Jack's home twice to the same client tells me she may be bringing in an offer. On a whim I call Dania Bellington, the agent who brought in the first offer. I knew her client had to sell a property before they bought one—so maybe this buyer was still around. Once they hear that someone else is considering buying, that may spike their interest. My hunch proves to be correct. Their second choice fell through, because Dania's buyer couldn't sell their home in time. Knowing another party was interested geared them into action. They offered $100,000 more than their initial offer and to counteract the sting of the higher price, asked Jack to carry the 10 % loan. Jack ended up getting more than he expected and was one happy camper. He still sends me referrals to this day.

Chapter Eight

EMPATHY
Understanding Others

AT THE END OF MY FIRST YEAR of real estate in San Francisco I am the number one agent in our office. Confronting my fears, disciplining my mind, keeping positive and developing a strong sense of self help me change destructive patterns into success stories. No one cares that I am driving a Chevette, and not being from California, don't know anyone.

Tina Linstrom, a part time agent in my office, wants me to represent her and her husband in the sale of a house they just built. Tina is a tiny woman in her early forties, perky and upbeat. Her husband is a handsome, big Swede with thick, wavy, blonde hair and massive hands, reminding me of Paul Bunyan. He is a licensed contractor and appropriately named Butch. Despite the fact that she is a third his size Tina is the decision maker so I easily get the listing. They are a fun and outgoing couple. I'm excited, thinking this will be an easy slam dunk transaction.

A few months into the marketing, we obtain an offer on a cold, rainy night in November. Tina asks if I can meet them at their home. It is better to meet clients at the office, but wanting to please her, I agree. Besides, I tell myself, this is a spec home (a home they built for profit) and Tina and Butch Linstrom are sophisticated sellers.

Because it is the first heavy rain of the season, the roads are slick and there is a prolonged traffic backup. Running late, I am beginning to regret my decision. Not only is her house in an inconvenient location, but I won't have access to a copying machine and any forms I may need. Was I scared or just lazy when I agreed to her suggestion? Through the pouring rain, black night and dimly lit streets I strain to find the house number I have jotted down in my planner. After circling the block several times, I find their majestic contemporary home in Golden Gate Heights with the spectacular views of the famous bridge. I glance at my watch as I grab my umbrella. I make a hasty dash for the door, but still get drenched. Dripping, I ring the doorbell. Tina answers and ushers me inside. While taking off my raincoat, I can hear talking in the background. The other agent has arrived before me. Damn!

Tina introduces me to Ming Le, who I spoke to briefly over the phone this morning. Shouldn't it have been the other way around? Me introducing Ming Le to my clients? We gather around the dining table as Ming Le describes her client—a young Asian family (not too much of a surprise—Asians love new construction). The newly constructed home is perfect for their three children and also close to their family business, a laundromat, in Noe Valley. A perfect location for the burgeoning bourgeoisie neighborhood (Sunny and safe and convenient to the freeways and downtown, this location is perfect for small families). Since the buyers are not salaried employees, I am a bit concerned if they can qualify. Ming Le hands us each a copy of their prequalification letter. All appears to be in order. I notice Tina and Butch shifting in their seats. I need to move this process along. I extend my hand and ask for the contract. Ming Le hands it over as she explains the minor contingencies. My eyes scan downward, searching for the purchase price and am as unprepared as Tina and Butch when we see it.

Tina, unable to hide her disappointment, gives Ming Le a cold hard stare. "How could you be a guest in my house and insult me like this?" She starts to tear her copy of the contract in tiny pieces and throws the ragged shreds on to the table. I am speechless, unable to comprehend what is happening to my good-natured colleague. Butch puts his arm around his wife and gives me a reproachful look. Starting to sob, Tina points to the door, asking Ming Le to get the hell out of her house. I follow, whispering a hollowed regret with a promise that I will call her tomorrow.

I hesitate in the entryway, taking a deep breath to calm myself as I turn around to face the Linstroms, wondering what awaits me. I know I screwed up and now I have to take the consequences. I am in a foggy haze as I make it back to the dining room and sit down. Tina has put her head in her hands and won't look at me. Butch shakes his head as he leaves the room. I do my best to remain cool and collected all the while feeling my blouse clinging to my back with sticky perspiration. Surely, deep circles of water stains are forming underneath my armpits. I take a tiny sip from my water glass passing the time in deadening silence.

Tina looks up at me with a tear stained face. "How could you have allowed this to happen? Butch spent two years of his life designing and building that house. What do you take us for—fools?"

I mumble a few words about how excited I was to receive the offer that I didn't think of asking for the details. My excuse is having little effect on Tina. Her face is still squished up in pain as if she just got hit by a fast volleyball. I remember what Mr. Carrington told me when I first started. Give clients a good war story of what happened in the past and what you learned. People learn from stories. But I cannot think of any. I am too new in the business. There's also the three F's that work well in negotiating. The three F's are… are… I'm a freakin', f—— failure! *No, think positive,* I tell myself. All is not yet lost. I rack my brain. What are the three F's? Something about *feeling.* That has always been the hardest part for me—the empathy—understanding how other people feel. Feeling… Feeling… Ahhh! Now I remember! *Feel, Felt, Found!*

"I understand how you must be feeling," I say, still groping for what to say next. "I've felt… felt that way before."

"What do you mean you know how I'm feeling?" Tina's voice sounds accusatory. Maybe she knows I'm just reciting some sort of sales script. "Exactly what is it I'm feeling?"

"Well… ahhh… you must be feeling hurt and ahhh… betrayed… Yes. Betrayed." I hit a deep core truth. When all else fails, tell the truth—even if it makes you look bad, That's what Dad always said, not to mention my EST presenter. "Because… because… I didn't take care of you well enough." There. I said it. The truth is now out in the open. "I should have prepared you for the low offering price."

RULE #8-1: BE EMPATHETIC Since you are the conduit between buyer and seller, who will, in all likelihood, not meet each other's expectations, clients may misdirect their disappointment at you. You need to be understanding during the selling process as well as a supportive sounding board and their voice of reason.

Tina's face softens slightly, but her words do not. "It's over and done. I'm going to bed now." She stands up.

Feel, Felt, Found. What's the found?? I'm about to lose her. What's the found? "I've found that… " I hesitate, "it's… ahhh… not good to… ahhh… give up too quickly. Yeah, that's right… Let's not give up quite yet. Let's give them another chance."

Tina turns sharply around. "Paula, are you crazy? We're miles apart—Miles!"

"Yeah, I know," I say, forming the words slowly as they come to my head. "You're probably right—these buyers probably won't come up to our price—but what if we're wrong? That's right, Tina. What if you and I are wrong? What if they really want the house and have to have it? We will never know unless we ask."

"Goodnight, Paula."

I stay glued to where I sit even when she motions for me to get up.

Tina glares at me in amazement. "Whose side are you on anyway?"

I continue, knowing I am on to something. "One thing we know for sure is if we don't give them a counter, we definitely won't have a sale. Some of this is my fault. I should have spoken to the agent ahead of time and found out more about the offer so I could have prepared you. But, Tina, let's not take my mistake out on these buyers. It won't cost us anything—just a couple of minutes. It is worth taking the time to write something up, don't you think?" I sit with my hands folded neatly in my lap and wait.

Tina sits back down. The room is so quiet that I am tempted to fill the space with more talking, but that would interrupt the process that Tina is going through—trying to figure out what to do next. I stay with my uncomfortable feelings, knowing that this is one of the main reasons salespeople are paid so well. Butch looks in from the kitchen where he had escaped during his wife's tirade. He is also waiting.

"Okay. I'll do it. Just hurry and write it up. Butch, you can come in now. We're giving them a counter."

The next day I deliver Ming Le a verbal apology and a written counteroffer. By the end of the day her clients agree to all the terms we asked, giving proof that *it's not over till it's over.* I now explain to sellers that when an agent presents an offer, focus only on the financial qualifications of the buyer and the terms of the offer and don't take anything personally. They can ask the agent if the buyers can extend the close of escrow or shorten the contingency period of inspections or loan approval, but it is best to stay away from discussing value. "Wait for the agent to leave," I say, "then we can discuss the offering price on our own and counter what we think is reasonable. We don't want to be volleying back and forth with the other agent, who is only trying to represent her buyers in getting them the best possible price."

I also no longer make presentations at sellers' homes where they are liable to get too emotional. Even if sellers are motivated to sell, they are letting go of something that has had a lot of meaning to them. Who knows if they will be as happy in their new home? Maybe they have to prematurely sell for financial reasons. Or maybe they are getting a divorce. Or their children have grown and left. Whatever their reason for selling, sellers will most likely have conflicting feelings. I also make light of the bidding process, comparing it to a game of poker—one party makes a move, then the other and so on. Simply put, you've got to know when to hold, when to fold and when to walk away.

> RULE #8-2: PREPARE YOUR CLIENTS ON WHAT TO EXPECT No one likes to be put in a situation in which they do not know the rules of the game. Explain to your clients that there will be negotiation back and forth from both sides. Hopefully, they will meet somewhere in between where it can be a win-win situation for both parties.

Cindy Wilson is pretty, personable, and smart yet she has a hard time making enough commissions to pay her bills. She has been selling real estate for over fifteen years and reads all the positive thinking books she can get her hands on, takes all the newest seminars, and understands the basic principles of selling. But Cindy just can't seem to close the sale.

In my eight week training session I observed that Cindy talks too much and too often, appearing desperate. Coming from a strict traditional Greek family, Cindy confided to me that she has a strong need to be liked, but sales is about focusing on clients' wants and interests and not what we need. When she gets a floor call from a man who wants to sell his home in the Inner Sunset near Golden Gate Park, she asks me to help. It is a Marina style, built in the forties, and showing the beginning signs of wear and tear. In other words, it needs a paint job and maybe a new roof.

Mr. Chase greets us at the door with a quick handshake. My guess is he is in his eighties and now needs a retirement home. We head down to the garage first and work our way up. He shows us the burglar alarm system, the circuit breakers and the washer and dryer. We both nod our heads as he explains when they were installed and their warranties. Realizing we need to connect with Mr. Chase on a more personal level, I make my way past packed cardboard boxes to the oil paintings stacked along the sidewall of the garage. "Mr. Chase, did you paint all of these?"

"My late wife, may she rest in peace, was the artist of the family." He gingerly picks up one of the paintings and shows it to us. "This is one of the many bridges in Shanghai. Notice how Rose was able to catch the shadows of the afternoon sun. Just look at the detail. Every time I study this painting I see something new. She was quite a gal, my wife."

Cindy is the first to speak. "One of my girlfriends is a flight attendant and she raves about her visits to Shanghai. What is it about the city that people like so much?"

(Perfect! Even though Cindy has never been to Asia, she came from curiosity and asked an open-ended question to establish rapport.)

With eyes bright and shining, Mr. Chase shows us a few more paintings as he describes the background story of each one. When there is a lull in the conversation, I point to the large bolts in the mudsill partially hidden by the boxes.

"I see you've gotten some seismic work done recently—a buyer is going to love to see that! And look at how close the studs are—they just don't make houses like this anymore."

Mr. Chase continues to expound on the many virtues of his home as we take notes and listen for the reason he is selling. Since he also has a rental unit, I ask if the house and apartment are separately metered.

"Oh, yes, and we have 220 amp service to the kitchen and laundry room. Both units also have their own hot water heaters and forced air furnaces which are periodically checked and maintained."

"I'm assuming the apartment's legal?" I ask.

"Oh, yes, of course. I have all the paperwork if you need it."

"That would be great. While we're talking about the systems of the house, do you know the condition and age of the roof?"

"It's about ten—fifteen years old," he replies

Probably more like fifteen, I'm thinking. Sellers tend to be overly optimistic when talking about the house they love. To get to the bottom of the truth, I ask, "Have you ever had any leaks?"

"One about a year ago, but it's all fixed."

"Do you happen to have the invoice for the repairs? We will need to disclose this incident to any prospective purchaser."

Mr. Chase scratches his chin and his eyes are starting to glaze over. I need to set him at ease. "Don't worry," I say with a broad smile, "most buyers realize there is no such thing as a perfect house. Besides, they will trust you more when you tell them about defects upfront." Realizing that the conversation is becoming too serious, I glance around the garage until my eyes land on a tennis racket. "So, I see you play tennis?"

Mr. Chase's eyes brighten once again. "It's such a great exercise running up and down the court—even though I don't play that much anymore." He goes into detail about the technicalities of the game. I find myself nodding, recalling the time in the seventies when Billie Jean King beat Bobby Riggs. I make a joke about the tennis match and Mr. Chase laughs, outwardly pleased that I have taken an interest in his much beloved sport.

"Any place close by where you can play?" I ask, thinking this can also be a selling point.

"Yeah, by the high school—near the new Starbucks."

I jot down both these items as Cindy describes her morning walks around Stern Lake which she finds exhilarating. They continue talking as we make our way up to the main part of the house. Although neither Cindy nor I are artists, have ever been to Asia or played tennis, we are well on our way to forming a solid business relationship with a man whom we just met.

> RULE #8-3: FIND COMMON GROUND People want to do business with people who they like and trust. To connect with clients find some similar interests which you can talk about. In other words, make business more personal. The emotional bond will help you create a more solid relationship with them.

During the rest of the tour I make sure I ask the following four questions in between our casual chit-chatting:

Why are you planning to move?
(This will weed out the 'Not So Motivated Sellers' from the 'Real Ones.')

What's your timetable?
(This also will help qualify how motivated a seller is.)

How many agents are you interviewing?
(If I feel that a seller won't be offended, I ask who they are. If they don't want to share the name of the agent, they will usually share the name of the firm. Then I will know who my competition is and how to better plan my presentation.)

What are you looking for in an agent?
(I don't understand why more agents don't ask this question. When asked, most people will tell you what their expectations are. Then in the second meeting, you can mirror back what they told you. If you get the listing, the next step is to deliver what was promised.)

Before we leave we sit down at the kitchen table and show Mr. Chase samples of our company's advertising and history as well as background information on ourselves and a pricing and staging video. "We'll leave this for you to review at your leisure," I say. This accomplishes three things—it informs him of our qualifications without boasting, educates him on how to get the highest price and gives us a reason to meet with him again.

Of course, Mr. Chase asks the inevitable question every seller wants to know—"What do you think my house is worth?"

I hesitate to give him a number. Almost all sellers have a price in mind. When you come in too low, it is hard to back pedal. Even though sellers claim they don't choose an agent on price, they often do. I have lost many listings being right instead of listening to sellers' expectations.

I rephrase his question and toss it back to him. "Well, Mr. Chase, do you have any idea what your home's worth?" This is called the 'porcupine' or 'hot potato' close—a great way to find out what price he has in mind.

"At least a million—but I'm really curious what you think. A ballpark figure will be fine."

"Mr. Chase, your house is a valuable asset and this question deserves some thoughtful consideration. Why don't Cindy and I go back to the office and do a market analysis for you?" To soften my response I make sure I put my reply in the form of a question.

"Just give me an estimate." He smiles sweetly as he says this.

If we give him a reply right now, we may not have the opportunity to meet with him again. I think carefully before I respond.

"We'd love to give you an answer today, but I feel we would be short changing you if we did. We need to extrapolate all the data on similar type properties that have sold in the last six months plus the ones currently on the market to give you an accurate price."

I take out my calendar and using the alternative assumption close, ask, "Would Tuesday at five work or is Wednesday better?"

He tells us Tuesday works just fine. Like most sellers he is going to want to know two things—*what we think his house is worth* and *what we are going to do to sell it.* If we can convince Mr. Chase that we are capable of getting him a high price, plus eliminate the high stress of selling, we will have an excellent chance of getting the listing.

We present our three point plan—Pricing, Marketing, and Staging—paying close attention to Mr. Chase's body language and letting him guide us to how much detail we give him. If he starts to fidget and look away, I know he's losing interest and I need to speed things up. If his eyebrows crunch closely together, he's probably getting confused. Then I either need to slow down or not go into so much detail. If his body is relaxed and he asks questions every so often, my pace is just right.

When we talk about getting the property ready for sale, I do my best to present the changes he needs to make in such a way that he won't feel overwhelmed. "You really don't have to do much," I assure him. "We'll organize everything. We just need to paint a little bit here and there, rearrange some furniture and store away some of your personal belongings." I point to family photos prominently displayed on his fireplace mantle.

Mr. Chase has the typical reaction and starts to object. "Why is all this so necessary? I enjoy my things and house just the way they are."

"That is why we need to make some changes, Mr. Chase. This is your house now, but once you decide to sell it begins the process of letting go. Your house is going to belong to some buyer out there soon." I make a big arc with my arm, pointing outside.

His face morphs from being soft and open into more angular and stern. Empathizing with what he is going through, Cindy says, "This transition is difficult for most sellers. Think of your home as a means to getting onto your next phase of life—a place which better suits your current needs." Then she adds in a soft soothing voice, "Remember, we'll be here to help."

I pause a few moments while he ponders Cindy's comforting words, and then ask a pointed question to get his commitment. "You did say that you wanted the highest price possible for your home didn't you, Mr. Chase?"

He nods his head.

"Well, de-personalizing your home will get you a better price. Prospective purchasers can better imagine themselves living in a house that has a neutral, yet warm atmosphere. We can help you create that feeling by doing some minor modifications. Keep a special photo or two in your bedroom if you like, and if there is something else you really don't want changed, just let us know."

Mr. Chase takes his time to answer. "I don't have to remodel a kitchen or bathroom, do I?"

If we were talking with a young, energetic couple who wanted to make the most of their house investment, we would say, "Yes." The stress it would cause Mr. Chase would be too much so we tell him we don't think it necessary. "We'll simply hire a professional interior decorator to place the furniture—using mostly yours of course. She may bring in a few pieces of her own, such as bed linens, pillows and maybe a chair or two to tie everything together. If you agree, maybe we could replace the rusty bathroom cabinet and the hallway sconce which is a bit dated."

He agrees, providing we do all the coordinating. He also insists we leave one of the photos of his wife and all the paintings in the dining and living room exactly where they are. It is not the perfect scenario, but feasible.

It is now time for us to go in for the close once again. "I feel we have a good rapport going on here, don't you agree?" I ask, watching his face as I talk.

He gives a small smile as he nods in agreement.

"Do you feel comfortable in making those small changes we recommended so that we can get you the highest price?"

He agrees to that as well. I purposely build up agreement on the smaller items first to get him used to saying *Yes*. "With those agreed changes then we would recommend a list price of $1,300,000 to $1,400,000. Is that in the price range you were thinking, Mr. Chase?" (I always like to give a range and then ask what price other agents gave. If I can get that information up front, so much the better. In any case, I do not write the price range on the market analysis I give clients. If the market changes, or if I am overly optimistic, it is easier to get a price reduction later.) Again, I watch closely for his reaction.

He confides to us that one agent came in much higher, but four other agents were in agreement with us. "So I'm not sure what that means," he says.

"Do you want my opinion?" I ask, knowing I am on sensitive ground.

His facial muscles are relaxed and his voice soft as he says, "Yes, I'd be curious what you think."

"Well, the agent who came in higher probably hoped you would go with the highest bidder, but that's not the best way to choose your agent," I say. I give him the MLS statistics which show that the majority of activity is in the first six weeks a property is on the market. After that the chances of getting the list price or higher is greatly diminished. And if a property is listed too high initially, the seller will probably get less than if he had listed more realistically in the beginning.

Mr. Chase nods in agreement. "That makes perfect sense," he says.

Now Cindy and I need to follow up with all the positive reasons for listing with us. "As I'm sure we've proven to you, we're knowledgeable in your area, have an aggressive marketing plan, and a good name behind us with a trusted client base. We also have the contacts to help you spruce up your property and stage it so it shows to its best advantage." I pull out the Exclusive Right to Sell Agreement from my briefcase and ask, "Why don't we start this process and move forward?"

Mr. Chase says nothing. Cindy starts to talk and I shoot her a look that closes her mouth so fast she almost bites her lip. Thank goodness—she remembered that the person who talks first loses! Several more seconds pass. It feels like forever. Mr. Chase appears as if he is deep in thought, pondering what to do. Cindy shifts uncomfortably in her chair and fiddles with her purse. Meanwhile, I pretend I have all the time in the world.

Mr. Chase finally speaks. "I'm not ready. Let's wait."

I know I have to proceed cautiously. "What's there to think about?" I ask as I lift my eyelids to see how he is handling the pressure. I notice he has folded his arms neatly over his chest and his mouth is curving downward. He is withdrawing. I need to change tactics—and try a softer, more subtle approach.

"Mr. Chase, I understand your hesitancy. Selling a home is a big decision. Just know that we love your house, and want to represent you. Fortunately, we came prepared and filled out the paperwork ahead of time. Why don't we leave it with you and you can go over it at your convenience?" I graciously back away and given him some space so he can think this over.

His austere expression softens as he takes the paperwork. Cindy and I get up from where we are sitting and give him a warm hand-shake. "Please feel free to call us if you have any questions."

That afternoon Cindy sends Mr. Chase a handwritten note thank-ing him for considering us as the representatives for his lovely home. She takes the letter to the post office herself, knowing that we need to keep our name in front of him as much as possible while he is mak-ing his decision.

We call Mr. Chase a few days later to reconnect. He has a long list of questions. We're helpful, but not too much so—we want him need-ing our expertise. We also need another face-to-face meeting. Rarely can one close a deal over the phone.

"Mr. Chase we can answer these questions better in person," I say, talking slowly so he can hear over our speaker phone. "Every home… in fact, every sale is different. We are going to be in your neighbor-hood this afternoon. Why don't we stop by?"

There is a long pause. It is probably obvious to Mr. Chase that we will be asking him to sign the listing, but there are other agents calling him. We do not have the luxury of being patient. Persistent yet pa-tient pressure is what is needed now. He agrees. I have another ap-pointment, but rearrange my schedule. Something could always come up to prevent him from signing with us and I do not want that chance.

He welcomes us inside with a strong handshake. I return the hand-shake with an equal amount of pressure. He shows us into the dining room and asks if we would like a cup of coffee. Normally, I'm not a coffee drinker, but when I see he has a cup, I say yes.

"I take sugar no cream," Mr. Chase says, handing us the sugar bowl. "How about the two of you?"

"That would be perfect, thank you," Cindy answers. I agree.

"Do you plan to hold open houses?" Mr. Chase asks as he crosses his right leg over his left. His voice is low and his speech slow.

"We were planning to have both Broker Opens and Sunday Opens if that's okay with you," I say. I make sure I do not speak too quickly or loudly, wanting to follow Mr. Chase's speech pattern.

Mr. Chase leans closer as he says, "I'm concerned about security, especially the paintings I have stored in the garage."

"We can always keep the garage door locked and interested parties can make an appointment to come look at a later time. This way we will be able to determine the serious buyers from the 'Lookey-Lous.'" I slowly cross my right leg over my left mirroring his posture.

RULE #8-4: CONNECT THROUGH BODY LANGUAGE People give off non-verbal signals all the time, indicating what they are feeling. Observe your clients carefully to obtain clues on how to communicate more effectively with them. Whenever possible subtly mirror their posture, facial expressions and gestures. This will insure connection.

"Explain to me again what you'll be doing to market my property." Mr. Chase looks at me directly as he says this and holds a pen ready to write.

I meet his gaze as I take my pen in hand. "I've listed all the magazines, newspapers and online sites where we will be advertising with the approximate publishing dates, but feel free to take any notes if you wish." I explain that we will put his home on the MLS, in which all the 3,500 agents in the city will have access, as well as my company's website, my own website, Cindy's, Realtor.com's and his own website with his address. I give him examples of 'Just Listed' cards, invitations to the first Broker tour and Sunday Opens and a promise of a professional photographer for the color brochure.

"What will you do differently from other agents?" he asks, his posture erect.

I make sure I am sitting straight as I answer. I tell him that either Cindy or I will personally accompany all showings and follow up with a phone call to the agent. "That way we'll know right away their feedback and communicate with you after each showing. Most agents will just put on a lock box, hand out a key or have their assistant show your home. With us you will have two full time agents working for you 24 hours a day, seven days a week. We will be 100% available. Who knows? That one person we accommodate which other agents can't because of their heavy schedule could be the perfect buyer." I take a long pause and then ask, "So, do we have the listing?"

"If you're this persistent with me," Mr. Chase says, "you're going to be persistent with buyers. I like that."

We wait while he ponders our request.

"Yes, you can have the listing," is his final answer.

Cindy and I let out a cheerleading-like whoop of happiness. We shake Mr. Chases's hand, telling him we will take excellent care of him. I make sure to have the Agency Disclosure signed first, then the Commission Agreement, and then the MLS Information Form. There are at least twenty other disclosure forms and instead of just leaving them with him to sign—sellers usually are too overwhelmed to fill out these forms themselves—I ask if now is a good time. "It will take a least an hour to complete the rest of the paperwork, but we can always come back at another, more convenient time." I say, making it an easy process for the client.

Mr. Chase gives us a wink. "Now that we've come this far, let's do it." He gets another cup of coffee for each of us and we spend the next hour filling out disclosures. Right before we leave, I offhandedly ask why he chose us instead of the five other agents he interviewed. (If we hadn't gotten the listing, I would have also asked the same question. I find this information invaluable in helping me fine-tune my presentations.)

"All the others told me about how great they were and what they've done, but you and Cindy were different. I felt you really cared about me and would not only get me a high price for my house, but also would support me throughout this whole selling process. That was more important than any Million Dollar Club or how long I knew someone. One guy, who is the top agent at Prudential and lives down the street will be very disappointed, but I felt I had to go with my gut instincts."

Establishing rapport had gotten us his trust and in turn we got the listing. Sales may not be that academically difficult, but it is challenging in a more significant way—emotionally. To be successful requires that you develop a firm anchor of who you are so that you can handle a parade of situations. That is why I like real estate so much. It is not the typical nine to five, but requires constant learning.

I am putting away my exercise mat when my Pilates teacher, Deborah Knox, approaches me. "Paula, I heard you are in real estate."

"Yep. Been doing it for almost thirty years now," I answer.

"Do you ever sell in Oakland? My daughter, Roberta, needs some real estate advice. She bought a condo there nine months ago and she and her boyfriend are breaking up." Deborah looks up at me, doing her best to steady her voice. "She needs to sell yesterday."

Oakland does not have the best reputation, because of all its crime statistics, unemployment and high school dropout rates. On the upside, parts of it are beautiful, they had a great Mayor in Jerry Brown and it is affordable. When clients get discouraged with the high prices of San Francisco, they often decide that the short commute—in spite of the congested traffic of the Bay Bridge—is the answer. Besides, there's the Bay Area Rapid Transit system (BART), the usually efficient subway system to the financial district, Union Square, Civic Center and airport.

I put my hand on Deborah's shoulder. "There's a gal, Dona Fuller, in my office who lives in the East Bay and sells in Oakland. She can help me do a market analysis." I usually do not sell outside the area of my expertise, San Francisco, because I do not think it is fair to the client. Plus, it is immensely time consuming to learn a whole new market. I find that specializing in an area is best. However, from the tone of Deborah's voice, I sense that her daughter has gotten herself into a difficult situation and I did not feel comfortable passing this off to someone else. I write down the address of Roberta's condo as well as her phone number.

As soon as I get home I call Dona. "How busy are you these days?" I ask. "I have a lead for a listing. Roberta Knox, a daughter of a friend of mine, bought a new condo with her boyfriend less than a year ago and now needs to sell. They're breaking up."

"Uh-oh. I know the market is still streaming along in San Francisco, but in Oakland it is not quite so rosy. Especially if these clients just bought and especially if they bought in a new development. You know what the developers are doing over here, don't you?"

"No," I say, not trying to get alarmed. "What are they doing?"

Dona speaks with an authoritative tone in her voice. "They are offering people these phenomenal terms so first time buyers can qualify. You know, no money down and a 4% interest rate for the first year. It is probably the only way these developers can sell all the new condos that have glutted the marketplace recently. So although people can qualify, they cannot afford to own long term, especially if something unforeseen happens—loss of a job, a pregnancy or divorce. And let's face it, in life, shit happens."

Call me conservative or old fashioned, but I am very skeptical of the 100% financing mortgage companies have been offering buyers the last few years. There was a good reason why lenders used to require 20% from buyers—they wanted some of their cash in the property so the buyers would be a committed partner in their investment. It would insure that they would make their monthly loan payments so as not to lose their down payment. I never understood why, all of a sudden, their strict rules of qualifying changed. In many cases lenders no longer required a credit report or payment stubs. People could just state what their income was and they would lend. It seemed so shortsighted on their part.

"I hope Roberta didn't agree to a negative amortization loan too," I say, "because then this will most likely be a short sale." A negative amortization loan arises when the mortgage payment is less than market rate which causes the loan balance to increase rather than decrease. These loans are also called "teasers," because the buyer is not paying the full amount of what he owes. A short sale is a sale in which the lender allows a property to be sold for less than the amount owed and takes a loss.

I had been *almost involved* in a short sale years before. One of my clients put a large second mortgage on their home to pay for their son's college. She was a nurse and her husband a civil engineer, but they knew nothing about finance. They probably would have been able to pay the loan back had it not been for the back breaking 17% interest rate. Perhaps their credit was not picture perfect or their combined income too low or they were just naïve and got the easiest loan offered to them—from one of those telephone solicitors. But whatever the reason, now they were stuck. Although taking out this second loan solved their short term problem, the exorbitant interest rate ended up being a major problem. A big portion of their monthly payment went to interest and not to principle so they were like indentured servants working their ass off for this greedy home equity lender. These companies should be banned from lending money. They prey on naïve, unsophisticated consumers. Ten years later and my clients were forced to sell their home. They had to rid themselves of their crushing debt, which felt like a weighted boulder on their chest. After two months on the market, we got an offer which was $25,000 short of their closing costs and the balance of their two mortgages. I did my best to negotiate with both the first and second loan. Both banks insisted my clients made plenty of money so they would not help. Over the next several weeks, I begged and begged, but neither bank would budge. Bankers tend to be very conservative and, although knowledgeable at lending, they don't know much about real estate. The buyer got impatient of waiting and bought something else. I put their house back on the market, but received no more offers.

My clients, who were respectable people with good values, became disillusioned and no longer felt an obligation to make their mortgage payments. Instead, they started saving money for a new rental which they knew was inevitable. Four months later the second lender called, ready to take our offer, but the buyer was long gone, the real estate market had softened, and both my clients and I were exhausted by the whole process. The lenders had to foreclose, fix up the house which my clients left in a state of disarray and take a price much less than our offer. My clients were forced out of a home in which they had raised two children. I received no commission for eight months of hard work and the bank got a house they did not want. That experience taught me to be leery of short sales.

"Why don't I do a market analysis and I'll get back to you?" Dona says.

"No matter what the answer—and it doesn't sound good—I owe it to my friend to meet with her daughter," I say.

> RULE #8-5: DO THE RIGHT THING Real estate is a service industry, on par with a teacher, nurse and firefighter. Our clients trust us with one of the major decisions of their lives and how we act has far reaching effects.

Dona calls me the next day with the news: the development project in which Roberta bought still has brand new condos up for sale—even less than what Roberta and her boyfriend paid.

"Yep, she's in trouble. Want to come with me when I deliver the bad news?" I ask.

"Sure," Dona says, "glad to help."

Dona meets me out in front of the condo the next day. It is a bright and sunny afternoon, but on this particular block of MacArthur Avenue, I find myself looking over my shoulder. I would not want to be here at night, I tell myself. Why do people make these dumb decisions? I shudder. Walking up to Roberta's unit, we notice large alluring signs pointing to the sales office, claiming no money down, phenomenal interest rates and no homeowner payments for a year. The whole manipulating scenario makes me want to gag.

We ring the doorbell and are buzzed inside. There is a long narrow staircase which leads us to the top where we shake Roberta's hand. She is a beautiful young woman with coffee colored skin, short dark hair and almond shaped eyes. She is dressed in an expensive business suit and tells us she is on her lunch hour. She shows us around the ultra modern condo with its eye popping granite, cherry cabinet kitchen, sky lighted living/dining combo area and marble bathroom boasting European fixtures. So this is how the developers hooked them.

One of the bedrooms is filled with toys. "Don't worry," Roberta says, "we'll clean all this up."

"You have a child?" I ask incredulously.

"Oh, I guess Mom didn't tell you. I have a seven year old daughter from my first marriage. The light of my life and the reason I want to quit my corporate job. I just don't have the time to be with her."

So, here we have a situation in which there is a relationship falling apart with a child involved, a mother who wants to quit her job and both adults being overextended financially. This is going to be one big headache.

I suggest we go over the comparables. Dona lays them out on the cold grey stone counter while Roberta and I get comfortable on the bar stools. She describes the current listings and recent sold properties. She points to prices hovering around $640,000—$10,000 less than the price they paid. Roberta is visibly upset. "What about all the curtains I put in? And the washer/dryer? They are brand new."

"Yes, they are—as are the two units on the market in your development which are still being sold by the developer." I soften my voice when I add, "Buyers like new. That is why they will buy the never before lived in units the developer has on the market before yours. For a buyer to buy your unit, your price will have to be lower than what he is offering. Especially, because you cannot offer buyers the terms the developer is offering."

"You mean, I am going to have to come up with money to sell this condo?"

"It looks like it," Dona says.

"Do you have your closing papers and mortgage information I can look at?" I ask. I had told Roberta we would want to see this paperwork to help advise her. I look them over. "It appears you only had to put down $6500 for closing costs," I say.

"That's right," Roberta says. "Buying here was about the same as renting. Plus," she waves her hands around, "you can see for yourself how beautiful it is."

I smile softly. "It certainly is and you have done a wonderful job of making a lovely home." Breaking more bad news is going to be painful. I just reviewed her promissory note which states the terms of her loan. "Who was your real estate agent?" I ask.

"We didn't have one. We just walked in here one day and the person on site showed us how we could afford this new home. We jumped at the chance to finally own."

"I see," I say, "—*the American Dream.* That explains it then."

"Explains what?"

"Are you aware that your payment is going up $570 next month?"

"What?" she screams as she reaches for the papers out of my hand.

"The first year's monthly payment is what they call in the business a 'teaser rate.' It is just a way to help you get started in owning a home."

Roberta thinks a moment. "Yeah, now I remember. They did mention that with increase of appreciation and the fact that our salaries would be increasing would make everything all work out."

"Unfortunately, they sell you on only the best case scenarios," Dona says.

Roberta starts talking again. "The truth is neither of our salaries has increased and, like I might have mentioned, I am tired of the corporate world. The hours are killer. I never get to see my baby girl and Ralph is not into taking care of a child who is not his. Plus, we're fighting a lot."

She seemed wistful and withdrawn. I wonder if there is some domestic abuse going on. Not unlikely, especially when there are financial woes thrown into the mix. I am in a thoughtful mood when Roberta asks, "Well, do you think you can sell it?"

"Sure," Dona pipes up, "but not at the price you need. I don't see you getting the price you paid for it—you will probably get $20,000 less in spite of all your upgrades. Plus, you need to pay commission and transfer tax. Even if we lower our commission to 5% to help you out, you will still have to come up with another $20,000 for a total shortage of $40,000."

Roberta looks down at her hands folded neatly in her lap. She doesn't say a word.

I am the first to speak. "Since your monthly payment is going up another $570 this month, I suggest you talk to your lender. Unfortunately, they are not that fast moving. So you need to be prepared for another six months of staying put while we market and try negotiating with your lender. Does that work for you?"

Roberta fidgets in her chair and takes a long time to answer. "Probably not. Ralph, my boyfriend, doesn't want to talk to the lender about our problems. He and his family are big into responsibility and paying back what you owe."

"Even if it's just impossible to do so?" I ask incredulously. "The truth is you were naïve first time buyers, who were not represented by an agent and you fell victim to developers' and lenders' greed. And it doesn't sound to me like anybody fully explained the ramifications in obtaining a negative amortization loan."

"No, they didn't. They kept emphasizing all the appreciation we would get in owning."

As Realtors (meaning we are a member of the National Association of Realtors (NAR)), we are trained never to speak of what the future brings, but just what has happened in the past. One can never predict what the economic climate will be in a year or two years from now. Whenever my clients ask what I think their property will be worth, I tell them I am not a fortune teller with a crystal ball, but a real estate agent. I always advise them to be prepared to hold on to a property for at least five years. Speculators who want to flip and make a fast buck, I don't want to work with.

I pick up the closing statement. "You have only put in $6500 besides twelve months of mortgage payments. Think of the later as rent. Plus, you got some tax breaks. I know it will hurt your credit if you take the route we are suggesting, but what is the alternative? Stay in a relationship and job that aren't working? Attempt to pay back a loan that will eventually require one of you to take a second job? What about your health? Your baby girl?" I want to throw in the word, *safety*, but think it best not to. "If I were in your situation, I would walk. You made a really bad decision, but I don't see paying for it the rest of your life. Sure, you won't be able to get a substantial loan or buy a house for seven to ten years... "

Roberta interrupts, "I don't want another house—ever. This one has been one big problem. I would agree to what you are saying, but Ralph will not. I just don't know what I am going to do."

She looks so stressed, I feel compelled to ask the question that has been looming in the back of my mind since we got here. "Can you move in with your mother while you sort all this out with Ralph?" I ask.

"Yeah, maybe that's for the best."

She shakes our hands as we leave. I wouldn't want to be in her shoes for anything. I turn to Dona. "I wouldn't feel comfortable having an open house here, would you?"

"No way," she says.

"We'll have to do some research and find a real estate agent who specializes in short sales," I say.

"Yeah, a big, brawny, broad shouldered guy who has taken a lot of karate would be helpful too." We both laugh and get back into our cars. I head home to my beloved 'City by the Bay.'

> **RULE #8-6: LEARN TO SAY NO** It is important to know your priorities and what you do best. Sometimes the best advice is to refer business to someone who is a better match.

A few weeks later Roberta and her daughter have moved in with her mother. Ralph wouldn't sell and lose money so for a few months Roberta sent him half the mortgage payment, telling him she could not do it forever. She also told him he would have to cover the increase in loan payment. He eventually got a roommate and Roberta asked to be removed from title.

Roberta and Ralph's situation is not an isolated case. They are just one example of our current mortgage crisis, but folks, let's call it what it really is—a mortgage scandal. Unscrupulous developers, bankers and some agents sold houses to people who should not have owned one in the first place. They all got their money up front and left the poor homeowner holding a loan which they could not afford to pay off. The bankers made double digit profits by selling their loans to Wall Street, who wanted in on the sweet deal, but then it all crashed (Does Bear Stearns ring a bell? Why not look up what their profit was in the second quarter of 2007—a whooping $2.5 billion. And Merrill Lynch's profits up nearly a third). Our government, true to form, bails out the big money guys while homeowners are left without a home, but with strained relationships and bad credit. Well, I digress. My book is about sales, real estate and the American dream and not about greedy corporations, self-indulgent CEOs and a disempowered government failing to act on behalf of its people.

PART TWO

The Eight Potential Vices

CHAPTER NINE

CODEPENDENCY
Honoring Yourself

YOUR BROTHER'S MISSING." I look up from my arithmetic homework which is scattered across my bedroom floor. Peter is not even in kindergarten.

"You have got to find him. I've looked everywhere," Mother says as she starts to cry.

"Don't worry," I say, jumping up, "He has got to be around here somewhere." Running outside I check our front yard—a mini forest with big fluffy fir trees three stories high and a mixture of shrubs, ferns and small maples. I look in between the trees, my eyes glued on the ground. I get down on my hands and knees to peak underneath the brush, thinking perhaps Peter is playing some hide and seek game. But I don't see him. I get up, rubbing the brown dirt off my legs and arms, and walk on. My feet make loud crunching noises as I step on the dry brittle pine needles. I wonder if perhaps the lush green lawn of our backyard would make a better playground for a four year old. I leave the woods and its cool damp air with its musty smell and make my way to the opposite side of our house. The bright heat of the afternoon sun feels good on my face. I squint to see the full expanse of our yard, hoping to find him. The yard is deep and long with small groupings of white birch trees with splotches of black spots. I walk past the rectangular perimeter of a demolished chicken coop, making sure I don't trip on the concrete foundation sticking out amidst the green grass.

Daddy told me he had bought our land from a bankrupt farmer who sold off lots in his desperate attempt to get out of debt. Since Daddy was the first bidder, he got the best. Well, if it was not the best then, it was now. Daddy had planted so many pretty trees, blossoming bushes and colorful flowers that our house was a real showpiece. At least that is what people said. Plus, the long winding stone walkway up to our house on the hill and the huge retaining wall surrounding it, made everyone 'oohh' and 'ahh' when they visited. I beamed proud.

Proud of our house and proud of Daddy. Remembering to look for Peter, I decide to check out the vegetable garden—maybe he got hungry for a sun warmed tomato—so tasty when picked straight from the vine. I walk in between the golden haired corn stalks, hoping tonight for dinner we'll have corn on the cob. Fresh, sugar-sweet and delicious. Maybe Daddy will grill London broil. Of course, we'll have a cucumber and tomato salad, maybe with some lettuce, but it is the buttered salt and peppered corn on the cob I like best. My mouth starts to water when I think about it. Curious, I open one of the tall blonde stalks checking for weevils, like I'm looking for a prize in the Cracker Jack box—even the ugliest of creatures fascinates me. I find one and crush it between my thumb and forefinger. Yes, I am an avid appreciator of Mother Nature, but I love corn more. I continue on through the rest of the garden—the many rows of lettuce, cucumbers, squash, peppers, green beans and tomatoes—touching the plants with my fingers. Too many vegetables for a family of four, but Mother cans some and we give the rest to our neighbors. I walk to the edge of our property and into the empty field where the grasshoppers rule. The Queen's Anne Lace, Goldenrod and Wild Anise aren't that high, because it is not quite mid summer, so I can see far. But I still can't see Peter. I call his name, cupping my hands around my mouth to make my girlish voice louder. I wait, hoping to hear his voice. I call again. "Peter, Peter… Time to come hooo-ooomme." I take one last loop around the house to be extra sure. I notice my Schwinn with its shiny handlebars and pink trim propped up in the garage and hop on. Perhaps, he was more adventurous than this acre-large yard. I speed down our long driveway, ready to scope the entire neighborhood. Mother is depending upon me. I cannot let her down. "I'll find him," I say to myself. "I've got to—for Mother."

I knock on Melnick's door—our next door neighbor. Maybe Peter wandered over to play with Roger. "No," they say, "he hasn't been here." I take the bike down the road, periodically stopping to talk to neighbors. "My baby brother's missing," I say. I describe what he looks like, trying not to talk too quickly. "He's this high," I show them, flaying my hands this way and that. No one has seen him.

I continue on. I can't give up. I promised Mother. I ride my bike over the soft tar bubbles in the road because I like to hear them pop. I am tempted to stop and squish them with my heel, but am afraid of the gooey black mess getting on my white sneakers... afraid of Mother. That's why I have to find Peter. If only I hadn't been doing my homework, this would never have happened. This is all my fault. I should have been watching him. Poor Mother can't cope with any sort of problem and this was serious. Now my brother is missing. I've just got to find him. I pedal harder and say a Hail Mary. I need help. The long ride around the block does nothing. I have no clues where he could be. I feel a trickle of warmth down my chin and put my hand to my face. The back of my hand is red. I must have bitten my lip from worry. I stall in getting home, afraid of telling Mother the bad news. There is just no other place to look. I try to come up with something positive to tell her. That someone saw him recently? No, I can't—that would be a lie. Isn't there something I can say or do to make it all better? When Daddy gets home he'll be able to help. Everything's always better when Daddy's home. I look up at the sky and say another prayer that Daddy comes home early tonight.

I steer the bike down the driveway and lower the kickstand ever so carefully. I don't want it falling over and making a big crashing sound. I take as long as I can—forestalling the inevitable and wondering if I'll be punished because I couldn't find my brother. I can hear Mother's voice in my head saying how I disappointed her. How I'm to blame. If only I wasn't so preoccupied with my own life. Maybe then I would have paid more attention to what my brother was doing. As I make the climb up the stairs, I stop, wondering what to say to Mother. I chew on one of my nails till it's raw and hurting. I decide instead it is better to wait outside. As I make my way down the stairs, I hear Mother's voice. I tilt my head sideways to listen closer.

"Great News! I found Peter asleep under the picnic table!"

I let out a huge giddy gush of laughter. Now I don't have to come up with some silly story to make Mother feel better.

Even when I am an adult and living on my own, I notice there is an emotional cost when I become too immersed in other people's drama. I especially remember the referral I got from management on a four unit building in Pacific Heights. Blayne, a well-known San Francisco attorney, is selling. He is recently married and his wife, Angela, has just been diagnosed with breast cancer. Her wish is to move back east to be closer to her family.

As soon as Blayne opens the door, Puccini's bittersweet aria, *Un Bel*

Di, from *Madame Butterfly* floods into the entryway. Being an opera aficionado wannabe, I am entranced as Blayne invites me in to join him for his afternoon tea in the library. He and Angela live in a two level lavishly decorated penthouse above three other rental units. I pass through a customized Italian kitchen with dark-rich cherry cabinets, a large center granite island and grand glass doors opening to a wraparound deck. I can hear song birds and bubbling water. I take a quick peak outside. The Japanese inspired garden is a magical vision with fountains, tall bamboo, rock garden and a Koi pond in the center—a serene respite from the busyness of the city.

The library has a British flair with floor to ceiling bookcases, oversized leather coffee-colored chairs and dark mahogany paneling. A serving tray is already laden with elaborate petit fours, dates and cucumber sandwiches. Everything around me is well designed, impeccably placed and expensive. Blayne is as fastidious about his person as he is about his beloved house. He is partial to charcoal gray suits with black woolen turtlenecks and speaks in the matter-of-fact, clipped way which many attorneys do. If he hadn't told me he was married, I think I would have taken him for being gay.

Nine weeks into the marketing of his property and we have no serious buyers. Blayne wants me to meet with Angela who, he thinks, has some great ideas on how to market the house (she has been back east this whole time undergoing chemotherapy treatments). This is the early nineties, the economy is in a recession and real estate, even in San Francisco, is depressed. In addition, we have the added problem that this is income property located in one of the most prestigious areas of the city. I explain to Blayne that most of the homeowners in this area are into status and do not want the label of being a landlord. Blayne is not deterred, still determined to get an astronomical price for his property. Partially, I think for his wife. "She has been through so much—poor thing," is his response whenever I broach the subject of price.

Angela is a petite fashionable woman with a pretty face, pointed chin and painted, pouty lips. One would never guess that she is in the midst of the fight of her life until she speaks in her soft, wispy Jackie O voice which I strain to hear. I get tired of saying "What?" and "Pardon Me?" so I do my best to get the gist of what she is saying. She recites the many special amenities of the home—all of which I have listed on the statement sheet—yet I listen, giving her lots of eye contact while she talks on and on. She picks fault with my marketing plan, wanting more advertising. But I have come prepared. I take out the many sample ads I have already run.

"Obviously, it's not doing the job now, is it?" Angela whispers. "We still don't have a buyer."

"Which periodical do you suggest I advertise in?" I ask making sure my voice is neutral and calm. I do not want to give into the common trap of defensiveness.

Blayne's response is quick and to the point. "It doesn't matter to us. Just advertise in one that works."

"Well, it is a bit hard to tract exactly what ad will bring in the buyer for your property," I say, knowing price and not advertising is the reason for the property not selling.

Angela gives me an encouraging smile. "How about the *Nob Hill Gazette?* Surely they will have a buyer of the caliber we are looking for."

Of course, she would want an ad in the super exclusive (and expensive) *Snob Hill Gazette* where all the pages are filled with stories and photos of San Francisco socialites. "I really don't think a four unit building is appropriate for that magazine," I say. "Why don't we advertise in the *Marina Times* instead?"

Angela clasps her hands together. "What a great idea—we will advertise in both! Paula, don't you worry, when those buyers come in and see all the custom designs we have put into this house, they will be sold. Blayne, don't you agree?"

Of course Blayne agrees.

RULE #9-1: TELL THE HARD TRUTH Although it is important to be empathetic with your clients, they also need to hear the hard truth—no matter how uncomfortable it is for them to hear or for you to say.

"However," I add, "it is pricing—not advertising—that is the biggest determining factor in getting a property sold. We might want to re-evaluate… "

Angela interrupts in her ghost-like whisper, "We do not want excuses, Paula. We want solutions." I stop mid-stream. She continues. "We have a special property and want it presented as such."

"Of course, I understand." Right now might not be the time to talk hard truths, I tell myself, so instead I take out my new color brochure, omitting the high asking price so not to discourage potential buyers. "Well, what do you think?"

I am confident they will like it as I made sure to include Blayne in the decision process. He was there the day the professional photographer did the photo shoot and must have noticed me bringing in the elaborate flower arrangements and wood for the fireplace to create the warm ambience for the photos.

"Mediocre," Angela responds as she gingerly picks up the glossy booklet, staring at it at length, scrutinizing for any typo, I imagine.

"Yes, I agree—mediocre is the right word," Blayne replies, not once mentioning he was there and approved of all our decisions.

Angela looks at me with her eyelashes all aflutter. "Why didn't you show the beautiful etched glass shower door we custom designed for the master bathroom?" Her voice is soft and melodious yet her demeanor is ice cold.

How can I tell her that the majority of buyers are not into having naked etched wood nymphs in their bathroom? I hesitate for a moment and then reply, "I thought the other amenities of the home were more important."

"How unfortunate. I think that was a big mistake on your part," she purrs.

Not knowing what to say, I say nothing.

I am still hoping to discuss the comparable sales and sensing a lull in the conversation, start to say something when Angela stops me short with a flick of her wrist. "Let's hope this meeting has been fruitful, giving you some good marketing tools to get our house sold. We really are anxious for a buyer."

Wanting to state my side of why the property isn't selling, I say, "Well, more marketing might not be the only solution," I slide the recent sales statistics I have taken out of my briefcase across the table.

Angela pushes them back to me and stands up, offering her hand to me like she is a member of royalty. I have no choice, but to stand up and take her hand. "Thank you so much for coming," she says. "Don't forget to take everything with you." She is speaking so softly I can hardly hear her.

As I am being ushered out the door, I make another attempt to address the tough competition and what we are up against in a down real estate market. Angela interrupts in a firm voice I didn't know she had. "We are done now, Paula. There is nothing more to talk about. Blayne and I do not need to hear any negativity, what we need is a strong marketing effort on your part." She gives me a sweetly sickening smile. "It has been lovely seeing you again—just lovely."

In spite of all her elegance and social etiquette, I feel like I have just been kicked out.

Weeks go by and still there are no showings and no interest with Blayne calling me at least every other day. Most agents would just shrug their shoulders and understand that there is nothing more they can do. I forget all about disciplining my mind and being positive and start feeling depressed for Blayne and his situation. The least I could do, I think, is sell his house. Desperate, I convince a close friend to preview the property and pretend he is a potential buyer! (So much for telling the hard truth!) Of course, this plan does not work either, because now Blayne is pestering me about Ernie and how he seemed really interested in the house. Blayne now wants to know if he is going to write an offer and if not, why not. "Paula, I think we have a live one here and I want you following through. Did you pre-qualify him yet? What did you say he does for a living? How did he find out about the house?… "

My inability to tell my clients the truth makes me realize I need some professional help. On the recommendation of an agent in the office, I make an appointment with a psychologist to help me with my dilemma. The night before the first session I have a vivid dream:

A group of people approach me while I am walking my dog and point to a pile of feces lying on the ground, demanding that I clean up my dog's mess. I immediately agree and apologize—without assessing the situation first. As I start cleaning it all up I realize these droppings are too small—no way could these be an Old English Sheepdog's…

Dr. Black's office is in Mill Valley so I have to travel over the Golden Gate Bridge to get there. The traffic is not too bad, because I am doing the reverse commute. I also enjoy driving on the bridge. Its famous sloped golden-orange frame is spectacular to behold against the cloud-speckled sky and the rolling bay underneath. I look for the weather-beaten lonely tree on the ridge of Sausalito's coastline. I am always inspired by its resiliency to stand there alone day after day in spite of the heavy winds; winter's pounding rain and incessant chilly air. I sneak another look as I drive, careful not to cross the orange traffic cones separating me from the oncoming traffic. I roll down my window and take a gulp of the fresh, moist air as I go over in my mind what I want to get out of today's counseling session. So it is with high hopes and some trepidation that I enter Dr. Black's office early that misty morning.

Dr. Black is not what I expected. She has shoulder length corn-yellow hair, a round face, a full buxomly figure and a gay bubbly voice. Flashing me a wide open grin, she extends a warm hand and shakes mine soundly. It would not surprise me in the least if she gives me a big bear hug at that end of this session. It is just the type of person she is, and after all, she is from Mill Valley.

She glances at her schedule underneath a pile of scattered papers on her desk. "So Kathy Trapani referred you?" I have no idea how she could find that piece of information so quickly. Some special inner radar system, I guess.

"Yes," I say as I shift in my chair, trying to find a comfortable position.

"Just so you know, I have heard just about everything so don't be shy. Tell me what's going on."

I explain the situation with Blayne and Angela and then tell her about last night's dream. "Isn't it odd that I should have such a disturbing dream right before our session? I know the subconscious is powerful. Do you think it is giving me some clues to all this?"

"What do you think the dream means?"

I ponder the question for a moment. "Something about people blaming me for messes that are not mine?"

Dr. Black smiles with her whole body bobbing up and down. "You got that right! So how does that tie in with the problem you're bringing me today?"

"Well, Blayne and Angela keep implying that the reason their building isn't selling is because of me. Then I start blaming me too."

Her demeanor turns pensive. "In the dream you believed these people's accusations that the dog's mess was your responsibility when it was not the case. It appears to me you are repeating the same scenario with Blayne and Angela. From what you have told me, you are doing everything in your power to sell your clients' house."

I shake my head with a definitive yes.

"I imagine it was their decision to list their property too high?"

"Yes," I say, exasperated. "I've been doing extensive marketing for three months, but no interested buyers. Instead they keep insisting I spend more and more money on advertising. I've tried to give them the MLS statistics, newspaper articles on the current market and comparable sold listings in their area, but whenever I bring up facts, they tell me not to be so negative."

"So they won't even listen to your expert advice yet you blame yourself for their decision of asking more than the house is worth?"

"Yes," I say.

"Does that make sense to you?" Dr. Black asks.

I think a moment. "No, it doesn't make any sense. That is why I need your help."

"By pretending you had a buyer, you have prevented your clients from learning the truth—that there is no one interested in their home. You say you tried telling them that their property was listed too high, but there is another part of you that is protecting them. That part is your codependency behavior and the reason why you felt compelled to produce a buyer—albeit a false one. They hired you, because you are the expert. Give them advice, but allow them their process. Let them feel the frustration and pain of their house not selling. You have other clients, don't you? Focus on them. Don't be so invested in saving Blayne and his sick wife."

> RULE #9-2: ALLOW CLIENTS THEIR PROCESS You are the expert and can guide your clients, but you cannot make decisions for them. They are independent beings and will make their own choices.

I admit that the reason I put up with Blayne's intimidating behavior and Angela's aloofness was because I felt sorry for them. "It's confusing to me because they keep calling me, wondering why there are no showings, but won't even have a discussion about the dynamics of the down real estate market. Sometimes I think that maybe Blayne doesn't really want to sell his precious home. I know he is under a lot of pressure to sell from his wife, but I also know he loves where he lives. Or maybe Angela expects a certain price and Blayne wants to please her after all she has been through."

Dr. Black stops me mid-sentence. "It really doesn't matter. They may sell. They may not. They may agree to reduce their asking price and they may not. Again, you can only advise them. Don't try so hard in controlling their behavior. It is still Blayne and Angela's house and their life—not yours."

Dr. Black then leans back into her soft leather chair and swivels the chair back and forth a couple of times. "Have you ever noticed that your life gets entangled in other people's drama? That you have a hard time separating their problems from your own?"

I sit very still pondering this idea. I guess several minutes pass, because I hear an echo of someone in the back of my head talking, but I am having difficulty focusing on who it is or what is being said.

"Paula, are you all right?" Dr. Black asks.

Her question brings me back to the room. I look up from my hands folded neatly on my lap and shake my head up and down, still unable to talk. I am using all my energy to put the pieces of this puzzle together.

Dr. Black takes a long pause and then looking me straight in the eye, says, "What you are describing is a classic case of a codependent."

"That sounds great to me," I say, relieved that someone knows what is going on, because I certainly did not. "What," I ask, "is a codependent?"

My homework is to read *Codependent No More* by Melody Beattie. I can still hear Dr. Black's words as I left her office—"Realize that your job as a real estate agent is to give expert advice, but clients have the choice to follow it or not." Why am I so invested in Blayne and Angela? I wonder, as I drive to the closest bookstore. My mood is light and hopeful, knowing I am about to find an important key to solving my client dilemma. A thin rail of a woman directs me to the 'Self Help' section. The selection of books is vast, addressing a multitude of relationship problems. I spot the title I am looking for and practically tear the book off the shelf. Melody's definition of a codependent: "A person who has let another person's behavior affect him or her, and who is obsessed with controlling that person's behavior."

Hmmm… That sounds right. In the past I have certainly focused on other people's needs rather than my own, such as Mother's, Daddy's and all my loser boyfriends'. Now it appears I am doing the same with my clients. While I am at the bookstore I also pick up a set of audiotapes, *On the Family,* which I listen to in my car on the way home. The reader and author is John Bradshaw, a current leading psychologist on family dynamics. Bradshaw explains that codependency starts when, as children, we are forced into caretaker roles in response to emotionally unbalanced parent(s). Since our survival depends on them, our focus shifts from our own needs to theirs. I identify with a case study of a baby girl, who at only nine months, is the caretaker of her mother!

"The first step in changing the dynamics of codependency," Dr. Black says when I visit her the following week, "is to set boundaries by separating your feelings and needs from the other person(s). It is not your responsibility to solve Blayne and Angela's problems for them. Yes, be the expert, but know you cannot control what choices they make."

"So if they don't want to listen to my advice, I just stand by and do nothing?"

"Yes."

"But they keep blaming me for their house not selling."

"Well, then you need to start setting guidelines on how other people treat you. Have you ever heard the phrase, *'We teach other people how to treat us?'*

"No," I say, "but it sounds like an interesting concept. How do I do that?" I ask, my lower lip beginning to tremble. All this is so new to me that it is becoming overwhelming. "As soon as Blayne or Angela start interrupting, criticizing, blaming or avoiding you, tell them. In other words—Name What is Going On as soon as it starts to happen."

"Give me an example," I say.

"The next time Blayne interrupts you, stop him by saying, *'What works best for me* is if I can finish explaining my marketing strategy. After I'm done then you can make suggestions.' Or if Angela is ignoring you, say, *'What works best for me* is if I could have just ten minutes of your undivided attention. If right now does not work for you, tell me when a good time would be for us to get together.' Just be aware that since the relationship between you and Blayne and Angela has already been formed, you are going to have to train them to treat you differently. They may be very resistant—and resentful—to any sort of change."

"Kind of like teaching an old dog new tricks?"

"Yes—it is so much easier in the beginning of a relationship to form boundaries." Dr. Black takes a long pause, then adds, "And remember you can only change your behavior—you cannot control someone else's. Hopefully, you changing will be enough to shift the dynamics of the relationship, but you need to be aware it may already be too late."

> **RULE #9-3: SET BOUNDARIES** As soon as you notice a person(s) projecting their negativity on you, tell them. Then state how you expect to be treated by using the following phrase: *"What works best for me is...."* If they continue, follow it up with a consequence for their behavior.

I set up a meeting with Blayne to discuss what we should do next. I then compose a list of all the agents who have shown the property. I type out their clients' comments along with the accurate date and time shown. I compile all my ads and the comparable listings sold and available properties in their neighborhood. The written evidence will be more objective and powerful when I explain that it is price, not marketing, that is preventing their property from selling. Before I drive over to Blayne and Angela's, I go over the steps on how to set boundaries:

1) Be in touch with your own feelings, needs and wants *(Know thyself)*.

2) When someone transgresses your boundaries, tell them *(Name what is happening in the moment)*.

3) Ask for what you need *(What works best for me is...)*

4) If they continue their same behavior, tell them to stop or face the consequences *(Choices have consequences)*.

At the meeting Blayne is adamantly opposed to lowering the asking price. "Which properties in the comparable listings sold are you using to support your price?" I ask, making sure I look at him directly.

Blayne shoves them aside, ignoring my question. Instead he picks apart the new ad I had written for an open house. "It doesn't fully describe the Japanese garden with the waterfall and fountain. Look here—you abbreviated garage. Not everybody is going to understand what that means."

Remember to feel, I tell myself. I take a deep breath, recognizing that I am feeling intimidated. What's the next step? Ah-ha! *Name what is going on!* Crossing on unfamiliar territory I manage to pull myself together and say: "Blayne, we are not talking about the ads right now. We are discussing our current competition and the sold prices of other similar properties—information which any potential buyer will review before putting in an offer. Please let me finish and then we can discuss the advertising."

He starts off again, criticizing the poor wording. Now he has not honored my request. His voice is getting more pointed. As soon as he stops, I say, "This isn't working for me, Blayne."

"What isn't working for you?" I can hear the irritation in his voice.

"How you are talking to me." I remember to use *'I statements'* and state how it makes me feel. "I feel intimidated when you keep interrupting me. I know you have some good ideas, but I am having trouble hearing them right now."

"All I want you to do is to sell my house and it's not selling! I'm just trying to help!"

I speak softly when I say, "It works much better for me when we can discuss things calmly." There! I said it. I asked for what I needed. Step Three.

He picks up the ad again and starts restructuring my sentences.

Since Blayne is not honoring my request, I need to set up a consequence for his behavior. I'm almost there—this is the fourth and last step. "Blayne, if you continue focusing on just the ads, we might as well end the meeting right now. Like I said before, I am open to any suggestions you might have, but before we go over the ad, we need to have a discussion about what's currently happening in the marketplace. If not, we are just spinning our wheels."

Blayne sighs as he looks at his watch. "I don't have much time. Here's the ad with my notes. Please change it." He gets up from his seat.

I follow. "I am leaving the MLS statistics with you," I say, remaining calm—unaffected by his behavior. "Please go over them and we can have a discussion about reducing the price next week," I say.

"We won't reduce the price."

"Well, that's certainly a choice you can make. Just don't be surprised when we don't get many showings." I am no longer going to feel responsible for Angela and Blayne's property not selling. I cannot change them, but I can change how I feel about the situation.

In the following days I do not hear from Blayne or Angela and am noticing that I am feeling sad. I listen to the codependent tapes some more and get a massage to help me through this rough spot. Changing patterns is difficult and feels weird. The truth is I still feel some pangs of doubt—perhaps some of this is my fault. It is time for another counseling session.

"Guilt," Dr. Black says, "is merely a nagging fear that you have done something wrong. You are not operating in the present moment, but dwelling on the past. Worry is the flip side—a fear that you will do something wrong in the future. You seem to be doing a bit of both."

"So, how do I stop feeling bad?"

"Remember to separate your feelings from your clients' emotions. It is okay to feel empathetic with what they are going through, but do not become enmeshed with them. As soon as you start wanting them to do things your way, know you have regressed into your controlling codependency behavior."

My homework is to find something I love to do and lose myself in the moment. "When we are 100% occupied with what is happening in the present," Dr. Black says, "our mind does not dwell in the past or wander into the future." She suggests a form of physical exercise which requires mental concentration. It will keep my mind occupied plus release those happy endorphins to help me feel more positive.

I choose ballroom dancing. Now not only do I have a hobby I look forward to three times a week, I also learn to stay in the present. When my partner takes a step, my body needs to listen so I can make that split second later counter motion. I do not have the privilege of worrying about my real estate deals or my financial woes, because I have to focus on what my partner is doing. If I don't do my part, we are not in sync and we end up tripping over each other.

I become so involved in dancing that even if I have a bad day, I am able to have a good night's sleep and start the next day feeling positive. I realize that my life is no longer dependent on what is happening with Blayne and Angela. When they try to pull me into the drama of their house not selling, I keep reminding myself I am not responsible for their choice of overpricing. The only thing I can do is give them my professional advice and then let it go. I start focusing on prospecting and developing new business.

Whenever we do things for others at the expense of our own well-being we have crossed the line into the world of codependency.

CHAPTER TEN

FRUSTRATION, ANGER
AND VICTIM MENTALITY

Managing Your Emotions

I SLAM THE PHONE DOWN so hard it almost breaks. I continue unpacking the groceries I just bought—the fresh organic produce in the hydrator, the meat in the freezer and the dry goods on their appropriate cabinet shelves. I look at the dozen eggs and decide not to unpack them individually as I usually do. I just don't trust myself. Not right now anyway. Instead, I pace back and forth across my living room, recalling the conversation I just had with my neighbor, Dr. Larry Kessler.

I met Larry several years ago when he moved into his home on the top of our cul-de-sac overlooking downtown. He and I would walk our dogs together. It did not matter that he had a punctilious Pug and I had a sappy Old English Sheepdog. Being a Jewish doctor from Manhattan, we had New York, a medical background, and a love of San Francisco in common. He had traveled three thousand miles, as I had, for the adventure and the promise of milder weather. Sure we also liked the eclectic attitude and diversity of San Francisco, but what we really loved was the architecture. And San Francisco certainly offered a variety of that, whether it is Edwardians, Victorians, Tudor, Marina Style, Arts and Crafts, or Modern. Our houses, which were built by the same developer in the mid-eighties, were copied after the narrow Stick Victorians. Yes, they were narrow like sticks, but they got their name from the exposed trusses or "stickwork" on the exterior. We choose our houses because we liked the charm of a by gone era, but wanted all the modern conveniences of modern houses. We had the high ceilings, but not the cold draft coming in from the creaky old wooden windows. We had good practical floor plans—not the tiny rooms with big parlors which Victorians were known for, but good-sized bedrooms with walk-in closets. We had spacious bathrooms with plenty of room to navigate getting in and out of the shower, and we loved our gourmet kitchens with all the bells and whistles. Plumbing had not been introduced into houses until the early 1900's so kitchens and baths were awkward, back-of-the house additions. They did not have cars back then either so these Victorians had no garages. But we did.

Yet we still loved the older homes. I got my fix by selling real estate. Larry got his fix by drooling over the mansions in Pacific Heights during Sunday open houses. He told me he had compromised when he bought in Noe Valley. He just was not able to afford what he wanted in the more prestigious North of Market neighborhoods, so settled for the next best thing—to his constant regret. Since the first day I had met him, Larry had been compulsively saving until he could get into his first choice neighborhood—even if it meant downsizing to a condominium. He had approached me about three months ago and asked for my help in finding him something in the trendy upscale Cow Hollow area near Union Street. Not only was he compulsively searching for his ideal home, but also his ideal mate. I would have fixed him up with one of my girlfriends, but he wasn't into women. After he and his partner, Scott, got together, he was more determined that ever to find his ideal home in the most prestigious neighborhood. And now he tells me he found it—with another agent!

I, of course, immediately asked him for the address—3282 Filbert. Of course, I knew the property. In fact, it is our company who put the condo up for sale! I had previewed the condo weeks ago. Granted it is on a special block, utterly charming and spacious. But certainly not a match for Larry. Larry couldn't fix a thing and this condo needed tons of work. Tons!

"Larry, you looked with another real estate agent after all the real estate advice I've given you over the years, after all the times you've been to my house for dinner… "

"Paula—Stop for God's sake! I didn't do this on purpose!"

I say nothing, waiting for him to explain.

"I just asked a guy I knew at the gym. He's in real estate too and has been bugging me to give me a free appraisal of what my house was worth. Then one thing led to another."

"But Larry I told you what your house is worth. I gave you all the comparable sales in our neighborhood plus what is currently for sale." My knuckles are turning ghostly white, because I am gripping the phone so hard. I switch the phone to my other ear and shake out my cramped fingers.

"I just wanted to be sure—that's all." Larry lowers his voice (As if that will make all this easier for me). "Then when I told him what I was looking for, he told me he had the perfect place. You know, we've been looking for almost three months now, Paula."

"But you told me you could only spend up to a million," I say, trying not to panic. "The asking price is $950,000 plus all the work it needs will bring it up to a million plus."

Larry lets out a long sigh. "I really wish you had told me about it. Then we wouldn't be having all these problems."

Well, at least I have the listing on his house, I tell myself. My ears perk up. "What do you mean problems?"

"Well, H and L Realty also offered to list my house at a much lowered commission if they represented me on both the buying and selling end so I agreed. I can do a lot with an extra eight thousand dollars in my pocket."

I felt like I had just been hit by an eight hundred ton semi-truck. That's the point when I said goodbye and slammed the phone. Now I keep pacing the floor, wondering what to do next. I open the refrigerator door and look at the carton of eggs sitting placidly on the middle rack.

Underneath my professional exterior and need to help others, lies another person, ready to leap into a rage when I feel someone has taken advantage of me. The voice in my head is getting louder and louder, repeating *After all I've done for you!* I imagine throwing the dozen eggs I just bought against his new tri-colored paint job. I picture the yellow yolk oozing down the front of the building, making a terrible mess. It gives me some satisfaction, especially since he is such a compulsive neatnik. Do you think he'll figure out it was me who did such a dastardly deed? I slam the refrigerator door. I lift the telephone up from the cradle to call him back and tell him what a creep I think he is. But I can't do that either. I fling the receiver across the wall and watch as it crashes. I still feel frustrated so I batter the plastic earpiece into the floor until it is smashed. Wires are sticking out all over the place. I sit back on my heels and start to cry.

RULE #10-1: BE PREPARED FOR ANY POSSIBILITY Real estate involves a lot of money. People are unpredictable, fickle beings and are capable of a wide spectrum of behavior. Be prepared for your best, most loyal clients to act in ways you never thought possible.

After my knee jerk reaction to Dr. Kessler's betrayal, I spend most of the day in bed. That evening I am feeling better and, not wanting to be without a phone, go shopping for a new one. I am ashamed, but I do not know how to stop breaking things when I get upset. Despite my impulsive reaction, I do know what I need to do next. I relinquish my hurt feelings and remind myself that real estate is a service business. I call Larry back. "Sorry, if I seemed abrupt when you called me yesterday," I say.

"Hmmm… " is all I hear on the other end of the line.

I continue, knowing to get reconnected I must tell the truth. "My feelings were hurt." Silence. I persevere. "If you want the name of a few contractors who I trust to check out the condo you are considering buying,"—I try not to choke—"I can give those to you."

"That's nice of you Paula, but we had the contractor's inspection today."

"And?"

"I hate to admit it, but you were right. The place needs way too much work… and money. Money which I do not have."

"I'm sorry to hear that," I say with genuine concern as well as a wave of relief. I pause before I ask him the question I need to know. "Will you still want to continue looking with me then?"

"To tell you the truth, Paula, I'm pretty wiped out by this whole process. I think I need a break."

"But what if I see something really special—can I still call you?"

"Well, you know what I'm looking for… okay… sure."

Larry is no longer on the top of my client list, but if I happen upon something that meets his needs, I'll call him. I won't let this incident stand between me and a sale. It is mid-summer before I find that special property. I am brimming over with excitement when I place the call. Larry is ambivalent about looking. "I just bought an expensive couch and loveseat for my living room as a consolation gift to myself," he says.

"So? Bring it to your new home. This condo is one in a million, Larry. Right on Vallejo Street. It is a charming Edwardian with all the wainscoting intact, original light fixtures and a renovated kitchen with one of those center islands. And you know Edwardians have much more practical floor plans than Victorians. Instead of narrow triple parlors and tiny bedrooms you get wider, larger rooms with bigger closets and a good size kitchen with plenty of pantry space. Plus, the bathrooms are all located throughout the house, not just in the back, because these homes were originally built with plumbing. Sure, the outside of the Edwardians don't have all the intricate gingerbread molding like the Victorians, but inside they kept the wainscoting, hardwood floors, high ceilings and the crown and picture moldings. They also added boxed ceilings, stained glass and built-in china cabinets in the entertaining rooms.

"Well... "

"Besides," I say, "This condo has already been renovated. The kitchen's all granite with top of the line appliances including a Sub-zero refrigerator, wine cooler and cherry wood cabinets." Silence. "The cherry wood is smooth like silk to the touch and so rich in color, Larry, you will be amazed." I wait to see his reaction. He appreciates fine quality and good taste and this condo has both.

"I don't know... "

"It has a formal dining room with built-in leaded glass cabinets, space for your hutch and a window seat. Just take a look—you owe it to yourself." I wait some more. "The two bathrooms are Italian marble and when you glide your hands across... "

Larry acquiesces. "All right then—I'll see it!"

I bring a measuring tape to see if the new furniture will fit in the living room. The couch will, but the love seat will not. "What if we put the loveseat in the den?" I suggest. We measure it together. It will fit, but it is going to be tight. I wait for his response.

"I'm not sure," he says. "Can I have Scott take a look?"

"Sure," I say and the next day the three of us are back looking. "It's not perfect," Larry says.

"Is it because of the loveseat?" I ask. "Is that the only objection?"

He doesn't answer.

"Life isn't perfect, Larry and houses aren't either. Even millionaires don't get one hundred percent of their wish list," I say. "If you get 80% of what you're looking for, you're doing well."

I can tell from the glint in Scott's eye and his wide smile that he loves the place. I try to enlist his help in bringing Larry around. "What do you think, Scott?"

"I like it," he says. "I really like it." He starts feeling the smoothness of the Brazilian cherry wood cabinets in the kitchen with the palm of his hand, admiring the workmanship (good, now I have an ally).

"I'm just not sure," is Larry's answer.

I continue showing Scott the special features and do a lot of oohing and ahhing—all sincere of course. This is a great condominium at an affordable price. I know in my heart of hearts it is perfect for Larry. As we are headed down the stairs, the agent whispers in my ear, "You have the patience of Job." If only she knew the whole story.

"We need to make a decision before the Sunday open house," I say, as we get into our respective cars. "After that it will be a free-for-all and this flat won't last."

The following day Larry decides to pull the trigger. He has made up his mind. He wants the property. He offers at the asking price and the offer is accepted.

> **RULE #10-2: SAY YOU ARE SORRY** There will be times that clients will disappoint you. You may say things you regret. If that is the case, own up to it and say you are sorry. Most clients will forgive you.

Frank Woods is one of my most favorite clients. He decided his current house is too small for him, his new fiancée, Linda, and her five year old son. Frank is bright, witty and charming with a high profile job in the insurance business. He also has plenty of money and such an easygoing personality that it is a real joy to work with him. We have become good friends and even see each other socially. He is a great source of referrals. He sings my praises and lauds my merits to his influential circle of friends. In the span of a few months, I find him a magnificent (and very expensive) home in Pacific Heights. To make sure we win the bid (it's a seller's market), we get our inspections and disclosures done before the offer date. As I am driving to Yosemite to celebrate my birthday, I get a call on my cell phone. I'm in high spirits, thinking our non-contingent over asking offer is a sure thing. It is Darlene, the listing agent on the phone.

"Frank just called and withdrew his offer."

I gasp, searching for what to say. "He did what? What reason did he give?"

"No reason. You better call him and straighten this out. I am meeting with my sellers in an hour. You still have time."

I call him immediately. Although Frank is an astute businessman with a prestigious job, he is nervous. I feel exasperated. I expected much more of him. All the time we spent looking was for nothing. He's about to miss out on a great house. He tells me he could not sleep at all the night before. Instead of recognizing his buyer's remorse, I get irritated. "We've done our inspections. The house is in perfect condition and in your most favorite neighborhood. It is such an opportunity," I plead.

"I just can't go through with it," he says.

"But this is your dream house."

"I'm not ready," is his answer.

I start to get forceful. I tell him how embarrassing it is for me to withdraw an offer already in place. I remind him how prestigious an address it is. I know I shouldn't be thinking of my feelings, but I let him know how embarrassed I am letting down a top selling agent in my own office. As a professional, I should to be detached, but I cannot contain my disappointment. I feel the anger collecting at the bottom of my throat. Instead of throwing the phone, I do something worse. I attack him where he is most vulnerable.

"Did Linda put you up to this?" I can almost hear the venom in my voice.

There is silence at the other end of the phone. I have made a huge miscalculation. My bitter words hang like drawn daggers in the air. Cruel words which I cannot take back. He does not answer, but rushes a goodbye. I wonder if it will be goodbye for good. Will I ever be able to amend the hurt I just caused to my friend and client?

When I return from my vacation, Frank avoids all my phone calls. A few months later I notice his home listed with someone else and wonder where on Millionaire Row he lives now. I still write and call him occasionally, but never hear back.

RULE #10-3: FOCUS ON THE PRIZE This is a profession where you need to accept delayed gratification. If your clients are well-qualified and motivated, support them the best you can through their indecisions, whining and frustration, remembering there are big rewards at the end of the rainbow.

I could feel like a victim and beat myself up after ruining my relationship with Frank, but I chose instead to move on and help my other clients. I get past my frustration, although some agents cannot get out of their victim mode and seem to wallow in their self-pity for too long.

Herbert Hubbard wastes a lot of time by acting as a tour guide for 'Lookey-Loo' buyers. In other words, he does not qualify his buyers financially or emotionally. He does not ask the five basic questions which every newbie agent needs to know to determine a buyer's motivation:

1. *"Are you currently working with another agent?"*

2. *"Why are you buying?"*

3. *"Have you been pre-approved with a lender?"*

4. *"When do you intend to move?"*

5. *"How long have you been looking?"*

Instead, as soon as Herbert sees a live body, he shoves them into his car, hoping for the best. This sloppy business practice is always getting Herbert into trouble—financially and emotionally.

More than once, I have overheard agents in our office warning Herbert about Sarah, a client they see him counseling in the conference room. Agents who have worked with Sarah knew she had been looking for property for years, but could never make a decision. Herbert shrugs off their concern, insisting he has a special relationship with his new client and is confident that he will succeed where they have failed.

Several months after he began working with Sarah, Herbert comes to me for business coaching. He shares his disappointment that Sarah never purchased a home. Herbert tells me that he has written three offers, but each time they are accepted, Sarah backs out. When I ask Herbert why he didn't listen to the other agents, he becomes defensive. I continue, explaining why I see his effort with Sarah as a big waste of time. "Wouldn't your time be better spent prospecting?" I ask.

He doesn't respond.

I remind him of the popular saying—*if you really want something, you need to let it go.* "Then maybe it will come back to you. Trying too hard and forcing an outcome rarely works. Maybe Sarah needs some space to sort things out for herself." I give him the example of Russ, a well to do client of mine from Beverly Hills who bought a probate on top of Nob Hill, a block from the Mark Hopkins Hotel. A premium location for sure, but a four level home with no garage and no yard. Not a typical choice for most people. Russ considered himself an innovative marketer and felt he could turn this property quickly and make a tidy profit. After four months with no offers, he still was not willing to reduce the price, so I needed to let him go. He listed with another top Realtor in the city. I did my best not to take it personally, but Russ did not want to hear the truth. When the other agent was not able to sell it either, Russ came back to me. Why? Because now he was ready to sell. "Herbert, from what you have told me you've done everything you can to help Sarah. It is time to let her go. Sarah may never be ready. When she is, maybe like Russ, she will come back to you."

> RULE #10-4: KNOW WHEN TO LET CLIENTS GO You need to qualify your clients motivationally as well as financially. Ask how long they have been looking, when do they expect to buy and why do they want to buy now. If their time frame is six months or less, they are motivated buyers. If for some reason they cannot go through with the sale and it happens more than once, waste no more time and let them go.

Shortly after our counseling session, I notice that Herbert is no longer attending office meetings. Curious about what's going on, I call him at home.

"I've been in bed ill with some sort of bug the last couple of weeks."

Whenever I get sick myself I always look for some underlying emotional cause. My scientific training taught me that microbes are around us all the time. It is often in time of stress that we get sick. "Is something else bothering you?" I ask.

"Well, I think this thing with Sarah has gotten me a bit down. Could they be related?"

"They could be related," I tell him. "You've been working nonstop, trying to get her in contract. What do you think, Herbert?"

"For the past nine months I have been thinking that all I need to do is find the right house for Sarah, but now I'm thinking it is not the house—it's her—getting in the way of a sale. She just can't seem to make a commitment."

Herbert promises me he is going to tell Sarah that he is no long willing to work with her. If he has learned a lesson from his experience with Sarah about being more selective in working with clients, then I have done my job as his coach. Not long after our conversation, I pass him in the hallway. He looks miserable, so I ask him how he is doing.

"I've been working with this couple for over a year, but the transaction fell through because of their terrible credit."

"Wait, Herbert!" I say. "Didn't we discuss how important it is to establish the three signs of readiness in each new buyer? Why didn't you have them pre-approved by a bank beforehand?"

Herbert is not listening to me. He would rather blame these buyers for wasting his time. "You could be more selective, Herbert," I say gently. I was not going to buy into his victim mentality.

"You don't have any idea of what I am going through," he says as he stomps off. "Just feel lucky that you don't have loser buyers like I do."

CHAPTER ELEVEN

JEALOUSY, GREED
AND ARROGANCE
Letting go of Unbridled Ambition

STICKING TO YOUR PRIORITIES once you have set them is difficult. I discover this as I am writing this book. At the moment, I am involved in a very difficult real estate transaction with a friend of mine. What I learned from the following example is the importance of associating with people who have similar values. Doing so will save you a lot of time and heartache.

I met Carrie Mingleton, a title representative, through Kevin O'Connor, an easy-going, good-looking Irish lad and a San Francisco native, who sat across from me at work. Kevin kept me in stitches with his off-the-wall humor and endeared me to him by calling me "Honey." That he also called the other gals "Honey" as well didn't bother me, because his devil-may-care attitude and charming demeanor took the stress out of the intense daily grind. I think he had a crush on Carrie, who came by the office promoting USA Title and who frequently chatted with Kevin whenever she could, even though she had a boyfriend. Carrie was poised, soft-spoken, articulate and attractive—an alluring package. I am a genuine appreciator of beauty whether it is an antique Chinese vase, a violet pink sunset or a graceful demeanor. I appreciated Carrie's sense of style and after a few months of her politely pressing me to give her some business, I did. Carrie steered me to only the best and most competent escrow officers, who handled the small details of loan payoffs and demands, required city documents, arrangement of fire and title insurance policies, and the fine intricacies of balancing all the credits and debits from sellers and buyers with masterful precision. If they were too busy, I could always count on Carrie for following through, delivering time-sensitive paperwork and making sure the deal got done correctly. She and I made a good team. In spite of all her glamour and social connections, I think she wanted a friend who appreciated her good work. I filled that role.

I had gotten Carrie into her first real estate purchase, which, she repeatedly told me, was one of the best decisions she had ever made. During our friendship, I had been there for Carrie when she needed advice on her marriage, business pursuits and divorce. Over the years of our friendship, she had supported me when my when my sister-in-law discovered that her cancer had metastasized. I felt compelled to tell my brother the truth—that Janie was now on borrowed time, but Carrie advised me against it. "Let him have hope for as long as he can," she said. For that sage advice I felt indebted to her.

Carrie called me immediately when she noticed the For Sale sign posted on the upper flat of her two-unit building in the desirable Marina district. She loved her lower flat and thought it would make good economic sense to own the whole building. I had introduced Carrie to Robert LeCamp years ago in the hope that the two of them could form a partnership and buy the building together. I showed them how they could own near the hip-happening Chestnut Street—a popular haunt of the twenties and thirties crowd—where they both wanted to live. I explained that after they lived in the duplex for a year, they could then start the condominium conversion process. It would mean working together with an attorney to draw up the CCR's, (the Covenants, Conditions of Record, i.e., the rules of the condominium association) and the subdivision map, which would specify which part of the property, would be Carrie's, which would be Robert's and which would be the common area.

Once all the paperwork was approved by the Department of Real Estate in Sacramento and recorded, they could then refinance and replace their partnership agreement with their own separate recorded grant deed. At the time Robert was emphatic about having the upper unit and Carrie acquiesced, just thankful she could own something. Now, years later, each owned a flat and Robert LeCamp was selling his, because his company had transferred him to Boston. Carrie's divorce also had just been settled, which couldn't have been better timing. She could buy his upper unit with all cash, if necessary.

The first scheduled showing is to be the following Tuesday on Brokers' Tour. (Every Tuesday is caravan day when agents preview the new listings in the Multiple Listing Service (MLS). If they find a possible match for their clients, they then make an appointment with the listing agent.) I know the agent, Nina Hatvany. She is the top agent at TRI-Coldwell Banker and, besides this condominium, which is listed at $995,000, Nina has three other listings, all in the three to six million dollar range. I know she is really busy and because this is her least expensive property, Nina would want to close on it quickly.

I also know the real estate market is booming, and if Carrie waited until after the designated tour to place her bid, we would most likely get into a multiple offer situation. The price would be bid up so that Carrie might not even get the property. The MLS listing further states no pre-emptive offers, (meaning no offers before the customary two-week marketing schedule) a common practice in a hot San Francisco sellers' market. However, I was not going to let these obstacles deter me in getting Carrie this condo.

Since Nina is used to dealing with the highest echelon properties, I know she would not be interested in spending much time with a sale for just under a million dollars. We structure an offer which is a 'no-brainer'—all cash with no conditions and over the asking price. (Carrie Mingleton was in a unique position. She already knew the property, so she did not need any inspections.) Nina would not have to market the condo, coordinate showings or worry whether the escrow would close because Carrie offered to put up a non-refundable $40,000 deposit with a twenty-one day closing period. So just as I anticipated, Nina took the bait and agreed to present our offer to Robert LeCamp.

However, we were still on shaky ground. Robert LeCamp did not like Carrie. She had expanded her lower unit into her storage space in the garage and made an extra room, enhancing the value of her condominium. It infuriated Robert that, in spite of insisting on the top unit, Carrie had gotten the better deal. It takes some strong negotiating, but with Robert already relocated in Boston, and Nina, living up to her four-star reputation as one of the best agents in the city, our offer is ratified (accepted).

I appreciate Nina's candor when she explains we are to follow the contract to the letter because Robert is not willing to "give us a single inch of slack." I emphasize this to Carrie. It can be difficult to work with a friend. Sure enough, Carrie consults with her tax accountant, who advises her to get a loan instead of using up all her cash. Then Carrie decides on using an out-of-state lender who her new boyfriend, Craig, recommends. I explain to Carrie that a lender she's never met has just a superficial phone relationship with her. In these situations they often give the best scenario to get business, but are not always reliable. I relay war stories of how these lenders—who are looking for the best commission for themselves—push buyers into a less desirable loan program or simply not return calls when they cannot deliver what they promised. I hope she would choose my recommendation— a lender I've developed a long, close business relationship with over the years. My established contacts rely on my business and my referrals and will do whatever is necessary to close the deal. That's what Carrie needed. In the rare case when a lender I recommend cannot perform, because of a low appraisal or lack of available funding, s/he will tell me immediately and not leave me hanging. Being stranded with a buyer who is already packed with no place to move is a predicament I never want to experience.

I give Carrie a few more names of lenders and beg her to call one of them. Carrie's response is unexpectedly rigid. "I really want this 90% loan at 6% interest rate with no points," she counters (Points are the upfront fees a lender charges to keep the interest rate low). I am familiar enough with the current financial market to know that these terms seemed overly optimistic. That's when I say, "This loan sounds way too good to be true—what if this lender, who neither of us know, doesn't perform?"

"Craig got a loan from him with no problems," Carrie brags.

I feel we're taking an unnecessary risk. This mortgage broker is from Las Vegas and I'm sure doesn't have a clue to the exceptionally high prices of San Francisco real estate. Only a San Francisco-based appraiser will know what properties in the Bay Area are worth. If this lender doesn't use a local appraiser, the value of the property will never come in high enough. I try the back-door approach with Carrie to soften the information I'm about to deliver. Maybe this way she'll listen to reason. "How large was Craig's loan?" I ask.

She covers the phone with her hand and I hear muffled talking in the background. "$250,000," she eventually answers.

"Carrie, your loan is going to be much more. Anything over $417,000 is a jumbo loan and has entirely different guidelines. (The lower conforming loans can be sold in the secondary financial market and are much easier to obtain.) Plus, we don't have much time. Three weeks goes by really quickly." I pause a moment and suggest she use Michael Peck. He has been in the mortgage lending business for years and has done several loans for me. "All without a hitch," I add, "—not that your loan will be difficult—I'm sure it will be smooth as silk—but one never knows with lenders."

"Paula, you're such a Nervous Nellie. Will you stop it please?"

I beg her to reconsider.

"Okay," she says, "I'll call this Michael Peck and talk to him, but I'm telling you right now, I won't use him if his terms aren't as good."

"Thank you. Thank you," I say and then I'm off the phone.

Day Three—Friday morning. It's time to touch base with what's happening with the loan. I call Carrie.

"I talked to your friend Michael," she says. I thought I heard a sarcastic tone in her voice. "His terms aren't as good so I'm sticking with Craig's lender."

I bite my lip. What if the bank requires we get a termite inspection? This is pretty standard procedure for most lenders except for those based in the Bay Area. Then I'll have to get Robert LeCamp's permission and I am sure Robert will not cooperate. After all, the only reason he took our pre-emptive offer was because it was hassle free. Now our deal's starting to get complicated. I speak softly when I say, "Craig's lender is not from here. What if he can't get this 90% loan? What will you do then? You could lose your deposit and even the house—is it really worth the risk?"

"Don't you trust Craig's recommendation?" is her response.

I know there are some boundaries friends cannot cross and boyfriends are one of those. Yet I also know that if the lender does not come through, Carrie will turn to me to solve the problem. "Okay, then. Let's use Michael Peck as a back-up," I suggest, trying not to sound aggravated. Most lenders don't like to do this, because it is a lot of work on their part with a good chance of no reward. However, Michael is a good guy and I knew he would do this as a favor for me.

"Paula, I still haven't finished filling out the first loan application. I don't have time for all this nonsense." To quiet my fears, I give Michael Peck a call myself. I've been in this business long enough to know that *Wishin' and Hopin'* does not close real estate transactions. I want to know if this Las Vegas lender is for real. When I give Michael the quotes, he promises me he will call his list of banker contacts to see if he can match them.

Day Five. Michael calls me Monday morning, telling me he could not find any lender who can come close to the Las Vegas quotes—even for conforming loans under the $417,000 guideline. I thank Michael for all his time. "Would you still be willing to find a loan for Carrie?" I ask.

"Sure, Paula. In fact, I'll even meet with Carrie at her house to help her fill out the application."

"Thanks a bunch, Michael. I may take you up on that." Not only is Michael on top of his game, but he's generous as well. I make a mental note to myself to use Michael's services for my next transaction. His high standards of business practice make my job easier. I know the frantic last-minute stresses of closing, so I talk to Carrie's lender about his loan program. He is vague and non-committable. I then ask him to put something in writing and fax it to me. After a day and a half I call again. He does not respond. I know from long experience what this means. A value I hold dear is being truthful and Carrie needs to know the truth—that the phenomenal rates and terms she was quoted probably are not accurate.

When I explain the ramifications of the lender's unresponsiveness to Carrie, she does not believe me. "Why would he lie to me?" she asks.

"It's simple. He wants your business," I say. When I tell her Michael Peck will meet with her at her home, she tells me she is too busy. Busy doing what? She doesn't even have a job. Perhaps Carrie's and my values are not aligned. I promised Nina and Robert a smooth real estate transaction and want to keep to my word. Carrie's focus seems to be only on getting the best deal—even if it goes against the terms of our agreement.

Again I suggest she use Michael Peck as a back-up. I explain how the last-minute stress so characteristic of closings can take its toll—peace is another value I hold dear—but Carrie will not be persuaded. She is sticking fast to her guns. Not wanting to be the one who is shot, I fax and send Carrie's lender a letter confirming his quotes and a request for written confirmation.

RULE #11-1: FOLLOW YOUR VALUES Values represent who you are as a person—what principles you hold dear to your heart, what gives your life meaning. Hopefully, integrity, fellowship, honest communication and follow through are high on your list.

Reflect on what is most important to you, realizing that the choices you make will have consequences.

Day Twelve. Carrie's lender has not responded to my fax, my letter or my four telephone calls. I am getting nervous. I call Carrie. Carrie is aggravated with my nervousness and tells me—in not-so-polite terms—to back off. "Paula, you are being way too negative. If I don't get the loan, I'll pay all cash if necessary." I realize I cannot make Carrie do anything. I have to let it all go. I may even have to lose this deal.

Day Twenty. We are supposed to be closing tomorrow and the loan papers have not yet arrived. Carrie has been calling me every couple of hours for the last three days in a panic, trying to blame me. Instead of saying, "I told you so," I patiently remind her that Robert LeCamp accepted our offer, because he wanted the short escrow period and that she may have to come up with all cash to close this deal. Meanwhile, I am telling Nina Hatvany what the Vegas lender told Carrie—that the papers are due to arrive within a day or two (Or three? Who knows with this guy). I assure her and the title company that we will close with or without the loan papers, because Carrie will pay all cash if necessary. Nina gives us until Friday and moves on to her next transaction.

Day Twenty-three. Wednesday morning. The loan papers have arrived. Carrie is on her way over to sign them. I call Nina and tell her the good news—just a few days late—but it is finally going to happen. Then Carrie calls me from the title company. She is hysterical. Sure enough, the terms quoted to her are not the same as in the loan papers, so she is refusing to sign.

"That's okay," I say. "We still have time. Nina has given us an extension until Friday to close so you can bring in your cash today or tomorrow."

Carrie surprises me by attacking with the viciousness of a pit bull. "What?! All the money? How dare you even suggest such a thing!"

"Carrie, that's what you told me you would do if this loan didn't come through," I say, shocked at her line of reasoning.

"Well, do you believe everything I say?" she asks with an accusatory tone.

I answer, "Of course. Aren't I supposed to?"

"No," she says. "I must have been under duress when I promised you I'd use up all my cash. Now I've changed my mind." Instead, she plans to go to this bank directly and by-pass her dishonest lender, who she so vigorously defended in the beginning. I tell her that this will take time. I remind her that already we are three days late in closing and the seller, Robert LeCamp, is getting impatient. If he decides not to wait, she may lose all her deposit.

"I don't care," she says. "And don't think you can convince me to pay all cash which is not in my best interest. I thought you were supposed to be representing me!" Her voice is bitter and accusing; the words harsh.

I don't even attempt to answer. To save a few bucks, Carrie has forgone truthfulness, loyalty and friendship.

Day Twenty-four. I learn from Carrie that the bank is willing to work with her directly, which cuts down on some of the costs, but they want a new appraisal. Re-enter Michael Peck. With my tail between my legs, I ask him for another favor. Does he know of an appraiser who can write up an opinion of value ASAP? He makes a few calls on our behalf—all pro bono—and is able to find someone to do an on-site inspection and a written appraisal in two days—a record in the fast-moving San Francisco real estate market.

Day Twenty-five. Friday morning. Nina does her best to calm her client, but Robert LeCamp calls the title company directly and demands to know what's going on. When he learns that the first loan papers were never signed and we won't be closing for a few more days, he wants $5,000 for the inconvenience. Nina and I persuade him to accept the much-reduced fee of $2,500. I personally deliver a bottle of Silver Oak Cabernet to Nina and tell Carrie of the good news. Carrie hits the ceiling and demands that I pay the $2,500. Since I already agreed to give her a 20% referral fee, because this was supposed to be such an easy transaction, I refuse. Carrie then threatens to back out. I decide that losing my self-esteem is more painful than not getting paid. I tell her I will stand behind her decision of not consummating the deal.

She changes tactics, knowing that her $34,000 deposit is at risk. She now threatens a lawsuit, saying she did not understand the contract she signed (Not only had she bought the Marina condo I sold her ten years ago, but since then, a two-and-a-half-million dollar home in Tiburon as well as a ten thousand square-foot villa in Mexico with her ex-husband. Oh, yes, I almost forgot—before she married she worked for a title company for eight years. Carrie is no naïve young lady. Of course she understood the contract!) I listen, but again do not react. "Do whatever it is that you have to do," I say.

Day Thirty. Carrie pays the $2,500 penalty and buys the condo, but a huge rift has come between us—a rift that will not be bridged. Carrie has chosen money over a long-term friendship, honesty and fairness. I also feel badly about how she had used my good-hearted, knowledgeable business associate, Michael Peck, with not so much as a thank you. I had previously heard her divorce to her multi-millionaire husband, who she'd been married to for only a few years, had been extremely bitter. I didn't want to believe it before, but now I knew. Carrie would do just about anything for the almighty dollar.

> RULE #11-2: CHOICES HAVE CONSEQUENCES Every choice has a consequence. Know what your professional standards are because there are times you may have to sacrifice a sale or a friendship to remain true to what is most important to you.

Friendships are tricky. They can make or break a business relationship. In the case of Michael Peck, our friendship has brought both of us professional advantages. In a tough situation like the one I just described with Carrie, Michael helps both me and my client. While we are attempting to get answers from the out-of-state mortgage broker, Michael is available for advice and direction. He gets us in contact with a local appraiser who is able to give us an appraisal within two days. When we need a copy of the appraisal, it is Michael who facilitates it. Michael confides to me that Carrie is periodically calling him to check on the information she is getting from her lender because, although she wants this guy's rates, she does not trust him. Michael is not paid a dime, but does all this as a favor to me because of our solid business relationship.

Michael is a person with whom I want to do business with in the future. Carrie is not. As a Realtor, I know when a loan deal is too good to be true. I chose to let Carrie delude herself about her too-good-to-be-true loan by continuing to work with her even though I could see trouble down the road with the financing. But when she came running to me to take a lower commission, I refused. If I had to do this negotiation over again, I would make the same choices.

This transaction showed me the importance I place on good solid relationships, fair play and integrity. Being financially successful and being rewarded for a hard day's work are also important, but I will choose the former over money any day. I have never seen where money alone has made a person happy.

During this time Michael Peck told me how much he wanted to buy a home in Mill Valley. The real estate market in the Bay Area had been a Seller's Market for several years. Single family homes are selling approximately 10% over asking. Discouraged, Michael decides to wait until the market cools before starting his search. Am I surprised when he tells me that he bought a house from one of his neighbors!

He met Mary Thompson a few months before while walking his dog. They forged a strong bond because of their similar values. Mary recently left a corporate job for the flexible hours that real estate provided so she could be more available to her children—the same reason why Michael left his job as a stockbroker to get into the lending business. When Mary and her husband bought a larger house and needed to sell their current house quickly, she immediately thought of Michael's dream to own in Mill Valley. Mary figured that since she had gotten a great deal, why not offer Michael a good price. She could have an easy, stress-free sale and save herself a lot of time. Also, she could focus on other things that were more important—her family, the move and her new job.

That is how Michael got his dream house way below market value. A fluke? I don't think so. For both Mary Thompson and Michael Peck, strong relationship connections are one of their highest priorities. I share this priority, so I work well with them. Nina Hatvany is one of those rare business people who has that plus is at the top of her game. But not all of us can juggle several balls in the air at once. Few will be able to have a healthy personal life and reach the the apex of business success as Nina Hatvany has. Most of us will have to make choices. Realize that success can be measured by the amount of money one makes, the number of deals one brokers or the serenity that one feels in their relationships. The value with which you place these is a question only you can answer.

One year I listed a grand Victorian in Pacific Heights with no garage across from a bustling medical center. It had been Jerry and Jesse O'Neill's childhood home and they had inherited it from their mother when she passed on a few years before. Trustee Sales, which this was, can be tricky. The homes usually have not been lived in for several years and since the owners are either sickly or elderly, there is almost always deferred maintenance—leaky roofs, drafty windows, busted pipes, faulty wiring, out-of-date appliances and obsolete floor plans. In other words these houses are 'white elephants.' There is also a precise legal process and specific disclosures uncommon to the average sale. Did the person die in the property? Do you have all the correct signatures and a copy of the trust? Is there an appraisal of how much the property was worth when the person died? An appraisal when a spouse or other joint heir died? Is anyone contesting the will?

Besides the choice of a real estate agent, the sales price and how much work will be done on the property before it is offered for sale, there are the personal effects of the home which need to be sorted through, dispersed and given away. Decisions, decisions, decisions. What makes Trustee Sales tough, though, is not the paperwork, the condition of the house and all the work it entails, but the emotional baggage of a family besieged by grief, rivalry and petty grievances. The sale usually involves people who do not always agree, have their own demanding lives and do not have the time, energy or the money to deal with the mountain of details they suddenly face.

Homes are more than an investment, more than a place to hang our hat, more than a tax break. Homes represent family, love and security and, like most things in life, come up a bit short. These family homes are riddled with sentimentality and the overburdening sadness of what was or what could have been. It is a complicated, messy affair of personalities and emotions. The O'Neill's house was no exception.

Before Jerry and Jesse enlisted my help, they had made the choice of painting the exterior of the home a loud brick red with black trim and the stone walkway and wrought iron gate an incandescent white. The combination of the three stark colors with three different textures is what I would describe as alarming. However, what could I say? They just spent $20,000 on a new paint job and I did not want to insult them. Jerry was the younger brother who never married and lived in an apartment which the family owned around the corner. He was supposedly the caretaker of the property, but with the amount of fix up that this home needed he was a bit lax in his job. He kept telling me he would get this and that done, but never did. He was all talk and, from my observation, hitting the bottle pretty heavily. Jesse was slightly older, married and a lawyer who lived in the East Bay. He was introverted, quiet and soft spoken—not the typical attorney. He also was quite protective of his younger, troubled alcoholic brother.

A week before we planned to put the property on the market, Jesse called to tell me Jerry wanted to increase the list price from $1,295,000 to $1,595,000. "It's a historical home," his brother had said to me several times. "Mayor 'So and So' lived here. It has three bedrooms and a view. It has got to be worth at least a million and a half."

Can't they see that their mother's house needs at least another half a million to bring it into this century and another two hundred grand to put in a much needed garage? The top floor, which claims a city view of sorts, is really a converted attic. The deck is so dry rotted I am afraid if more than three people stand on it at one time they will fall through. The kitchen needs to be gutted. The house has only one bathroom. On and on and on...

"It is not just the money the buyer has to put into the property," I tell Jesse, who is the executor and the supposed decision maker. "But it is all the hassle the buyer has to go through to get the work done. Getting plans approved by the Planning and Building Departments is not easy. Plus, this house has the added complication of having an apartment where the garage needs to be." I explain how San Francisco is unusual in that a third of its residents are comprised of home-owners and the other two-thirds are renters. Since politicians side where the votes are, renters have a huge say in how our city is run.

"But my parents never rented out the apartment," Jesse argues. "It was just used for our family."

"It doesn't matter," I say. "The city doesn't like it when rental units are removed from the housing inventory. They will put up a big fight to keeping the apartment intact—even if it was never rented. This is going to be a big obstacle for prospective buyers. We need to give them an incentive to buy. Since we aren't investing a lot of money in the fix up, a competitive price is essential to get this puppy sold."

Jesse understands and agrees with me on the lower price when we review the comparable sales, but Jerry won't budge. He storms out of the room, hurling insults at both of us at how we are ganging up against him. It is obvious Jerry does not want to sell. He is very attached to the property. Having lost both his mother and his eldest brother in the past few years, he feels that selling is just another loss. Although Jerry's unrealistic stance frustrates his older brother, Jesse gives in. He is afraid Jerry may go on one of his binges and admits he is not up to having another casualty in his life right now. After all, Jerry is Jesse's only surviving family member. Since I want to make the selling process as easy as possible for Jerry and my direct presentation of the facts is not working, maybe a slower soft pedal approach will. So I change the price and add three months on to the listing period.

> RULE #11-3: CONCENTRATE ON WHAT YOU CAN DO There are some things you can control and some things that you cannot. Avoid interfering with family dynamics and be as flexible as possible. Time will wear down even the staunchest positions.

Getting agents inside the property is a huge challenge. Besides having no curb appeal, there is the added drawback of a busy street and no parking. I cater broker lunches, mail hand-written invitations to the neighbors, and distribute an elaborate color brochure to the top agents. I advertise in every magazine and newspaper I can think of— all with hardly a response. The one thing in my favor though is the shortage of big houses on the market. If someone wants a family home in a prestigious area and does not mind doing the work, this could be a definite possibility. Each month that passes make Jerry and Jesse less committed to their asking price. Thirteen weeks into the marketing of the property, an attractive preppy husband and wife, John and Muffy Winthrop, come through on one of the Sunday open houses with a small child. They are not working exclusively with an agent, but do not want me representing them since I am representing the seller.

"That's fine with me," I say, just wanting to get this albatross sold so I can go on with my life. After a long litany of questions, they assure me they will be back once they find an agent. A few days later they are back with Suzie Weinhammer and a licensed contractor. I go through the house with them once again, answering all their questions. Two hours later I hand them a detailed disclosure package, including the pre-sale inspections already done on the property.

It is almost seven in the evening on a Friday when my home phone rings. My husband, Greg, is due to return shortly from a week long business trip. We made plans to meet up for dinner and, since I am already late enough as it is, I have my assistant answer. Suzie Weinhammer of Sotheby's has an offer for me. I get out of the shower, still dripping, and take the call, asking if she can call me back in ten minutes. "I'm running late and have to meet my husband and a group of friends for dinner," I explain.

"No, I can't." she says, insisting I call her back.

"Fine," I say, thinking Suzie may be one of those prima donna egomaniacs. Realizing I am being negative, I cancel that thought and concentrate on the positive. Suzie Weinhammer is an established agent and this is the first offer we have received after several months of marketing. I look at the clock, knowing I am late and throw on a dress, some makeup and earrings. I make sure I grab my cell phone on the way out, and plan to call her on route.

I do my best navigating through pouring turrets of rain, and suddenly realize I do not have Suzie's telephone number. That means I have to retrieve her number from my voice mail at work by punching in my extension, security code and going through all my other messages. I decide it is just too dangerous and drive on.

The restaurant is small and intimate and spilling over with people celebrating the start of a weekend. There is no place I can go to make a phone call. I order a glass of wine and relax, enjoying dinner with my husband and his friends. On the way home water is still spilling from the sky in sheets. When it lessens I pull over, but with the rain pounding my convertible top, I cannot hear my messages. Unfortunately, it is also getting late. "Well," I reason to myself, "they waited a week to write the offer, they can wait a few more hours."

When I call Suzie early the next morning she does not answer. I notice a contract came through the fax machine, but it is light and hard to read. I change the ink cartridge, read the contract, have breakfast, get dressed and wait for Suzie's call. Forty-five minutes into my yoga routine the phone finally rings. I ask if she can meet with my sellers to discuss the offer. "The price is a bit low," I add.

I hardly get these words out of my mouth when she shoots back at me, "Great! Now you're telling me that you have difficult sellers who aren't motivated! I don't know how thoroughly you read the offer, but you'll have to hurry because we expect an answer by five tonight!"

"How do you expect me to do that? It's Saturday and almost noon!" I answer without thinking, ready to meet her forceful energy. Catching myself in a power play, I look at my Buddha sitting comfortably above my desk and change my approach, remembering my 'Empathy Rule'—maybe Suzie had a really hard week. In my softest, most understanding voice I say, "I will do my best to get a meeting with at least one of them today, but I know Jesse has an appointment in Santa Rosa. Hopefully, it is later in the afternoon and I can meet with him before." I did not want to meet with Jerry and certainly did not want this agent to know I had a difficult seller—an overly sentimental, alcoholic seller to be exact.

"That's better," she says.

Once again I make a plea for her to be at the presentation, using team language and her name so she feels acknowledged. "Suzie, if you're there you can push harder for your clients than I can. You know them much better than I do."

"I already told you—I can't." Her words sound bitter and cold.

"It is a seller's market," I remind her and lightly laugh. "You know how sellers can be." I then take a deep breath, waiting for her response.

Suzie gets more agitated and belligerent.

My approach does not seem to be working. I wonder if by being direct and naming what is going on I will get her to be more cooperative. In a quick ten second analysis, I decide that telling her she is too aggressive will only add more fuel to the fire. A pointed question is probably best. "Why don't we work on this together and make it a win/win for both our clients?" I ask.

She ignores my question.

I use more empathy to build rapport, and once again ask for her help. "I would really like to make this work, Suzie. Are you sure you can't take a half an hour out of your day to meet? You're a great agent and I'd love to sell my listing. How about at your office?"

Her voice is tight and gritty. "I already told you I can't. Aren't you listening, Paula? You also should know that these buyers are considering another property so if your sellers aren't interested we will just move on. You have by five tonight or we walk."

I can feel red hot anger surging up from my chest like a volcano about to explode. *How dare she speak to me like that!* I want to tell her what I really think, but stop myself. That is an old pattern that never works. I need to get into a more positive frame of mind before I talk to my clients. A few quick stretching exercises and I am ready. I reach Jesse on his cell phone. Unfortunately, he is already on his way to Santa Rosa.

"By the way," he says, "before I left the house, I did some checking on our buyers online."

"Really?" I never thought of doing that. "What did you find out?" I ask, impressed he had taken the time in his busy schedule.

"Both the husband and wife are from wealthy well-established East Coast families, and John is a graduate from Harvard with a top notch position at a local law firm. They certainly have the money, whereas the proceeds from our mother's house are our main source of retirement."

"Does that mean you won't negotiate on price?" I ask, aghast. "Remember our list price is higher than we originally agreed."

"Sure. We'll negotiate some—we still have to sell, don't forget. Why don't you meet with Jerry today since they want an answer right away? The earlier the better. Hopefully, he won't have started drinking. He's waiting for your call."

I am frustrated that Suzie Weinhammer put me in this position. I could not very well tell her what I was up against, because she did not want to hear about my seller's situation and why they were selling. Knowing that my sellers had issues would only drive her away. So here I am being forced to negotiate with an irrational alcoholic who does not want to sell. If only Suzie was willing to work with me, I might have had a chance. We could have played good cop, bad cop, or presented the Winthrops to Jerry in such a way that he would want them to get the house. Better yet we could have waited until Monday to meet with Jesse, who would be more realistic. But, no, Suzie did not want to hear my side of the story so I had to go it alone—with the alcoholic brother who had plenty of time—not with the busy attorney whose input would have made a difference.

> RULE #11-4: WORK AS A TEAM Selling homes is complicated. The more people who work together to get the job done, the easier it will be. Enlist the help of the other agent. Find out information of why the other agents' clients are buying/selling. Real estate deals are best accomplished when it is a win/win situation.

Looking closely at the offer it becomes clear that neither Suzie Weinhammer or the Winthrops have read the disclosure packet I had given them. They did not follow the guidelines of a Trustee Sale, nor had they signed off on any of the inspections. I do my best to convince Jerry to give them a counter, but Jerry decides against it. "What about them going to another property?" I tell him what Suzie told me, but in more delicate terms.

"Let them. They don't seem like serious buyers to me. Besides, I don't like ultimatums."

I typically like to give a counter, because I feel constant dialogue is key to a successful transaction, but Jerry is adamant. I fold up my paperwork with a sigh—a low offer which does not work is better than nothing. Perhaps Jerry and Jesse will consider lowering their asking price soon. I make the courtesy call to Suzie, and leave her a message, thanking her for the offer and wishing her luck with the other property, because we are not going to respond.

The following day Suzie Weinhammer leaves a message on my voice mail telling me how unprofessional I have been. (The perfect compliment to convince me to want to work with her.) In the next breath she tells me she is willing to extend the expiration time and for us to counter her offer. I am left to wonder if the Winthrops ever had another property they were considering. I spend a good part of my morning weeding my backyard and watching for hummingbirds as I take in all the beauty around me. I do not want to be reactive when I speak with Suzie. With my mind clear, I return her call, suggesting we start fresh by having the Winthrops approve the disclosure package first and then resubmitting a new offer.

"NO! That is not how we're going to do it! You already have our offer—you MUST get back to us. That is the only way we will work with you."

Her energy is like a cluster of angry gnats around my head. I am getting tired of all her threats. "Well, Suzie I guess that is your choice," I say.

I take a long shower trying to wipe off the emotionality of our interchange, refusing to let myself get pulled into her drama any longer. I feel the pent-up frustration drain out of the soles of my feet through the tile flooring to the ground outside. I imagine the negative stream moving far away from me into the center of the earth. When I feel I have cleansed myself completely, I call Jesse and Jerry, relaying my conversation with Suzie in a light off-handed way. We laugh together, agreeing that none of us want to work with controlling people like these.

The next day Mike Greenland, my current manager, calls me into his office. Suzie Weinhammer has called and complained. I dig my heels in, becoming more persistent than ever that she is not going to win by intimidation. At the same time, I know the importance of remaining calm. Mike has seen me get emotional in the past and hates it. I think of my yoga practice to keep my voice steady while I explain that we were not given enough time to respond. I add, "The O'Neills are reasonable people and not opposed to working with the Winthrops. We are only asking the buyers to follow the standard protocol of a Trustee Sale with the disclosure package approved beforehand. Then they can submit a new offer."

Mike suggests we play the game the way Suzie Weinhammer wants. "After all," he says in his most convincing tone, "she is the number one agent in her office."

So whatever Suzie wants, Suzie gets—while she mistreats everyone else around her? Now is the honeymoon phase of the negotiating process when the selling agent does everything possible to please the listing agent. Once her offer is accepted, I can only imagine Suzie Weinhammer's difficult behavior escalating. Why would I want to put myself, or my clients, through all that drama? It is time to start setting boundaries now—not later when she feels she can get her way through force and intimidation.

I remind Mike that my loyalty is to my clients who hired me—not to any agent—no matter who she is.

"I don't feel comfortable trying to convince my clients to counter an already expired offer, which is way below their asking price and full of loopholes, because no one bothered to read the disclosure package," I say. "Let them do their due diligence then my clients will entertain their offer." I leave Mike's office feeling calm, with my self-esteem intact. I reward myself by having a long walk by the Marina Green.

> RULE #11-5: YOUR DUTY IS TO YOUR CLIENTS The Agency Disclosure is the first document you have your clients sign—even before the Purchase Contract. It describes your relationship as a "fiduciary duty of utmost care, integrity, honesty and loyalty in all dealings" whether you represent a buyer, a seller or both.

A week later we hear from Tracy Bingsley, an agent who works in the same office as Suzie Weinhammer. She tells me she has a new offer from the Winthrops on Sacramento Street.

"Have the Winthrops approved the disclosure package yet?" I ask. She answers that they have. "You understand then that this is a Trustee Sale?" I want no misunderstandings this go around.

Tracy says she knows that too and adds, "They've also been pre-approved by a lender."

This is how offers should be done. I suggest to Tracy that she do a face to face presentation so we can start fresh, admitting that the first offer got off to a bad start. "I find it always helps if the clients know a little about each other so they can relate better during the transaction. With you present the O'Neills can ask you questions about the buyer that I can't answer," I say. Tracy agrees and we set up a time to meet at my office. When Jerry suggests we meet at the property instead, I stand my ground, knowing we need a neutral place. I use the excuse of having access to all our forms and copy machine.

Jerry and Jesse arrive a few minutes ahead of time so we can strategize. "Feel free to ask the agent any question you wish," I advise. "Just don't get hung up on price. Keep in mind that a buyer wants to negotiate the lowest price possible so don't be insulted. We can always counter their offer after Tracy Bingsley leaves."

"Since the Winthrops have already given us an offer, won't it be better this time?" Jesse asks.

"I would think so, but it's hard to second guess. We'll just have to wait and see." I look at my watch. "We'll know soon enough. Tracy should be here any minute." I offer them a cup of coffee and get my notebook out with the counter form, thinking I will probably need it. If it is another low price, I hope Tracy Bingsley brings some MLS statistics to show how they arrived at their offering price. Although Jerry does not want to hear what I have to say about price, he may listen to someone else if they can substantiate their figure with some facts.

Tracy is right on time and is dressed in a Chanel powder blue suit. Her hair is blonde and long and she is a bit younger than I had expected. Despite her age it is easy to see she has put forth some effort into looking professional. She extends a warm handshake to each of us. She has photos of the Winthrops and a nice letter from them, which is a good idea, because Jerry and Jesse may have some preconceived, not so nice notions about these buyers. She also has a copy of their credit score from their lender—another item we never got with the first offer. So far so good.

I glance over at Jerry and Jesse. Both are alert with open body language. Jerry even asks Tracy about what the Winthrops plan to do with the property and actually leans over the table to listen to what she has to say. It is obvious he has not been drinking. I secretly applaud myself for scheduling an early morning appointment. He gives his own opinion what he thinks can improve the home. Things that he always wanted to do, but never found the time.

This is the perfect opening for Tracy who has a cost breakdown of improvements which she hands out to both brothers. Maybe not what they expected, but something that they need to hear. She then discusses other similar properties which have sold. Since she is not representing the O'Neills, she can be more forceful (Whenever I previously talked price, I had to be careful not to offend them lest they think I did not like their mother's house). Even though the Winthrops have not changed their low offering price, Jesse and Jerry remain cordial. They ask Tracy a few more questions, and tell her how much they appreciate her meeting them.

Although the Winthrops have already had a contractor's inspection and the disclosure package has copies of termite, geological and energy inspections, they still include a ten day contingency period to get more inspections. Jerry and Jesse are apprehensive. "They already had their inspections. Why should we give them more? It's just a loophole."

Yes, I also see this clause as a possible out, but I want to get this process rolling along. So what if this offer doesn't work? Maybe the O'Neills will be more open to the next one. So I respond by saying, "The buyers have the right to do as much discovery as they wish. They want to be secure in their decision and as sellers, I suggest you allow them to make any inspections they want. Let's concentrate only on price. Remember, if this offer does not work, I can tell other agents we received an accepted offer. Having an accepted offer will encourage more interest, because the adage, 'People always want what they can't have' also applies to real estate." I push a pen towards them and wait.

Neither Jerry or Jesse pick up the pen.

"If the Winthrops ask for more money after their inspections," I say, "We can always tell them no."

Jerry and Jesse look at each other. Jerry speaks first. "We still want more money though." Jerry and Jesse look at each other. Their eyes lock. Their hands are closed with an air of rigid determination.

One step at a time, I tell myself. I can only persuade so much. "What's the verdict?" I ask. I make sure I am smiling.

"We'll counter only on price," Jesse says. "We'll come down $20,000, but that's it."

It is not much, but something. I call Tracy Bingsley to tell her we are faxing the counteroffer to her office, explaining that my sellers would be open to a response. Jerry and Jesse did not tell me that, but I want to keep communication lines open.

The Winthrops do not respond. A week goes by. I continue marketing the property. Another week. And another. We still have not heard from the Winthrops and there have been no other buyers. I wait one more week, then call Tracy to see if the Winthrops found another property. They have not.

"Would they consider submitting their absolute best offer on Sacramento Street?" I ask. "It would have to be a better than their last offer, but I think the O'Neills are ready now."

Tracy comes back with an offer only slightly better and still with the same ten day inspection period. The O'Neills are disappointed, but have been worn down after almost five months of having only this offer. They grudgingly accept it, emphasizing they will not negotiate a penny less—no matter what the Winthrops find in the contractors' inspections.

> **RULE #11-6: TAKE ONE STEP AT A TIME** When it comes to negotiating, each day is a new day. Each step taken—no matter how small—is one step closer to the goal of closing the transaction.

We are in contract, but the following Sunday I still hold an open house. I have learned that one never knows what the outcome will be. A dowdy slightly overweight woman in her forties rushes through, bubbling with excitement, declaring that she has finally found her perfect home. *It always happens this way,* I muse—*feast or famine.* I tell her that the house is already in escrow with an inspection contingency. She runs to get her husband who is sitting in the car with two small children. He previews the house, also agreeing that this is the house for them. Chris and Macy Remy leave their number and ask me to call them if I know of any similar properties. That week I show Macy three other houses. She did not like any of them.

"Please promise me you will call me if the other offer doesn't work," she pleads.

"It's doubtful," I say as I hand her my cell phone number. "But feel free to call me Saturday if you wish. They had two inspections yesterday and it went well. They are supposed to remove the inspection condition by end of this week." Too bad they didn't come by a few weeks ago. It always seems people want what they can't have.

Thursday late afternoon I call Tracy. She had been out of town for a few days, but was expected back today. I get no call back. I call twice more the following day. Still no response. I am wondering why the delay in getting me the removal of the inspection contingency. I call her manager—he is out of town. It is now time for me to contact Jerry and Jesse and ask if they want to give the Winthrops a 'Twenty-Four Hour Notice to Perform.' They do. I send the fax to Tracy's home and office and call to tell her what we are doing. This time Tracy calls back in a matter of minutes, requesting an extension of the contract. I am thinking that the Winthrops want one more pass at the new listings open this weekend before they fully commit to buying this house. So it appears the inspection condition was a loophole after all.

I call Jesse and ask what he wants to do. He does not want to extend the contingency period. Why would he? The Winthrops have had six weeks to think about whether they want the property or not. The '24 Hour Notice to Perform' still stands.

Saturday morning comes and goes. The Winthrops have not responded to our request and are now out of contract. Chris and Macy call Saturday evening to check on the status of the house and are thrilled to learn that they have a chance. They have no agent representing them and want me to write up the offer. I meet with them the following day which is Mother's Day and Macy is beside herself with happiness. "This is the best Mother's Day present I could ever have," she says. "What ever happened with the other offer?" she asks.

"Well, the most curious thing happened. We did not hear from the buyers all yesterday and then this morning their agent calls to tell me they want $135,000 credit. Can you imagine? Of course, my clients said no."

Chris and Macy shake their heads. "You'll find we are easy buyers. We'll stand behind our contract and what we sign." They eagerly reach for a pen and sign every page without hesitation. They had brought a pre-approval letter and credit report from their lender as I had requested and a 3% earnest money deposit. Macy hands me a hand written note to the O'Neills as a way of introduction, praising their mother's home. I can see nothing that could stand in their way of purchasing their dream home.

I am just about to call Jesse to let him know the good news when my phone rings. It is Tracy. She is checking to see if the O'Neills would consider crediting her buyers half of their initial request—just $67,000. "No, they are not interested," I say, now self- assured with my hand on another contract. "In fact, we have another offer."

Tracy is aghast. "You can't do that. We had a contract. Let me call my clients. I'll call you right back."

The phone rings less than a minute later. It is Tracy. She sounds out of breath. "Ok, then. The Winthrops will stick with their original offer."

"Tracy, we can't do that now," I say slowly, choosing my words carefully. "There's another offer."

"But, Paula, you know how hard I've worked on this. I had to come back from my vacation in Mexico early to get this done."

"But the truth is you didn't get it done. The time elapsed yesterday at ten in the morning. You received a 'Twenty-Four Hour Notice to Perform' and you ignored it. It is now Sunday evening and there is another offer. If you want to resubmit your offer, I will present it again to the O'Neills, but you are now competing with someone else."

The next morning the O'Neills and Mike Greenland and I discuss the two offers. The O'Neills do not trust the Winthrops anymore, thinking they may find some new angle to wrangle over. They accept the Remy's offer unequivocally. It was an easy choice.

Twenty-one days later I deposit a whopping $55,000 commission check into my bank account—a direct result of me not slipping into my usual pattern of resentment and anger, and instead focusing on getting the house sold.

CHAPTER TWELVE

IMBALANCE
Learning Temperance

AFTER A TEN DAY SPAN of twelve to fourteen hour workdays I drag myself out of bed when I hear my phone blasting in my ear—another *Manic Monday*. I take a quick glance at my appointment book crammed with showings, inspections and offer presentations, half wishing I had gotten the few extra hours of sleep I needed instead of going out last night. *But when was it that I went out last?* I could not even remember. Besides, my night dancing at the Metronome had been terrific.

I prepare one of my antioxidant energy breakfast drinks. Deciding this is a two scoop day, I swallow the murky pea-green concoction down with a handful of vitamins. *This should do the trick,* I say to myself—all the time wondering how I will ever make it through the week that has just begun with three ready to buy clients and a listing on which I had just received an offer. After my sixty-second shower, I check the messages on my cell phone, the ones left on my home recorder and the ones in the office. It is eight in the morning so I call Steve Bellos, the fast talking stock broker, to get his final signature on a counter offer— "the sophisticated buyer" who assured me he would be reachable all weekend. As soon as he picks up the phone he tells me he is thinking about asking the seller to pay for his inspections.

"I wouldn't recommend doing that," I advise. "Another agent showed 1998 Filbert yesterday and probably will be bringing in an offer."

"They can't do that," Steve insists.

"In fact, they can. I don't have your final signature, Steve. Remember—time is of the essence when we are in the midst of negotiating." I answer, doing my best to remain calm as I have practiced so many times before. "By the way, where were you all weekend?

"On the golf course. I work hard during the week."

"Don't you turn your cell phone on at all?" I ask, bewildered by his lackadaisical attitude. We could lose this sale.

"Not when I play golf. What is this anyway—the Inquisition?"

Against my better judgment I return the volley. "Gee, I wish I had some time off once in a while." Being right is becoming more important than the money now. *See what happens when I'm overtired,* I say to myself, promising to go no further. I take a deep breath, remembering when Frank Woods refused to return my calls after I made the blunt remark about his fiancé.

"Did Paul Bishop sign the counter yet?" Steve asks. Paul is a past client, who brought Steve Bellos in on this deal in the first place. All the condo needs is a new kitchen and bath and can be flipped in a year or two for a tidy profit. Even if the market were to head south, they could rent it out and break even, because of its close proximity to Union Street, the Marina and public transportation.

"Yesterday morning. We are just waiting for you."

After a harrowing list of questions Steve finally agrees to sign, but insists I come to his office way across town, because he wants to have the original.

"Fine," I say, not wanting to argue. His faxed signature seals the deal, so before I leave, I open up an escrow with a title company, order the preliminary title report and arrange to have the good faith deposit money delivered. I then coordinate what needs to happen to remove the contingencies of the sale, such as setting up the termite, contractor and geological inspections, and organize the mound of disclosures which will need to be signed. A partial list for sure, but at least it is a start.

In the midst of all this craziness, I get a call from one of my 'Gotta Buy Now Clients' who wants to write an offer on the condo I showed them Saturday. Then the other 'Ready To Go Buyer' calls to tell me he found the perfect house when he was out looking at open houses yesterday. In the olden days I would have been out of my seat excited, but I find myself getting depressed—not knowing how I will ever be able to handle all the tasks in front of me. My office phone starts ringing madly, so I beg to get off the line and call him right back.

The phone call is from the agent who has been saying he may be writing on the listing I just put in escrow this morning. I then call the seller, Mr. Yang, who presses me with why I did not present the offer yesterday. "Because I just got the call today—this minute," I answer, double checking that my voice remains even though his accusation is like a knife in my gut. Fortunately for me, the first offer is the better of the two and this second one will be a backup. Still, I feel like I am on the firing line and Mr. Yang does not speak the best English. I get off the phone as quickly as possible, promising him I will call him back later to discuss his concerns. I get back to typing one of the offers while the fax machine rings loudly in my ear and decides to jam. *On this of all days?* While I try to pull out the crumpled paper, the machine lets out a huge screeching noise as if it is alive and I am purposely torturing it. Then the phone rings once again, disturbing my concentration. After stalling all weekend, Steve now has silly questions that he deems urgent. I think they can wait until tomorrow for answers. I explain I am swamped, but he does not understand. He gets irate, because he is a 'Right Now' kind of guy. He threatens to call Paul when I tell him I will get back to him later. Sure enough Paul calls shortly after. Now I have to do damage control. This is how my day goes—high stress to the max.

I am overworked, overtired and although well paid, I am wondering if all this is worth the money I will make. I grab a cup of coffee to keep me going and hop in the car to meet Steve, hoping to patch some of the damage caused by not giving him enough attention. I look at my watch and notice I am running a bit late. So what else is new. An intense coal-hot heat takes over my body, causing my blood pressure to rise and my heart to pulsate. If I were a car, I would be ready to blow a gasket. *I should never have drunken that caffeine-laden coffee.* Too preoccupied with what I need to do next, I ignore the police car at the intersection monitoring cars rolling through the stop sign. Looking in my rear view mirror, I see a spinning red light and an officer following me in his patrol car motioning me to pull over.

A square-shouldered uniformed man approaches my car with brusque steps. "Didn't you see the stop sign? Let me see your license, registration and insurance."

Unable to utter a word in my defense, I give him the feeblest of smiles.

"Come on, move it. I don't have all day." He already has a pen and paper in hand.

I fumble in my purse, hoping I can locate what he needs quickly.

The policeman starts talking again. "I am sick and tired of people ignoring signals as if they don't exist. I guess this is not your day, because you are getting a ticket!"

I want to go back to bed and pull the covers over my head. Add going to traffic school on my never-ending task list. *When is this hectic life ever going to end?*

> **RULE #12-1: MAKE YOURSELF YOUR NUMBER ONE PRIORITY**
> Make sure you schedule time for yourself in your appointment book. We all need time away from our jobs to recharge so we can operate at our optimum. Rest is important, because when your body and mind are well taken care of, you have energy to make decisions, juice to be creative and the pizzazz to be charming.

Yes, sales can be exciting, but at the same time, very seductive—taking over your whole life if you are not careful. I sometimes forget all about determining what matters most, because I get so caught up in the adrenalin rush of being successful. Balance is a constant juggling act. I sincerely believe that we are not meant to live these frantic frenzy lives where productivity, money, and success at any cost are our only values. In choosing such a limited scope of reality we lose the richness and expansiveness of life experiences around us... the smile of a child, the smell of fresh-cut grass, the sound of crashing waves on the beach, and the vividness of a scarlet sunset...

I had accomplished what I had set out to do. I had become a top salesperson, was recognized in the real estate community and had all the material necessities one could ask for—my own house, an apartment building, blue chip stocks, a BMW convertible, designer clothes and five ball gowns for my competitive dancing. Yet I was yearning for something more—and it was not about finding my soul mate. Finally, I got a subliminal clue when I started having dreams that I was living in Europe again.

In my waking life, I then manifested a boyfriend from Poland (I met him in a health food store of all places!) We dated a few months and shortly afterwards spent the summer in his small country town near Czestochowa. Although Marek and I did not make it as a couple, I received some valuable insight from him of what I needed to do to be happy. Europeans took time to enjoy the small pleasures of life—casual conversation, cooking, gardening, walking in nature—instead of the American way of focusing exclusively on making money. The European M.O. was: *Work to Live* rather than *Live to Work*. Embracing that idea, when I heard of 'Balance for Life,' an Australian-based holistic approach to healing, I volunteered to sponsor their program in San Francisco. We learned all about the benefits of food combining, basic yoga postures, herbs, essential oils, and acupuncture points. We then followed up our learning with an advanced month-long course in kinesiology and anatomy in Melbourne, Australia. I started to get in touch with the core of me—that I was more than just my real estate and dance achievements, my travel experiences or who I was dating at the time.

During this same period, my company, Premier Real Estate, in honor of their 75th Anniversary, sponsored four charity events. I volunteered to organize a benefit for breast cancer. Since the statistics in the Bay Area had jumped from one in nine women to one in eight for this deadly disease, my friends and I were concerned. Breast cancer was still hush-hush at the time—a topic not to be discussed in public. That did not deter me. Through a friend, I met Matuschka, an artist who was famous for her startling self-portraits after undergoing a mastectomy. She was portraying herself, although scarred, as a woman with her beauty, pride and dignity still intact. Amelia Davis, a native San Franciscan artist and Annette Porter, a photographer from Seattle, were also featured in *The Invasive Art Show* which I held at the Spectrum Gallery. All proceeds went to the National Lymphedema Network. It was a spectacular success (Little did I know then that in a few short years my sister-in-law would be one of the statistics, dying at the young age of forty-six).

RULE #12-2: CONTRIBUTE Real estate can be a very lucrative profession, but just making money cannot make a person feel rich. Giving can.

After I sponsored the Australian-based *Balance for Life* Workshops and *The Invasive Art Show,* I started to feel whole again. I was feeling more balanced, but I could still sense something was still out of whack. What was it?

Premier was—and still is—the top-notch real estate firm in San Francisco. It had taken me almost ten years to get there. I was proud to be affiliated with them, but lately the cut-throat competitiveness there was having a negative effect on me. I could deal with the snobbery and elitism in the good-time eighties, because there was enough business to go around. But the nineties were tougher financially and the cliquish prima donnas, who were the San Francisco social set, ruled at Premier. I was beginning to realize *sell at any cost* was not my style and never would be. I liked representing first time buyers, quirky artists and my past, true blue loyal clients. But Premier's main objective was to be the biggest, the strongest, and the best. And, of course, to sell, sell, sell.

My projects at Premier were beginning to go bad for me in many different ways. The previous year I had listed a great house in Jordan Park, near Presidio Heights, which was a referral, but now my contract had expired. We had planned to put it back on the market in a few months, but I was surprised to find that one of the super agents, who sat behind me in the office, listed it two weeks later.

Then, shortly thereafter, one of my past clients, Doug Haskins, was being transferred back to Houston and thinking of selling. I brought a sales manager, Art Mayfield, and a few other agents through to price his home. Obviously, Doug Haskins was not happy with our price, because he ended up listing with another top agent in my office at $50,000 higher than what my colleagues and I quoted.

Now a 'For Sale by Owner,' whose house I had put an offer on, promised me I would get the listing if he could not sell it on his own by the end of the year. Wouldn't you know it—when I returned from Christmas vacation, it was listed by one of the favored pets of the office. Surely, the seller must have called the Premier office looking for me. I assumed management, instead of contacting me, referred him to one of the chosen ones. Still I stayed. What was I thinking? Well, for one thing, I knew I was not being singled out. These unfortunate events happened to several of us. But my closest associates urged me to talk to management—this type of business practice was demoralizing. I agreed and made an appointment.

Mr. Beltham listened to the three different scenarios, nodding in acknowledgment. After I was done, he smiled, "So what's next?"

"Next?" I paraphrased back, not understanding what he meant.

"That is all in the past Paula. It's time to move forward. What are you going to do now for business?"

I shrugged.

"You could always take Lifespring and get a new attitude," he suggested with a smile so broad it felt insincere.

"I've done that route," I said. "Lifespring, Actualizations, EST, Affirmations, Positive Thinking, Meditation. What I think I need from you is a referral to make up for all these unfortunate situations," I said.

"Yeah, you probably do," he said and wrote himself a note. From the look on his face, I doubted I would ever get anything from him. The only referral I got in all the years at Premier was Blayne Ritter. Not a transaction action I would like to repeat. Yes, I finally did sell their property, but only after they slashed my commission in half. Truthfully, these were the type of clients I would never want to do business with again. Was the universe trying to tell me something? It was time to see Dr. Black again and get some clarity on what to do next.

Still her same blonde, bubbly self with maybe a few extra mid-life pounds, Dr. Black's first question to me was: "Why aren't you with a firm which is more aligned with your values?"

I countered her argument. "Premier is a well-respected firm with a good brand, and they represent prestige properties. I spent a lot of energy reaching the top and I am not willing to let that go."

Besides, I really did not want to move again. In the fifteen years I had been selling real estate in San Francisco I had been with three companies: Saxe Realty, my start-up in the Mission, Pacific Properties, my upwardly mobile years, and now Premier, the pinnacle of success. Each time I made the move I wanted a company which was more prestigious so I could sell more architecturally interesting, prestigious properties.

"But, Paula, you aren't happy. Isn't that what's most important?"

As usual Dr. Black was upbeat and positive. Her ubiquitous, jovial self was beginning to annoy me. What was she so happy about all the time, anyway?

"Why don't you make a horizontal move instead?" she suggested. "There must be other good companies selling properties in the better neighborhoods of San Francisco. What about that company you recommended to your friend, Helen Clawsen, a few months back?"

"Oh, Taylor Properties? She never went to work there. Helen decided to go to Coldwell Banker instead." I took a sip from my water glass and continued. "I know I would never be happy with a corporate franchise. I like the local independent real estate firms. San Francisco is special and those big companies just don't understand our unique city. Also, as I'm sure you've observed, I'm no corporate gal—too many rules and restrictions. I like the boutique San Francisco companies."

"Well, isn't Taylor Properties one of those family run boutique companies?"

Boy, Dr. Black sure is persistent. Why doesn't she let up? "Yeah, but—" I stammered, "—not as competitive."

Dr. Black, with that wide open smile of hers gave me a playful wink. "I guess my suggestions aren't what you want to hear today, Paula."

I pondered for a moment. "Certainly, Taylor Properties is as respected in the real estate community as Premier," I said, trying my best to be open-minded, "and they're known to be team players. Like me, many them have their Broker's License, so they are definitely a cut above the average… " Hmmm… Maybe Dr. Black was onto something. I continued, "Plus, there are no prima donnas working there that I know of and, the manager, Linda Walters, is one of the smartest real estate managers in the business." I felt my heart beginning to expand in my chest.

"Well, then. It's obvious. Go there."

I did not say anything. I was still thinking.

"Paula, what's wrong?"

"Well, the truth is I don't know if they would take me."

Dr. Black looked at me with sincere concern. "Why not?"

"Well, you know how I have been complaining about Premier being a bit competitive and hard-edged? I think, in the past I have been a bit like that myself. I don't know if Taylor Properties would want me."

Dr. Black looked at me directly. "Paula, you have been seeing me off and on for three years now. I can see a change in you. You are much more empathetic and caring and would make an excellent team player. I think Taylor Properties is a perfect match for you. Just tell them the truth—that you have changed. It is obvious that Premier is no longer a fit for you."

I leave her office, still unsure. Changing offices means telling my client base I am moving again. The universe does not let me off the hook, though. The following week on Broker's Tour I stop to view a large home in Laurel Heights. The agents are out in full force and as usual there is no place to park. As is the custom, I park for a few minutes in a neighbor's driveway, making sure to put my flashers on. I barely have entered the house when I hear loud footsteps behind me. "You just parked in my driveway!" The voice accompanying the noisy entrance is hinging on hysterical.

I turn around to see a face pinched in pain. "Yes, I did," I say. "I'm very sorry to have inconvenienced you." I grab the keys out of my purse as the woman steps forward with one of her hands raised. I step out of her way and make a hasty retreat to move my car.

She shrieks after me. "What is your name?" Her voice is reaching a high shrill while I do my best to ignore her. "I just asked you—what is your name?" As I open the door to my car, I can hear this woman asking the listing agent for my business card. I pray that Marianne Stein has enough sense not to give it to her.

I am back at my desk only a few minutes when now the President of Premier Properties motions me into his office. "I got a very disturbing call from a woman called Mrs. Pitts on Palm Street today, Paula."

"Oh, that. I parked in her driveway when I was out on tour today. I moved my car immediately, but she still went ballistic on me," I say, standing uneasily on my feet. Stay grounded I tell myself. This is just a minor inconvenience.

"Paula, you have to call her and apologize."

"Do I have to?" I ask, pleading with him now. "She was crazy. She almost hit me," I say.

"Paula, you have to. We cannot afford to have anyone upset with Premier Real Estate, especially in such a high status neighborhood."

High-status? Well, maybe, but certainly no class. I made sure not to say that thought out loud.

I am given a stern look. "Really, Paula, you should not be parking in front of people's driveways."

"You know we all do it. How can we preview forty-fifty properties in two and a half hours?"

"Paula, you must apologize. End of story."

I leave his office with my shoulders slumped. I knew I would not call this crazy woman—no matter how much money she had. This was just the excuse I needed to call Taylor Properties. I try to sound upbeat and positive, although deep inside I am wrenching anxious. "Hi, Linda," I say. "This is Paula Pagano of Premier. I was thinking of making a change and wondered if I could come in and talk to you." I tell her that Taylor Properties represents the team player coopera-tion I now craved rather than the competitive atmosphere at Premier. "Perhaps, you have an available desk?"

Linda answers in the affirmative. This is a good sign. At least Taylor Properties is open to speaking with me. Linda sets up a clandestine meeting early one morning for us to talk. It is done this way so not to jeopardize my relationship with my Premier.

Linda behaved like the consummate professional she was and did not hold my previous edgy competitiveness against me. She recognized that I was a hard worker, had a good reputation and solid client base. At the end of the short interview she said what I had hoped for—that Taylor Properties would love to have me on their team.

Losing a top producer is not something real estate companies relish, but it was clear that Premier and I were no longer a match. Not wanting to burn bridges, I explained to management that I wanted to cut back on my work hours and Taylor Properties was willing to accept my more laidback approach. The transition to Taylor Properties was quick, easy and seamless. I just needed to get clear what it was I wanted. Once I made my decision, I never looked back.

> RULE #12-3: ADJUST YOUR LIFE TO CHANGING VALUES Our lives consist of several stages. In the beginning of any career it is necessary to focus on developing the skills necessary to be an expert in your field. Once the foundation is built you may want to shift some of your attention to other areas, such as family and friends, hobbies, spiritual practices or contributing to help you feel balanced.

Twenty-five years to the day after I received my first Top Selling Agent Award, I sat down to write this book. I no longer yearned for the bigger sale, recognition as the 'Agent of the Month' or all the other accolades that come with being a top producing agent. In those twenty-five years I have shown properties to celebrities such as Danny Glover, Nicolas Cage, Michael Tilson Thomas, Bobby McFerrin, Alice Waters, Tracy Chapman, Pat Montadon, Jill Eikenberry, Michael Tucker a few well-known sports stars—whose names have escaped me—and a famous Hong Kong playwright. Some bought. Some did not. During this time I remained a member of the top ten producers in San Francisco, won two trips to Mexico, one to Hawaii, one to Australia and earned three diamond pins, a fourteen carat gold bracelet, two designer watches, lots of expensive dinners and numerous gift certificates to Nordstrom, the Ritz Carleton and wine country resorts. I even won a week-long sailing trip aboard an eighteenth century ship docked in Perth for the America's Cup! But it is not the perks, it is the people who make doing real estate so rewarding. My days are full of surprises, sometimes very pleasant ones, like the day I held an open house one damp, foggy Sunday afternoon.

It was the early nineties. The Bay Area real estate market, like the rest of the country, was deep in a recession. I had a great listing—a home in the Haight previously owned by Graham Nash—but with no activity for six months. That day, like many days before, I dressed for success, put on a positive attitude and told myself there's a perfect buyer out there somewhere who wants a home just like this one. I was rewarded when a casually dressed short black man appeared at the door and extended his hand to me with such self assurance that I thought, "Hmmm—am I supposed to know who this guy is?"

"Hi, I'm Bobby," he said.

"Hi, I'm Paula," I said, shaking his hand.

After a quick walk around the first level, I took him downstairs to the sound studio which Graham had built in the seventies when he owned the home. I usually guided people upstairs to the bedrooms, but had a hunch that this guy would appreciate this special feature.

Bobby was enthralled. "Do you mind if I test out my voice in here?" he asked.

"No... ahhh... not at all... sure go ahead," I said.

Bobby proceeded to sing—not in words—but in varied combinational vowel sounds. I moved to one of the back rooms to give him some privacy. Who is this guy, anyway? I wondered.

After about twenty minutes he was ready to see the rest of the house. Bobby breezed through it while here and there I gave him gossipy tidbits of information to keep him interested. I showed him the hundreds of popsicle sticks on the sloped attic ceiling. "These were supposedly glued on by the band members of Crosby, Stills, Nash and Young," I chuckled, "after their jamming sessions." I then pointed to the huge Georgian Colonial on the double lot next door, telling him it had once been owned by the 'Sugar' family. "By the way," I continued, "I just sold that house to Danny Glover a few months ago. I understand he's doing a huge remodel and putting in another full level for a gym. He could have bought anywhere and he bought here." I hoped this gentleman, whoever he was, could see the value of this location—directly across from San Francisco's beautiful Buena Vista Park.

The next day at the office I asked my fellow officemates who he could be—this short black man with long dreadlocks, who sang in weird vowel sounds, and whose first name was Bobby.

"Bob Marley," Kevin O'Connor answered, always the Irish smart aleck.

"Come on, really! This guy came into my open house yesterday. He was singing in all the rooms."

"Sounds like some impersonator deadbeat to me," he rallied. "After all, Paula, it is the Haight—all kinds of riffraff there."

"Nope—you're wrong," I answered. "This guy is someone famous— I can just feel it in my gut."

My colleagues walked away, shaking their heads, probably thinking what a nut I was for being so gullible. Well, I thought, I will just have to wait for him or his agent to call me. He did seem really interested.

Sure, enough, his agent calls later that day, thanking me for taking such good care of her client and not fawning all over him, because of his fame.

"And your client is... ?" I asked sheepishly.

"Bobby McFerrin of 'Don't Worry Be Happy' fame."

"Really? That is one of my most favorite songs. I use it kind of like a mantra."

"Well, he wants me to bring his wife through tomorrow. And just off the record," she snorted at her pun, "he's very excited to live next door to Danny Glover."

A few days later we sealed the deal. I secretly thanked my body for telling me that this person was a well-known artist. If I had not taken my hunch seriously, I might have treated him like some Haight Street bum, who just liked to sing on a whim at open houses, driving agents crazy.

> RULE #12-4: PAY ATTENTION TO BODY CLUES Your body absorbs information just as the mind does. Pay close attention to what it is telling you, because it may make a difference in how you communicate with clients and may even secure a sale.

As I continue to work selling real estate, I find that the skills I have honed are noticed by others and viewed as gifts, not just abilities that I have developed. Remember Mr. Chase? When I first worked with him, I had taken a break from real estate and was easing back in. I had limited myself to working with only two clients at one time. Therefore, Cindy and I had the leisure to stage his house successfully. So

successfully that we got eleven offers! Eleven! Before we started opening the sealed envelopes, I predicted to Cindy which offer would be
the winner. Cindy was astounded that I was right. She talked about my
ability to see the outcome as a special gift.

"What special gift are you talking about?" I asked.

"You know—your ability to see the future. You've always had it. It
is what helps you be so successful."

"It is not really a gift Cindy. It is just that I observe people's behaviors. I make a habit of being well-rested, so I am always in the present," I stamp my foot on the floor of our conference room for
emphasis. "I simply sit back and watch what is happening around me."

It was easy for me to predict that Annie Lim's offer would be the
winning bid. The word around town was that Annie, alias Dragon
Lady, came from Hong Kong royalty. It would not have surprised me
if it was true. It was impossible to ignore her as she rode around town
in her flashy Jaguar, was decked out in expensive tailor-made suits
and wore eighteen carat gold jewelry. When she entered a room, she
filled it with her regal presence. To add to her status at the top of the
San Francisco real estate hierarchy, she was married to a prominent
developer. Well-connected, fiercely competitive and as tenacious as a
boa constrictor, she guarded her status of Queen Bee.

Annie had tried bullying us to accept a preemptive offer, but we
had promised Mr. Chase two open houses and two broker tours. Since
it was a strong seller's market with few listings, we wanted to make
sure his house got optimum exposure. We required that she and any
other interested parties sign off on all the disclosures and inspections
ahead of time. The only possible contingency would be an appraisal,
but savvy agents and buyers were waiving those as well. We also did
some detective work and learned that Annie was not just representing any buyer—but her niece. The apartment was conveniently located in the north side of town, close to the Municipal Transportation
Agency, and had a garden apartment for her in-laws. There was no
other building like this. So Annie simply did what she had to do to get
her offer accepted—going way over the list price with no conditions.
Knowing her personality and the circumstances, the gift that Cindy
noticed in me was actually no more than a rational assessment of this
aggressive woman. Annie Lim would not let anyone other than her
beloved niece get this desirable property.

RULE #12-5: BE IN THE PRESENT MOMENT By being aware of what is happening in the present moment, you can develop your sixth sense of intuition. This will help you solve and circumvent problems as well as communicate more effectively with others. Intuition is simply being present and observant while combining rational analysis with creative thinking.

Whenever I list a property I do a thorough inspection of the house. I make sure to take lots of notes and ask many questions. Before I show a property to a buyer, I do the same. I get as complete a picture as I can, but no matter what, some unforeseen circumstance usually arises and the sooner one deals with it the better. Like the time I listed Bill Peterson's house. We are halfway through the escrow period finishing up on some paperwork when my eyes rest on the large entertainment center in the family room. "That's going to be difficult to move," I say.

"Yeah. I've decided to sell it to the neighbor down the street," Bill says. "He'll come get it after we sell."

Back at the office I go over the detailed list I made of what I need to accomplish to get Bill's place ready for sale. My eyes focus on the large piece of furniture going to the neighbor. Something in my gut is uneasy. I call Bill, compelled to ask, "By any chance did you cut the carpet to fit the entertainment center in the house?"

Bill admitted he had.

"You understand that the buyers are going to expect the den to be fully carpeted. You are going to have either re-carpet or offer them the entertainment center."

Bill objects at first, giving me all sorts of reasons why he does not think it necessary that we do anything. I listen to all his reasoning. When he is finished, I ask if he wants to get the highest price possible.

"Of course."

"You do understand, don't you, that to get the highest price, your house needs to be in impeccable condition," I say.

He agrees.

"That includes the carpet."

Bill suggests we simply disclose that a piece of the carpet has been cut.

"These current generations of buyers are busy people. They don't want to deal with details. Why give them an excuse not to buy?" I ask Bill to think it over, allowing him his process. We have time after all. I still need to order the reports and prepare the disclosure packet.

A few days later Bill calls, saying he will agree to install new carpet. He trusts my instincts. He knows that paying attention to the minutest details can make a difference. At the last minute, the missing piece of carpet could have been a deal breaker.

Intuition helped me again in this same transaction. A family came through at one of the open houses, speaking very little English. They stayed a long time, walking from one room to the next, speaking with excitement. I showed them the house the best I could, sure of myself that they were really interested. I took them downstairs to the patio and gestured to where the lot line ended. They walked around, peering over the side fences and observing the adjoining yards (A good thing to do if you want to learn something about your neighbors— many buyers don't do this). They then tested the water pressure in the two bathrooms, opened and closed the windows and peered into each and every closet. At the end of the tour, a good-looking young man with a flashy smile and tousled black hair introduces himself as Juan Chavez, pumping my hand in a vigorous up and down motion.

So when an agent presented an offer with only one signature I was not too surprised. But later that evening something in my gut did not feel quite right. I sat uncomfortably for about an hour, contemplating what was bothering me. Finally, it came to me: Coming from another country with seemingly strong family ties, I had a hunch that the bidding gentleman was married (In California the wife needs to either sign the contract or a quitclaim deed, relinquishing any rights of ownership). I needed to find out the details of his martial status. I call Carole Lynn, the agent representing Juan.

"Yes, he is married." Carole Lynn admits. "But his wife is still living in Argentina. Only he will be on the deed so what's the big deal?"

"California law will require that she either be on title or sign a quitclaim deed," I say. "I'd like this to get resolved as soon as possible."

"No problem," Carole Lynn says in a voice sounding too nonchalant for my liking. "We'll take care of it at close of escrow."

I remember what Tim Brown, my manager, used to say: *If someone keeps saying no big deal—no problem—that's the time to pay close attention. It very well may be a problem or a big deal.*

I speak in a measured controlled tone when I say, "Some spouses sign these deeds no problem. Others refuse, causing delays, and in some cases, a transaction to fall apart. We don't want that to happen, do we?"

"Of course not," Carole Lynn replies. "I've been working with Juan for four months. This deal better go through."

"The sooner we get the paperwork, the better. Don't you agree?" I ask.

Carole Lynn lets out a small nervous laugh. "Of course. I'll get working on this immediately." Good—she's on my side now. I breathe more easily, knowing this small, but important detail will be handled.

Carole Lynn follows up with a reassuring phone call a day later. Juan's wife has agreed to sign the quitclaim deed and the title company is expressing it to her today. We get it back a week later—in plenty of time. Once again another possible obstruction to the sale is solved easily by being grounded, balanced and observant in the moment. Thank you, intuition!

PART THREE

Pulling It All Together

CHAPTER THIRTEEN

SUCCESS
Creating Healthy Patterns

I'M THAT LITTLE KID AGAIN on a balmy summer evening. Our family has just finished dinner. "You know what it is you have to do before you go to bed tonight," Mother says as I tiptoe to my room, hoping she forgot.

"I told you I can't," I say. I feel the tears in my eyes.

"Oh, yes, you can. Tonight's the night."

"I've tried, Mother! Really I have! I just can't." I bend down to show her my scrapped knees with the crusty brown scabs from my previous attempts over the last week. Getting no sympathy from Mother, and hearing the nightly news blaring from the den, I ask in a mouse-like squeak, "Can Daddy help me? Please?" I'm hoping she'll soften, but if Daddy's settled into his chair and smoking his pipe, it's probably too late.

"No, he's busy," she says. "Don't bother him."

I pause for a moment, thinking of what to do next. "Well, I'm not going!" I declare, stamping my foot. I start wailing. I am ready to throw myself on the floor, kicking and screaming.

"Don't you dare have one of your tantrums!"

"What's going on in there?" It's Daddy calling from behind his newspaper. "Stop all that racket this minute or I'll get that belt out so fast you won't know what hit you!"

Mother grabs my arm and pulls me down the back stairs to the garage. "We got that nice Schwinn bike for you and it's just sitting here. Do you want to be the only one in your school who can't ride a bike?" I wrestle away from her and look down at the bike I wanted so badly with a defeated look. Why can't they help me like other parents help their kids?

After several minutes of sulking, I decide to give the bike riding another go. I clench my teeth and hold tightly onto the handlebars, while hopping on one foot with the other on the pedal. It feels so unsteady that I'm afraid to let the second foot off the ground. I remember the fall I took three days ago. Gravel embedded in my skin, my knees so bloodied I'd thought for sure I'd have to get stitches. Mother hadn't bothered taking me to the Emergency Room. Instead she had brushed my knee with soap and loaded it up with iodine. "Owww... that hurts," I screamed. She had assured me that if it did scar no one would ever notice. Who's ever going to be looking at my knees, anyway?

I keep hoping and hoping this bike riding will all work out somehow. It doesn't. Minutes later I collapse in a heap on the ground with the front wheel spinning madly and tiny pebbles piercing my skin. "I don't want to do this! I hate you!" I scream as I hit the seat of my bike with my fists. I keep hitting the pink cushion until I lay exhausted on my back, wishing I had never asked for a bike. I walk up the back stairs and pound on the door. "Let me in," I say.

"Did you get on yet?" Mother asks.

"No, I can't. Can I come in now?"

"Not until you learn to ride."

"It's getting dark outside, Mother." She doesn't answer. I jiggle the doorknob. She's locked the door again. I let out a huge cry. I throw myself as hard as I can against the door, but still no response. I go back outside.

I glare at my once precious bike which has now turned into my arch enemy. I give it a couple of good kicks till it falls with a loud crashing sound. "You miserable piece of crap! See how you like it!" I say as I stomp on the spokes once or twice for good measure. There, that feels much better.

Some behaviors are hard to change. I am an adult now, but I still act like a little kid when I get frustrated. I smash and break things. I'm sorry to say this is not my only self-defeating behavior. When my feelings get hurt I often strike back and say things I should not—as was the case with Frank Woods. I have learned much, but there are still many things I don't know. I share my rules with you, knowing they sometimes fail me as they will fail you—after all, we are only human. If you can exhale, step away and accept that your bad wolf will get in your way now and again, you will be well on your road to success. Also, in dealing with the 'wolf' part of ourselves, I find it helpful to understand how our brain chemistry works:

The brain is like a gigantic computer coordinating hundreds of intricate everyday tasks. It does this by producing 'feel-good' biochemicals, called neurotransmitters, which attach onto our cells in the same way a key fits into a lock. This locking mechanism encourages us to repeat tasks necessary for our survival, such as breathing, eating and moving. We want the pleasurable feeling these neurotransmitters produce, so we create a continuous cycle of habits.

Many of these automatic survival behaviors have helped us cope over the years, but some of these habits have become actual liabilities. Like smashing phones. Sure, it relives stress when I feel overwhelmed, but most anyone would agree that hurling insults or throwing things is not a constructive coping mechanism. Intellectually, I know it is destructive, but when my back is to the wall, when I feel taken advantage of or betrayed—like I often felt in childhood—the anger inside me looms large. I feel I will literally burst unless I am able to let off some steam.

Just look around you. Notice how much we are all driven by our engrained habits. Fat people gorge on pizza; drunkards down bottles of scotch; snobs flaunt their McMansions; victims cry over bad business deals and rageaholics rant. These examples commonly exist in everyday life. We are so intent on getting the fix we need that we are unaware of what we do to ourselves and to others. Getting our biochemical rush is our primary goal, like a junkie trying to score. That is why repetitive behavior can be so destructive.

Herbert Hubbard lives in a fantasy world of thinking that somehow his deadbeat clients will change and buy something. When they let him down, he denies that his poor screening has anything to do with it. He is so attached to being a victim that he takes no responsibility for wasting his time with losers. Cindy Wilson's pattern of being a people pleaser and making promises which she cannot deliver, gets in the way of her establishing a trusting bond with her clients. Suzie Weinhammer, in spite of her external success, is so self-centered and arrogant that most people can't stand her. Brian Rinsom, in spite of his inspiring ideas, is the epitome of the procrastinator and never really applied these universal laws in his own life. At fifty-two he is still a street artist. And me? When I feel that someone has taken advantage of me, I express my anger—even if a million dollar sale is at stake! That is the power of neurotransmitters.

So how do we disable an engrained destructive neurological pathway? First of all, you will never be able to completely disable it. Although I have achieved a high level of success, I still struggle with my automatic reactions. What has helped me is my willingness to stop, consciously look at my behavior and then fix it as soon as I can. I have also set up my own personal radar to avoid situations that can trigger my destructive, self-protective patterning. Even as I am writing on this topic of creating healthy habits, I find myself embroiled in a power play which has escalated in a drama of operatic proportions. Since it is so timely, let me share it with you:

I have just come back from a two week vacation in Italy. What was supposed to be some down time turned out to be six days of hiking with a wrenched back and a weak ankle. Even when we rested, it was torture: sleeping on a bed that was a lumpy abomination, schlepping two bags of luggage up and down narrow stairways, logistically demanding train rides and two stormy days in touristy, smelly Venice.

Since my husband, Greg, likes to get to the airport in plenty of time, we had three and a half hours before our flight back home. I decided to use that time to check my email. Four hundred and twenty-seven messages had come in while I was gone. The good news is that a loan approval had come in on my big deal. I had expected that. The buyer had a credit score in the mid-seven hundreds, a well paying job and was putting twenty percent down. I had felt confident going on vacation with that detail still hanging, because I knew she would be approved. Sure enough, it had happened. Her agent, Ernie Bristol, had emailed me that she had gotten her loan. The bad news was that, scrolling through the messages, I could not find confirmation that the closing papers had been sent out to my seller.

I wondered why Marcie Lasser, the escrow officer, had not emailed me (In California we don't use lawyers in transferring ownership from seller to buyer as most states do. Instead, the title companies set up an escrow account to disperse funds and act as a neutral intermediary, making sure that the scores of documents are signed). Before I left San Francisco, I had given Marcie precise instructions to get these documents to my seller, Peter Greene during my absence. Since Peter was working for the u.n. in a remote part of Bosnia, and would have to travel to the American Consulate to sign, I wanted to be assured that he would have enough time for these challenging logistics.

When Greg and I finally entered the threshold of our home it had been twenty-one hours since we left our hotel in Venice. Ever the compulsive professional, I just have to check my emails again. It is only nine in the evening, Pacific Standard Time, but six in the morning Italian time. Still no message from Marcie. Maybe she didn't want to disturb me on my vacation. That was thoughtful. Still—maybe I should shoot her an email—just in case. "Marcie, did you get the closing papers back from Bosnia yet?" (I want to say "Did you do as I asked and send the papers out?" But to avoid sounding accusatory, I use tact. Maybe she had gotten the papers out and just hadn't emailed me. Give her the benefit of the doubt, I tell myself.)

My body clock is so off that even though I take a sleeping pill, I am still wide awake at three in the morning. I get up and start opening mail, doing bills and unpacking, all the while keeping a watch on my email. It is after nine when I finally get an email from Marcie through her Blackberry. I'm skeptical. Isn't it common practice for escrow officers to get to the office early before their signings to check messages? The email says:

> *Paula,*
> *Welcome back. I sent an information sheet over to Peter a few days ago. Have you heard anything from him in the past week? Do you have another email address for him?*
>
> *Marcie*

Why would I hear anything? I was on vacation in Italy. My response is quick and to the point:

> *Marcie,*
> *Please call me back as soon as possible. I am not clear if closing papers went out or not. I have heard nothing.*
>
> *Paula*

I mark it high urgency with an exclamation point. Since I left the file with a business associate, I do not have Marcie's direct telephone line. I check her email—no telephone number. I check five or six old email messages. No telephone number on those either. I know she prefers email, but I am getting nervous. Marcie finally emails back:

> *Paula,*
> *Peter has not returned his payoff information so closing papers have not been drawn. Seller's papers are very minimal and we still have a*

comfortable amount of time before closing—again I am confident that things will be completed in a timely fashion. You haven't mentioned if you have heard from Peter? I will call you as soon as my closings are completed this morning. Thanks!

Marcie

Again—why would I be hearing from Peter if I was on vacation in Italy? I can not stand procrastination. I don't do it myself and I don't like people who use, "we have plenty of time," as an answer. Marcie's lack of direct contact, her needing information which she should have gotten before I left and her delay in responding to my requests drove me crazy. However, I needed Marcie's help in getting the job done so I had to put those feelings aside.

> RULE #13-1: SELF MANAGE YOUR EMOTIONS Concentrate on your goal first and foremost. Next when events or people drive you crazy do whatever you can to take care of yourself: talking out your frustration with a friend, taking an exercise class, or even yelling in the car if you must.

Now I'm anxious. Closing papers not sent out? If I bit my fingernails, now would be the time. Peter does not have any of his loan information in Bosnia that's for sure. It is a war zone over there. Why didn't she tell me before I left what she needed? I do some of my own research and send it over to Marcie, asking politely in my email, "Do you need anything else?"

I get an email back confirming receipt, but why isn't she calling me? Isn't this a high priority? I wait for her signing appointment to be over, but wonder why it is taking so long. Marcie came highly recommended to me, I tell myself. No need to worry. Debbie Richards, the Public Relations Manager for Trumbull Title, tells me Marcie is the best in the business. Debbie wouldn't steer me wrong, especially since I'm a new client whose business Trumbull Title wants badly. Besides, hadn't I emphasized that I'm a thirty-year business veteran? I had been so emphatic about how important it was to have a good team behind me. I do more paperwork, run an errand and look at my watch again. It has now been almost two hours and still no telephone call. I get the main number of Trumbull Title on line and call, telling the receptionist it is an emergency. They ring me through and Marcie picks up the phone.

"When are you planning to send the closing papers out?" I ask, almost breathlessly, trying to cover the angst I'm feeling. To soften the brittleness in my voice, I add, "It sounds like you've had as hectic day as I've had. It's hard getting back to work after two weeks away."

"Oh, yeah." She sighs. "I've been really, really busy."

"We've got to get these closing documents sent out to Peter as soon as possible," I say.

"Oh, yeah. Maybe I can get on to it later today." She sounds really tired like me or maybe she's just bored.

I'm doing my best not to antagonize her. Something inside me is saying she gets ticked off really easily. I continue with my pleading, "I really think this is high priority." It's already after one in the afternoon and we've lost another day since the first email. I continue, "We're due to close next Friday."

"Paula, you're not telling me anything I don't already know." Her voice is pointed like the tip of a dagger.

Great! Now I've pissed her off. However, I can't risk her not getting the urgency of my request. In a soft soothing voice I say, "Peter's way off in Bosnia. Who knows how long it will take. Promise me you'll get the papers out today."

I thought I heard a loud sigh at the other end. "I'll do my best," she says. "I need to go now." Click and she's off the phone. I keep checking my email until five and still nothing. Hoping she had time to express mail all the documents to Peter in Bosnia, I send one more pleading email before I head to bed. My body clock is still on Italian time.

I'm up and wide awake again at three in the morning. It is Friday. We have exactly one week to get the papers back from Bosnia. Will we close on time? I wonder. Nothing to do, so I open my email. I have an email from Marcie. It says:

Paula,
I am out of the office tomorrow, but will be able to get to every thing else on Monday. I emailed Peter the Grant Deed so that he can sign and have it notarized and returned. The rest can be faxed.

Marcie

How dare she not mention to me yesterday that she was planning to take the day off today! It is becoming clearer and clearer that we probably won't be closing next Friday. I need to alert the other agent and make other arrangements. When it's a decent hour I call Ernie Bristol and tell him we may be delayed. "Why don't we just close the following Friday instead?" I say. "That way your buyer will still have a weekend to move in. Her loan papers haven't arrived yet anyway," I say. "Let's go with the flow and avoid all the stress."

Ernie agrees to talk to his buyer. He doesn't anticipate a problem.

Boy, am I relieved. I decide to call Debbie Richards anyway. Didn't she know that Marcie was this incompetent? I feel I owe it to her (and me) to tell the truth. "Debbie, you know I love you and want to use your company, but I have to be honest. I am really disappointed in Marcie Lasser. She didn't send out the closing papers as I instructed her to do while I was on vacation so now it looks like we won't be able to close on time. Although I pleaded with her to get it done yesterday morning, she waited until after five with an email saying she would be out of the office all day today." I take a deep breath. "Between you and me, I'll never use her again."

Debbie sounds shocked. "I can't believe she did that to you."

Why would she be so shocked? She recommended her. "By the way," I ask, "how long has she been working for Trumbull Title?"

"How long has she been an escrow agent?" Debbie asks.

I sense she is avoiding my question so I repeat it. "How long has Marcie worked for Trumbull Title? How long have you known her?"

"Six months. But she's been in the business a long time."

I'm beginning to love Debbie a little bit less. Debbie recommended her to me four months ago. I had stressed to her I wanted an efficient, experienced escrow person.

I cannot do my job without good team behind me. A good team ensures success. That rule, I had learned in my early days from Napoleon Hill's *Think and Grow Rich*. So now talking with Debbie, I'm feeling that knotty anxiousness inside my belly again. It's the bad wolf. I don't want to feed him so I make Debbie promise not to tell Marcie of our conversation just yet. "I still have to work with her, but I am too angry to talk to her today," I say. I'll put off talking to Marcie until Monday. That will give me time to pull myself together and deal with the logistics of changing the closing date. Focus on the solution, I tell myself. Feed the good wolf. Still, Marcie's incompetence makes me anxious, annoyed and angry. Just as alco-

holics need to avoid going into a bar, I need to avoid any confrontation with Marcie.

> RULE #13-2: AVOID SITUATIONS THAT TRIGGER NEGATIVE
> PATTERNS When you feel that pang in your gut, the fluttering of
> your heart or the sweat on your brow, you may be in the middle
> of a survival pattern which can trigger negative emotions. It is
> best to remove yourself as quickly as possible and get grounded so
> you can problem solve.

I'm about to make some other calls when the cell phone rings again.
It's Ernie Bristol. "Bad news. We *have* to close next week. My buyer already gave notice to vacate her apartment. I advised her not to do
that, but she didn't take my advice, unfortunately."

Well, how many times has that happened to me? I'm thinking.
Clients don't take our advice, get into a pickle like this, and then want
us to solve everything. That's why allowing plenty of time, thinking
ahead and having backup plans is so valuable.

Ernie starts speaking again. "If we can't close on Friday, she wants
the seller to pay her hotel bills."

Just great! Well, Peter did get a good price for his loft. But it is not
his fault we can't close on time. "Let's see what I can do," I say. Keep
pushing yourself forward, I tell myself. Marcie has taken advantage of
me, but I am hoping my Higher Self can keep me from indulging in
my anger over it.

I call Debbie Richards at Trumbull Title. "The buyer gave notice to
her landlord and has nowhere to go. She expects the seller to cover
her hotel expenses." I go straight to the bottom line. "I do expect
Trumbull Title to pay for Marcie's mistake." Like Greg tells me—*If
people don't feel the pain of their mistakes, they'll never change.*

I can feel the resistance over the phone. "I'll have to check with
the County Manager," Debbie says in her best Public Relations voice.
"She may want to talk to you." Typical PR rubbish. Promise your
clients the moon and when there's a problem be vague. All I want is
for the hotel bills to be paid. I can't with good conscience ask Peter
to pay and, if Trumbull Title won't pay, then it will be me who pays
out of my commission, which I've already worked so hard to earn over
the past five months.

When Peter decided to sell, I had to get his tenants out. With San

Francisco rent control, this was no easy matter. Since tenants have all the rights, I took a subtle approach. Telling the tenants the property might be coming on the market, I made an appointment for our office to come through and help me with an 'Opinion of Value.' Having fifty agents tromp through your living space can be pretty intimidating. Especially when you're lousy housekeepers, as these tenants were. How embarrassing it must have been for them! Next, I asked when it would be convenient for the painters and handymen to get the place ready for sale. Both of them worked at home. What a hassle that would be! But it was clearly stated in the lease that the landlord has the right to make any repairs he deems necessary. They had no choice.

Then I had the ingenious idea to call the tenants all enthused—Peter would give them the opportunity to buy the property before it hit the market! What a deal! Again, this showed he was serious in selling and not just trying to get them out so that he could get a higher rent. I am sure they envisioned several months of intruding strangers invading their private space, so they decided it would be best to move. I got their Thirty Day Notice To Vacate, pleading with me not to do any painting or fixing while they lived there. Of course I agreed.

The tenants left the place in a shambles. Although the lease stated no smoking, the gray dust was imbedded so deeply into the paint that the walls needed three coats instead of two. The carpet and window blinds were ruined. There were two broken windows. The refrigerator, stove and cabinets were so filthy I was amazed that there weren't rats. We spent five thousand dollars to have the place looking nice for the new buyer. It took a full month working every day.

Another $4900 and this tired loft was transformed. In addition, Peter was resistant to paying for anything he deemed a frivolous expense. It took lots of patience, persistence and pleading on my part. The stager, Valerie Sadler, did a great job staining the concrete flooring a rich brown and finding new floor-to-ceiling drapes to match. A yellow accent wall in the living room leading up to the loft bedroom brightened everything up. Then we added in the modern furniture, some green plants, classy mahogany floors for the upstairs and an inviting patio set for the deck. Close to the 280 Freeway, the condo is perfect for Silicon Valley "Gen Xers" who want San Francisco. I wanted buyers to drool when they walked in.

The marketing was next. I decided to spend the money to design a website dedicated to this property. I then hired a professional photographer who worked with the designer to create a visual tour. Then I hired an illustrator to create an etching of the exterior for large newspaper display ads. And since detail is the name of the game in real estate, I took out classified ads in both *The San Francisco Chronicle* and *The San Jose Mercury News*. Since the loft is only five blocks away from the UCSF Medical Center, which will soon be employing 30,000 people, I took out ads in their local newspaper as well.

I also like to show all my listings personally. For brokers' tours, Sunday open houses and private showings, I was there ahead of time to open the windows, turn on the lights, and put on soft music. By the time buyers arrive, I was ready to point out all the special amenities. My attention to detail can determine whether a listing sells or not. Even though Peter's sale gets sidelined toward the end of the selling process, I had gone through five months of complications and crises without losing it, because I had allowed enough time. One advantage of being in the same business for thirty years is that I know what to expect. Precise scheduling may not be the way to make the most money in the shortest time, but it is a good insurance policy for maintaining sanity.

> RULE #13-3: ALLOW PLENTY OF TIME TO ORCHESTRATE ALL THE DETAILS Because the sales process requires a lot of coordination of events and people, it is essential that you give yourself plenty of time to accomplish even the simplest of tasks. If you are too busy, hire an assistant to help you. It is well worth the money spent.

My thoughts are interrupted when I hear the phone ring. Sure enough, it is Gail Grishny, the County Manager of Trumbull Title. "Hey, Paula, Debbie Richards says you have a problem with one of our escrows."

"I do," I reply. Less is more, I remind myself. I don't let myself spill the whole story of Marcie Lasser's stalling and spoiling my closing date. Instead I give her the bare basics, looking for a solution instead of blaming.

"Have you talked to Marcie about all this?" Gail asks.

Noticing that my anger is getting lit up like a Christmas tree, I do my best to not feed the bad wolf. "Several times. I have also tried to accommodate her schedule, but today she's out of the office all day. Each minute counts in this escrow." I explain that I have a seller who is working in a remote part of Bosnia and can't always be reached. "We need to get Peter the closing papers as soon as possible," I say. "The problem is, if we can't close by next Friday, the buyer will have to stay in a hotel." I can hear the whine in my voice. Again, giving Marcie the benefit of the doubt, I add, "Well, Marcie did say she was really busy."

"Paula, I wish that were the truth," Gail says. There it is—even in a situation where she is protecting Trumbull Title's interests against mine, Gail tells the truth. That's why I liked her so much. I focus on this instead of how furious I am with Marcie.

"You're not really busy?" I say, barely able to grasp that concept. Why wasn't Marcie available? Put a lid on it, I say to myself. Remember the wolf story. Give the energy to the good wolf—the one that's full of passion to get the job done; the one that wants to focus on the solution and not the problem.

"Let me see if I can get a hold of the file," Gail says. See, she's on my side, I tell myself. She is going to see if she can find a way to settle this.

> RULE #13-4: ACKNOWLEDGE THE PEOPLE WHO HELP YOU
> One of the reasons I like real estate is the great people I meet. I have huge respect for those people who—no matter what the situation—focus on problem solving and getting the job done.

It's my turn to speak. "Gail, thank you so much for handling this." I try my best to stay on the bright side. "Since the grant deed didn't go out until late last night, will we get it back in time to close Friday? I'm concerned because the buyer gave notice to her landlord and has no place to live."

"It's going to be close. However, since it is the end of the month, City Hall will let us do an afternoon recording on Friday."

"So if we get the grant deed returned to us by next Friday morning, we can close on time?"

Yes is her answer and the one I've been waiting to hear.

"And since none of the other papers need to have the original signature, you can fax them on Monday?"

"Correct," she answers.

Now I need to ask the million dollar question. I do so with baited breath. "And if we don't get the papers back in time will Trumbull

Title agree to pay for the buyer's hotel bills?"

"Let me see what I can do," is Gail's response. I may not get everything I want, but Gail's genuine concern is like a breath of fresh air. I thank her profusely, saying how much I appreciate her taking the time out of her busy day to help me. Like a spaced-out zombie in one of those science fiction movies, I go back to the file and the pile of paperwork in front of me. I'm putting the pieces of this gigantic puzzle together when the phone rings. I pick it up.

"Debbie just called me." It's Marcie Lasser.

"Oh," I say.

"What does Debbie mean when she says everything is spinning out of control?" The voice on the other end of the line is accusatory.

Damn it, Debbie! What did she think she was accomplishing by contacting Marcie on her day off? I am in the very situation I tried to avoid.

Marcie continues in rushed run-on sentences coming at me like darts. "I sent you an email last night. Didn't you get it? The grant deed went out. What's the problem?"

The problem is I have lost confidence in Marcie. I am wondering what other papers Peter needs to sign and will he get them in time? Is she planning to send them piece meal—some on Monday perhaps, some more Tuesday? She had two weeks to gather all the documents together and get this process rolling. I'm frustrated. "You did not follow my instructions, Marcie. Why didn't you send all the documents when I asked you before I left on vacation?"

"I wanted to wait until we got loan approval."

"I told you the buyers were pre-approved before I left. Even if what you say is true, the loan was officially approved Monday and today is Friday. And why didn't you express mail all the documents yesterday? Why does everything have to be the last minute?" I head to the enclosed conference room and close the door so not to disturb my other co-workers. "Marcie, can you tell me precisely what paperwork needs to be signed before we close?"

I am at a definite disadvantage here. I know that the title company needs the FIRTPA (the federal government's insurance that the seller's income tax has been paid), the city tax affidavit and the final accounting statement, but I could be missing something. Marcie isn't telling me, because she's too much into defending herself.

I feel my blood pressure rise. The bad wolf is out and getting bigger with each passing moment. When there's a gap in her sentences, I say, "Marcie, you and I are done," and hang up the phone. But the bad wolf wants to be fed in spite of my best efforts to keep him at bay. My body is shaking from the outright denial, the jet lag, and the broken promises. I rush to make the next call to relieve all the pressure I'm feeling inside me. Fortunately, Debbie doesn't pick up.

I leave a message. "I just got off the phone with Marcie. I thought you weren't going to talk to her. You promised." My voice is reaching an all time high pitch. "We still haven't solved the issue of the hotel bills and I'm the one being held responsible for the predicament we're in!"

> **RULE #13-5: CHANGE REQUIRES FOCUS, PRACTICE AND RE-WARD** Focus on what your goal is. If you get off tract, make a self-correction and be sure to reward yourself for your good effort.

I know I am upset and that, until I regroup, my best course of action is silence. I focus on resolving the issue at hand so I let my voice trail off and end the conversation. I think it best to leave it at that so I do. I had kept the bad wolf at bay in my conversations with Debbie and Gail, but that last call from Marcie was sending me into my old destructive anger pattern. I fold up my paperwork. I am going to reward myself by leaving early. On the drive home I try not to beat myself up. I tell myself anger isn't necessarily a bad thing. It warned me that something was amiss and that I needed to take action. I have made progress over the years. I know when I'm in danger. I can hear the wolf banging at the door before he gets too out of control. That's why I warned Debbie and Gail how I was feeling. That's why I got off the phone with Marcie. I just wish I hadn't been so angry when I called Debbie.

I look at my anger from another angle. Like Carl Jung, I know that my impassioned enthusiasm and my impetuous temper are interconnected somehow. If it wasn't for my anger, I wouldn't be as successful as I've been. My anger fuels me. It helped me pay for my college education by giving me the energy to work two jobs in the summer and a part-time job during school. It helped me find a research job right out of college although I had no guidance, no car and no money. It gave me the courage to leave the medical field and get into real estate. It gave me more courage to move to San Francisco. Anger propelled me to the top even though I didn't have the business skills.

I don't want to kill my wolf. He warns me when things aren't right. But I don't want him ruining relationships by running amok either. The trick is to notice when my bad wolf is at the door so I can avoid situations that trigger my negative anger patterning. The number one way the bad wolf gets in my way is when other people do not follow through. But things come up. People forget. People make mistakes. That's why if you want to be a professional, whether you are a real estate agent, escrow officer or mortgage broker, it makes sense to be flexible, allowing sufficient time to get things done, and work with people who are accountable. That way, when life gets in the way you are covered.

> RULE #13-6: TAKE ACCOUNTABILITY Action, not words, is what accountability is all about. To keep clients coming back to you, be sure you listen to what they want and deliver what you promised them. When you make a mistake, own up to it and correct it, doing your best not to let it happen again.

The following Monday I transferred the file, along with two other opened escrows, to another branch of Trumbull Title. After Marcie Lasser's outburst, I could no longer work with her. We closed a week later than scheduled, but because the buyer's loan papers were late, she couldn't blame the delay completely on us. I was able to convince Peter to let her move her belongings into the vacant unit (after I verified that the movers were bonded and insured) and she was able to stay with friends until we closed. I never heard back from Gail Grishny. I cancelled the lunch date I had scheduled with Debbie Richards to celebrate the closing when she refused to take responsibility for her bad recommendation. I have since found another title company.

I have related my experience with negative patterns to show how to look inside and see where you can self-manage your emotions. Be aware that whatever you do not acknowledge, you cannot change. Also, know that you can create healthy patterns through intense focus, practice and reward.

HOW TO BE YOUR BEST

A S A SCIENTIST, I have been fascinated how we get ourselves
hooked on something that is not immediately pleasurable.
Even if the reward is delayed for a few weeks, as in a cold call,
we eventually learn that the pleasure of a sale is related to the hell of
calling a stranger. First you need to find an existing healthy habit—
no matter how weak—that you can start strengthening. Knowing your
strengths gives you a way of identifying the behaviors you already
have. For instance, I know I get obsessive about details when I am
making a sale. Many people find this an annoying trait, but I am just
as detail-minded about people as I am about things. I size up people
very fast and recognize their insecurities. That's how I was able to say
to Marcie, "I guess you are very busy," even though she probably was
just sitting around. I knew to say to Peter's tenants that he was willing
to accept an offer from them, even though they could never afford
the place. I knew that asking for hotel money would get the attention
of a person of power to step in and perhaps save the day.

So if one of your strengths is establishing bonds with people, think
about making a new friend when you make your cold calls. If you love
houses, call on the particular neighborhood you like most. This common bond will be enough to get a conversation going. If you are a curious person, interested in what other people do and how they think,
do a survey. *How long have you been in your home? Have you ever thought
of trading up? Is your home convenient to your work? Do you have any children at home?*

Then you need to focus on your goal. Know the statistics: one in a
hundred calls will produce a potential client (The statistics of turning
that client into a closed sale are one in three). Think of it this way—
every time a person hangs up or says no you are one step closer to the
person who will say yes. When you get someone on the phone, you
have about twenty seconds to get his or her interest. I offer them my
assistance in determining the market price of their home as well as
refinancing, remodeling and relocating options. This soft-sell approach of helping rather than getting works wonders.

The next step is consistency. Practice, practice, practice. It takes about three weeks for the brain to start producing neurotransmitters, so that is how long it will take for your new behavior, such as making cold calls, to become an engrained habit. It is the same twenty-one day rule whenever you start an exercise program, learn a new language or take up a new hobby.

Last and most importantly, we need to trick our body into getting our 'feel good' rush. Therefore, it is vitally important that you reward yourself after all your hard work. The sooner the better, so the body connects this new activity with those pleasurable feelings. If I get off a particularly rude call, I get up from my seat and make myself a cup of tea with lots of honey. The honey is a good symbol for me. If I feel I need more support, I'll have some chocolate on hand—a sure fire way to feel better.

When you do not want to make your calls, remind yourself—*Ah-Ha! After I'm done I deserve a night out with the guys/gals to do whatever my heart desires! A hike in the mountains when I'm done! A day at the beach! A scrumptious dessert!* So it is three weeks of concentrated focus and practice along with instantaneous rewards to create new neurological pathways and healthy habits.

Since real estate involves many people, each with their own unique personality, it is a very fragile mechanism. I like to compare each person involved in the sales process to the spoke of a wheel. If one of the spokes is out of alignment it can affect the stability of the whole wheel, causing the ride to wobble and even fall apart. It is an interdependent process and relies on everyone doing the absolute best job they can. Just because our biochemistry makes us addicted to destructive patterning, such as anger, excess people pleasing, victimization or procrastination, does not mean we are not responsible for our actions. Laziness is the common excuse thread of mediocrity. Change requires intense focus, practice and reward. It is an ongoing process. Keep plugging away. If you do your best every day to change patterns, in twenty-one days you will begin to see results. That's *every* day. You don't get weekends off.

Paula Pagano was not a natural-born salesperson. After graduating from Oswego State College in New York, Paula became a medical researcher. It was not until Paula had to experiment on animals and actually kill them that she realized she needed to find another profession. She traveled to California looking for some answers. Someone suggested real estate. Paula thought she would give it a try. Her father was an architect and she loved houses, so she got her real estate license #592260.

However, real estate is not about houses. It is about sales and those sales come out of solid healthy relationships. Ironically, Paula, who is proud to be of mostly Sicilian descent with a bit of Irish and Mohawk Indian thrown in for good measure, found relationships to be her biggest challenge. Yet in spite of the emotional obstacles before her, she became the top agent in her office during a recession and remained a top real estate leader for three decades. Paula believes if she could become successful, anyone can.

All the situations in this book are viewed from Paula's point of view. Some of the names have been changed to protect people's privacy.

To learn more about Paula and her secrets of success go to
www.SecretsofaTopSalesperson.com.

Made in the USA